A Register Of All The Christenings, Burials And Weddings, Part 2: Within The Parish Of Saint Peters Upon Cornhill

Granville W. George Leveson Gower

A Register

OF ALL THE

Christninges Burialles & Weddinges

WITHIN THE

Parish of Saint Peeters vpon Cornhill

BEGINNING AT THE RAIGNE OF OUR MOST SOUERAIGNE
LADIE QUEEN ELIZABETH.

EDITED BY

GRANVILLE W. G. LEVESON GOWER, F.S.A.

PART II.

CONTAINING THE CHRISTNINGES AND BURIALLES FROM
A.D. 1667 TO 1774 AND THE WEDDINGES FROM
A.D. 1678 TO 1754.

LONDON:

1879.

THE

𝕻𝖚𝖇𝖑𝖎𝖈𝖆𝖙𝖎𝖔𝖓𝖘

OF

𝕿𝖍𝖊 𝕳𝖆𝖗𝖑𝖊𝖎𝖆𝖓 𝕾𝖔𝖈𝖎𝖊𝖙𝖞.

ESTABLISHED A.D. MDCCCLXIX.

𝕽𝖊𝖌𝖎𝖘𝖙𝖊𝖗𝖘.—𝖁𝖔𝖑𝖚𝖒𝖊 𝕴𝖁.

FOR THE YEAR MD.CCC.LXXIX.

A Register of all the Christninges Burialles and Weddinges within the Parish of Saint Peeter's vpon Cornhill.

CHRISTNINGES.

Years.	Month.	Day.	Names.
1667*	March	29	Geo. son of Henry Mosse, Merch^t tayler, & Juliana his wife
	April	5	Mary dau. of Tho. Child, Apothecary, & Anne his wife
	May	19	George son of John Alder, Vpholder, & Mary his wife
	June	2	John son of William Broman, Victualler, & Margaret his wife
		16	Anna dau. of James Blatt th'elder, Draper, by Elizabeth his second wife
	July	21	Ann dau. of John Mason, Fruiterer, by Ann his wife
		25	John son of John Gase, Baker, by Jane his wife
	August	1	John son of Robert Clarke, Victualler, by Ann his wife
		18	Martha dau. of John Knap, waxchandler, by Mary his wife
	September	19	John son of John Price, Skinner, & Elizabeth his wife born same day
		22	Elizabeth dau. of Walter Young, Sexton, & Bridget his wife born the 10th inst.
	October	14	Henry Peters a foundling left vpon Mr Henry Jordan the Tallow chandlers in Bishopsgate street
		20	Ann dau. of William Merrill, Innholder, & Ann his wife
		20	Elizabeth dau. of the s^d William Merrill & Ann his wife
	November	5	John son of Richard Hobson, Mercer, & Rebecca his wife
	December	7	Elizabeth dau. of George Grigman, Victualler, & Susanna his wife
		19	Richard son of Richard Fripp & Adry his wife
	January	5	Elizabeth dau. of Robert Russell, Innholder, & Ann his wife
		23	Henry son of William Clay, Grocer, & Sara his wife
		29	Mary dau. of William Tighe, Leatherseller, & Hanna his wife
	February	16	Thomas son of Owen Price, Fishmonger, & Sara his wife
	March	3	Martha dau. of Thomas Sawyer, Clothworker, & Martha his wife
		10	Tho. son of Samuell Wickins, Haberdasher, & Anna his wife
1668	April	14†	Ralph son of William Tronckett, Draper, & Elizabeth his wife William and Gerrard (twins) sons of Gerrard Whorwood & Jane his wife

* The Register from March 29, 1667, to March 10, 1667-68, is subscribed "Mr William Hillersdon, Churchwarden."

† The Register from April 14, 1668, to Feb. 23, 1668-69, is subscribed "William Parker, Churchwarden."

Years.	Month.	Day.	Names.
1668	April	27	Elizabeth dau. of Thomas Wickersham, Fishmonger, and Elizabeth his wife
	May	24	Elizabeth dau. of Tobias Garbrand, Fishmonger, & Margaret his wife
	July	16	John son of John Tassell, Goldsmith, & Susanna his wife born June 29
		22	Elizabeth dau. of Tho. Persehowse, Fishmonger, & Elizabeth his wife born same day
	August	9	Anthony son of Robert Clarke, Victualler, & Ann his wife
	September	5	John son of Lawrence Holker & Susanna his wife
		13	Jane dau. of William Parker, Clothworker, & Mary his wife born Aug. 30
	October	1	John son of John Alder, Draper, & Mary his wife
		22	George son of George Griggman, Victualler, & Susanna his wife
		23	Dorothy dau. of Hen: Mosse, Merch^t tailor, & Juliana his wife
		23	Richard son of Richard Palleday, Haberdasher, & Ann his wife born the 21st
		29	Mary dau. of John Roberts, Haberdasher, & Mary his wife
	November	1	Ann dau. of William Packer, Salter, & Mary his wife
		8	Jane dau. of Beniamin Maynard, ffishmonger, & Susanna his wife
		18	Eliz. dau. of Rich. Blackburn, Draper, & Eliz. his wife born ye 9th
		22	George son of Roger Rea, Mariner, & Katherine his wife
		29	John son of Samuell Wickins, Haberdasher, & Anna his wife
	January	8	Margarett & Rhodia, (twins) daurs. of Sam^{ll} Purchas, Vpholder, & Mary his wife
		9	Elizabeth dau. of Robert Rowland, Armorer, & . . . . his wife
		26	John son of John Metteijer, Haberdasher, & Mary his wife
		31	John son of John Mawe, Cook, & Eliz. his wife
	February	7	Robert son of John Adams, Cook, & Dorcas his wife
		7	Eliz. dau. of John Gayes, Baker, & Jane his wife
		23	ffrancis son of Wm Bragg, Merchant, & Ann his wife
1669	April	16*	Robert son of Robert ffinch & Mary his wife
		26	John son of Tho. Tatnall, Vintner, & Mary his wife
	May	19	Joseph son of Thomas Wickersham, ffishmonger, and Eliz: his wife born this day
	June	18	Sara dau. of John Price, Skinner, & Elizabeth his wife
	July	25	William son of William Tronckett, Draper, & Eliz. his wife
	August	13	Isaac son of William Brooman, victualler, & Mary his wife
	September	19	Robert son of John Mason, ffruiterer, & Anne his wife
		20	John son of Christopher & Bennet Colt
	October	31	William son of Tobias Garbrand, ffishmonger, & Margaret his wife
	November	2	Mary dau. of ffrancis Stairsmore, Haberdasher, & Mary his wife
		7	Martha dau. of John ffoster, Ironmonger, & Martha his wife
		10	Katharine dau. of Miles Ward & Abigail his wife
		14	Mary dau. of Thom. & Martha Sawyer
		24	Mary dau. of James Blatt elder
	December	4	Edward son of Edward North, Haberdasher, & Sara his wife
		6	Rowland son of Robert Wairing, Sadler, & Susanna his wife
	January	2	Katherine dau. of Walter Young, Sexton, & Bridget his wife

* The Register from April 16, 1669, to May 15, 1670, is subscribed "Timothy Rosse, Churchw."

Years.	Month.	Day.	Names.
1669	January	3	John son of John Roberts, Haberdasher, & Mary his wife
		5	Sara dau. of Jnº Cockeram, Grocer, & Sarah his wife
		6	Jnº son of Jnº Hobson, Haberdasher, & Rebecca his wife
		6	Sara dau. of Wᵐ Parker, Clothworker, & Mary his wife
		7	Wᵐ son of Edw. Rugby, Grocer, & Eliz. his wife
		30	Mary dau. of Robert Russell, Victualler, & Ann his wife
	February	3	Susanna dau. of Beniamin Maynard, ffishmongʳ, & Susanna his wife
		11	Sara dau. of Thomas Abney, ffishmonger, & Sara his wife, born Jan. 29 last
		27	John son of William Packer, Salter, & Mary his wife
	March	10	Sara dau. of Samuel Purchas, Vpholder, & Mary his wife
		24	John son of Richard Goulding, Ironmonger, & Judith his wife
1670	May	15	Mary dau. of Robert Rowland, Brasier, & Elizabeth his wife
	June	8*	Hannah dau. of Samuell Shenton, Sadler, & Elizabeth his wife
		12	Elizabeth dau. of Robert ffinch, Mealman, & Ann his wife
		18	Mary dau. of Nathaniell Redbourne and Martha his wife
		18	Mary dau. of Richard Shelly, Grocer, & Mary his wife
	July	12	Thomas son of Thomas Birkhead, Brasier, & Dorcas his wife
		9	ffrances dau. of Will'm Smith, Merchᵗ, & Bethia his wife
	August	10	William son of Richard Blackburne, Vpholder, & Elizabeth his wife
		15	Hannah dau. of Thomas Warren & . . . . . his wife
		23	Susannah dau. of Edward Rich . . . . & Susannah his wife
		28	Mary dau. of John Graves, Victualler, & Elizabeth his wife
	September	18	Susan dau. of John Tassell, Goldsmith, & Susan his wife
		18	James son of Thomas Lardner, Apothecary, & Elizabeth his wife
	November	15	Mary dau. of George Grigman, Victualler, & Susan his wife
		16	William son of Robert Waring, Sadler, & Susan his wife
		21	Anthony son of Elizabeth Player, A: B:
	December	4	Samuell son of William Brooman, Victualler, & Mary his wife
		18	Thomas son of Griffin Harvey . . . . & Sarah his wife
		25	Thomas son of Thomas Heycock, Porter, & Barbara his wife
	January	10	Henry son of Henry Palmer, Ironmonger, & Bridgett his wife
		29	Beniamin son of Thomas Wickersham, Linen draper, & Elizabeth his wife
	February	2	John son of Will'm Tighe, Linen draper, & Hannah his wife
		28	Thomas son of Will'm Trunckett, Oilman, & . . . . his wife
	March	16	A ffoundlin taken up at Mʳ Tatnell's door
		16	Samuell son of Samuell & Mary Purchase
1671	April	22†	Humphry Merriton son of John Merriton, Haberdasher, & Sarah his wife
	June	13	Mary Desborowe dau. of Christofer Desborow, Linen draper, & Sarah his wife

* The Register from June 8, 1670, to March 16, 1670-1, is subscribed "Jno. Smith, Church-warden."

† The Register from April 22, 1671, to Jan. 30, 1680-81, is subscribed "Will. Beveridge, Parson."—He was born at Barrow in Leicestershire in 1638; admitted to St. John's College, Cambridge, May 24, 1653; B.A. 1656; M.A. 1660; D.D. 1679-80; ordained Deacon Jan. 3, 1660-61, Priest, Jan. 31 following. On Nov. 22, 1672, appointed Rector of St. Peter's, Cornhill, upon the death of Thomas Hodges; Prebend of St. Paul's Dec. 22, 1674; Archdeacon of Colchester Nov. 3, 1681; Prebend of Canterbury Nov. 5, 1684; Chaplain to King William and Queen Mary; consecrated Bishop of St. Asaph July 16, 1704; died at his lodgings in the Cloisters, Westminster Abbey, March 5, 1707-8, buried in St. Paul's Cathedral. His wife Frances was buried here on May 10, 1680.

Years.	Month.	Day.	Names.
1671	July	8	A ffoundling taken up at Mr Knowles door
	August	6	Richard son of Robert Rowland, Brasier, & Elizabeth his wife
		22	Sarah dau. of Edward North . . . . & Sarah his wife
	October	31	Sarah dau. of John Metteyre, Victualler, & Mary his wife
		31	John son of Thomas Sawyer . . . . & Mary his wife
	November	5	Mary dau. of Robert ffinch, Mealman, & Mary his wife
		5	Jane dau. of John Roberts, Milliner, & Mary his wife
		7	John son of William Grimmett . . . . & Susannah his wife
		20	North son of Thomas Darleston . . . . & Ann his wife
	December	30	Sarah dau. of William Packer, Victualler, & Mary his wife
1672	May	21	Anne dau. of John & Heaster Potts his wife
		29	Jonothan son of Jonothan Terman & Elizabeth his wife
	June	30	Richard son of George Greigman & Susan his wife
		11	Ann daughter of Nicasius Russoll & Anne his wife
	July	8	Hugen son of Tho. Dorman & Mary his wife
		17	Anne dau. of Wil: Tye & Hanna his wife
		24	Robert son of Robert Rowland & Elizabeth his wife
	August	16	Elizabeth dau. of Edward Rugby and Elizabeth his wife
	September	26	Elizabeth dau. of Alexander Caster & Hanna his wife
	November	10	Nathan son of John Gase & Jeane his wife
	December	8	Joyce dau. of Anthony Hall & Joyce his wife
		8	Elizabeth dau. of Edward Atkinson & Margret his wife
		25	Theophilus son of Theo. Swift & Julian his wife
		31	Rebecka dau. of Henry Palmer & Rebecka his wife
	January	5	Cornelius son of Nicasius Russell & Ann his wife
		12	William son of Thomas Darlaston & Ann his wife
	February	16	Elizabeth dau. of Wm Sheppey & Mary his wife
		23	Wm son of Rob. Waring & Susanna his wife
		24	Thomas son of Thomas Sawyer & Martha his wife
		27	Elhana' dau. of John Alder & Susan his wife
1673	March	81	Thomas son of Thomas Tatnall & Mary his wife
	April	3	Heaster dau. of John Potts & Heaster his wife
	May	19	Elizabeth dau. of Tho. Wickersham & Elizabeth his wife
	June	1	Susan'a dau. of John Throgmorton & Elizabeth his wife
	June	3	Charles son of Samuell Purchase & Mary his wife
	July	1	Mary dau. of James Cole & Mary his wife
		17	Mary dau. of Richard Bartlett & Heaster his wife
		20	Mary dau. of John ffoster & Susana his wife
	September	11	Elizabeth dau. of Richard Nichols & Martha his wife
		12	Ann dau. of George Gregman & Susan his wife
		21	Debora dau. of Rob. Rowland & Elizabeth his wife
		28	Susana dau. of Wm & An'a Rycraft
	October	19	Wm son of Alexander & Hana Caster
	November	2	Richd son of Wm & Mary Parker
		30	Owen son of Lewis and Jane Wilson
		30	Wm son of Wm & Alice Coppinforth
	December	9	Tho. son of Thomas & Mary Dorman
		12	Sarah dau. of Antho & Joyce Hall
167¾	January	4	Hester dau. of John & Mary Meteire
		12	Ann dau. of Jno & Elinor Wickins
	February	6	Ann dau. of Edwd & Eliz. Rugbye
		8	John son of John & Eliz. Bowyer
		13	James son of John & Dorcas Adams
	March	10	Vrsula dau. of Wm & Han'ah Tigh
		11	John son of John & Sarah Thomas
		22	Susana dau. of John & Hester Potts

Years.	Month.	Day.	Names.
1674	March	26	John Peters a Foundlin left in Peters Ally
	May	1	W^m son of Thomas & Eliz. Lardner

Years.	Month.	Day.	Names.
1674	March	26	John Peters a Foundlin left in Peters Ally
	May	1	Wm son of Thomas & Eliz. Lardner
		17	Rich. son of Tobias & Margt Garbrand
		24	Will'm son of Samll & Mary Purchase
		25	Lois dau. of Nathaniel & Jane Thornbury
		29	Margarett dau. of John & Mary Thornebury
		31	George son of Wm & Mary Shippy
	June	15	Sarah dau. of Edwd Bull
		21	Charles son of Henry & Eliz. Creamer
		26	John son of Robt & Susanna Wareing
	July	20	Richd son of Richd & Martha Nicholls
	August	16	Rebecka dau. of Tho. & Eliz. Wickersham
	September	16	Paul son of Tho. & Mary Tatnall
	October	8	Charles son of Charles & Kath. Danvill
	November	1	Katherine dau. of Tho. & Jane Harper
		5	Tho. son of Samll & Eliz. Dighton
		20	John son of Robt. & Eliz. Rowland
		22	Jane dau. of Lewis & Jane Wilson
		22	Tho. son of John & Jane Compere
		27	Sara dau. of John & Sarah Filewood
	December	20	Mary dau. of Tho. & Mary Dorman
	January	17	Martha dau. of Theop: & Juliana Swift
		17	Elizab. dau. of Wm & Mary Parker
		31	Mary dau. of Tho. & Ann Darlaston
1675	March	25	Samll son of Antho. & Joyce Hall
	April	8	Deborah dau. of Thoms & Deborah Salter
		13	Elizab. dau. of Andrew & Eliz. Harrett
	June	27	John son of Robt & Rachell Paggett
	August	4	Wm son of Will'm & Hanah Tigh
		15	Hanah dau. of Alexand: Caster
		15	Elizabeth dau. of Rich: & Elizab: Williams
		26	Elizabeth dau. of Rich: Bartlett
	September	1	Tho. son of Richd & Arabela Tharp
		9	Mary dau. of Jno & Hester Potts
		16	Elizabeth dau. of John & Ann Mason
		19	Mary dau. of John & Mary Lloyd
		20	Mary dau. of Charles & Katherine Donvill
	October	7	Jane dau. of Benjn & Mary Thoroughgood
		9	Martha dau. of Rich: & Martha Nichols
		23	Tho: son of Tho: & Brigget Phipps
	December	14	Elizabeth Peters a foundling
		14	Mary Peters another foundling
		16	Susana dau. of Lewis & Jane Wilson
		21	Anne dau. of James & Mary Cole
	January	28	Henry son of Mathew & Katherine Chitty
	February	20	Lidia dau. of John & Dorcas Adams
	March	14	Elizabeth dau. of Tho. & Elizabeth Lardner
1676		26	Ralph son of Ralph & Elizabeth Smith
	April	12	Mary dau. of Tho. & Mary Thorneton
		16	Wm son of Edward & Ann Bull
	May	12	John son of John & Sarah Filewood
		13	John son of John & Elizabeth Morris
		17	Joseph son of Samuell & Mary Purchase
	June	27	Ann dau. of Tobias & Margarett Garbrand
	July	16	Antho son of John & Sarah Wiburne
		20	Christo son of Andrew & Elizabeth Heriott
		25	Alexandr son of Alexandr & Han'ah Caster

Years.	Month.	Day.	Names.
1676	August	27	Mary dau. of John & Elizabeth Graves
	September	15	Rich^d son of Rich^d & Alice Rowe
		17	John son of John & Mary Lloyd
		28	Bridg^t dau. of Tho. & Bridgett Phipps
	October	19	Charles Peters a foundling
		22	Elizabeth dau. of Robert & Rachel Paggett
		29	Anna dau. of George & Elizabeth Page
	December	3	Arabella dau. of Richard & Arabella Tharpe
		31	Henry son of Andrew & Bridgett Yates
1676	January	9	Robert son of Thomas & Debora Salter
		14	Samuel son of Samuel & Elizabeth Dyton
		21	Richard son of Richard and Hester Bartlett
		28	Elizabeth dau of Lewis & Jane Wilson
		30	Elizabeth dau. of Benjamin & Mary Thorrowgood
		30	Hanna dau. of David & Mary Jones
	February	2	Elizabeth dau. of Samuell & Margaret Clarke
		11	Anne dau. of Thomas & Anne Darleston
		16	John son of John & Anne Starkey
		18	Miriam dau. of Thomas & Mary Dorman
	March	8	Elizabeth dau. of Ralph & Elizabeth Smith
1677	March	28	Sarah dau. of John & Hester Potts
	April	1	William son of Ralph & Mary Palmer
		6	John son of Samuel & Mary Purchas
		8	Robert son of Barnabas & Sarah Scudamore
		24	Sarah Peters a ffoundling
		27	George and Rebecca son & dau. of George & Sarah Atwood
	May	1	Margaret dau. of John & Sarah ffilewood
		8	William son of Henry & Bridget Palmer
		14	John son of Richard & Elizabeth Williams
	June	10	Sarah dau. of John & Anne Young
	July	22	Mary dau. of William & Mary Shippey
	August	12	Susanna dau. of Charles & Katherine Domvill
		19	Hannah dau. of Alexand^r & Hannah Caster
		27	Ruth dau. of John & Susan Balding
	September	3	Joseph son of John & Sarah Wibourne
	September	18	Susanna dau. of Robert & Susanna Wareing
	October	4	Robert son of Robert & Elizabeth Rowland
		22	Robert son of William Spinage
		23	Catherina dau. of Mathew & Catherina Chitty
		26	Elizabeth dau. of Anthony & Joyce Hall
	November	13	Dorothy Peters a ffoundling
	December	16	Robert son of Samuel & Katherine Smith
		16	John son of John Pharoe
	January	3	Elleanor dau. of Thomas & Bridgett Phipps
	February	6	John son of John & Anna Allen
		24	William son of William & Mary Packer
	March	2	Mary dau. of Benjamin & Mary Thorrowgood
		21	Robert son of George & Jane Maynard
1678	April	21	Richard son of Richard & Ann Young
	May	27	Samuel son of Thomas Purchase
	June	14	Thomas son of Thomas Salter
		15	William son of John & Sarah Thomas
		23	Lewis son of Lewis Willson
		23	Robert son of Robert ffutter
		25	Ann dau. of John & Sarah Filewood
		27	John Peters a ffoundling
	July	5	Katharine dau. of Thomas & Elizabeth Orton

Years.	Month.	Day.	Names.
1678	July	7	Henry and Ann twins children of Henry & Ann Latham
		11	Jane dau. of Thomas & Mary Thorneton
		19	Elizabeth dau. of John & Ann Starkey
	August	2	William son of William & Hanna Tigh
		28	Samuell son of Richard & Alice Roe
		1	Elizabeth dau. of Thomas Knowles
		8	ffrances dau. of Andrew & Elizabeth Harriot
	October	6	Edward son of Robert & Elizabeth Rowland
		20	Elizabeth dau. of Alexander & Hanna Caster
	October	27	Samuell son of Samuell & Katherine Smyth
		31	George son of Richard & Arabella Tharp
	November	3	Paul son of Paul & Martha Peirson
		7	W^m son of Ralph & Elizabeth Smyth
		17	Elizabeth dau. of Thomas and Ann Darleston
		21	William son of John & Elizabeth Parrat
	December	1	Rebecca dau. of Robert & Rachell Paget
		9	Elizabeth dau. of Rowland & . . . . Curby
		17	Thomas son of Thomas & Elizabeth Lardner
	January	9	Anthony and Richard (Twins), sons of John & Ann ffaron
		12	Ann dau. of Andrew & Bridget Yates
		19	Elizabeth dau. of Samuell & Eliz. Dyton
		29	Susana and Helliena dau^{rs} of Thomas & Bridget Phips
	February	7	Jane dau. of William and Katherine Spinage
		14	William son of Anthony & Joyce Hall
		16	Hanna dau. of Ralph & Mary Palmer
	March	2	Vrsila, dau. of Thomas & Sarah Offley
1679		30	Katherine dau. of Richard & Easter Bartlet
	April	20	Grace dau. of Benjamen & Ann Grivell
	May	8	Mary dau. of Richard & Elizabeth Parrat
		13	Grace dau. of Richard & Elizabeth Williams
	June	22	George son of Henry & Rebecca Murrey
		26	Elizabeth dau. of John & Mary Lloyd
		29	Martha dau. of John & Elizabeth Radhams
	July	10	Sarah dau. of Charles & Katherine Domvill
	August	17	David son of George & . . . . Gray
	September	6	John son of Bartholmew & Sarah Pigot
		21	Elizabeth dau. of John & Elizabeth Graves
		23	Abraham son of Richard & Arabella Tharp
	October	16	Samuell son of Samuell & Katherine Smyth
		30	Mariam dau. of Richard & Ann Mariott
	November	2	Thomas son of ffrancis & Mary Simes
		20	John son of Alexander & Hanna Caster
	December	2	Ann dau. of Richard & Elizabeth Shaw
		16	Elizabeth dau. of Thomas & Mary Thorneton
		19	Daniell son of Daniell & . . . . Medows
	January	4	Margaret, dau. of John & Susan Potts
		25	Elizabeth dau. of Thomas & Debora Salter
		26	Ann dau. of Thomas & Ann Kinnell
	February	10	Richard son of Benjamin & Mary Thorowgood
		20	Peter son of Thomas & Bridget Phips
		27	Thomas son of Thomas & Elizabeth Lardner
	March	1	Susanna dau of Robert & Elizabeth Rowland
		4	Anna dau. of Agustus & Susan Swift
		11	Mary dau. of Charles & Mary Lane
1680		28	Elizabeth dau. of Randolph Vadre
		29	Ann dau. of Nicasius & Ann Russell
	May	2	Samuell son of Tobias & Margaret Garbrand

Years.	Month.	Day.	Names.
1680	May	13	W^m son of William & Mary Cox
	July	8	Mary dau. of George & Hanna Hale
		11	Thomas son of John & Sarah ffilewood
		11	David son of John & Sarah Thomas
		12	Elizabeth dau. of Charles & Katherine Domvill
	August	6	Andrew son of Andrew & Elizabeth Hariot
		29	John son of John & Elizabeth Perrat
	September	22	Mary dau. of John & Sarah Gwillym
		8	Anthony alias Andrew son of John & Elizabeth Baxter
	October	17	John son of Henry & Rebecca Murry
		28	Mary dau. of Ralph & Elizabeth Smyth
	November	7	Ann dau. of Nicholas & Ann Swingler
		25	Edmund and West sons of Paul & Martha Pirson
		28	Elizabeth dau. of Richard & Arabella Tharp
	December	1	Mary dau. of Edward & Martha Pitts
		10	Elizabeth dau. of Richard & Elizabeth Perrot
		12	Benjamin son of Lewis & Jane Willson
		25	Elizabeth dau. of Richard & Ann Marriot
		28	John son of John & Elizb^th Raddams
		30	Edward son of Richard & Heaster Bartlet
	Jan.	2	Margaret dau. of ffrancis & Mary Simms
		3	John son of John & Susan Potts
		4	Elizabeth dau. of James & Mary Sedownes
		5	Elizabeth dau. of Thomas & Elizabeth Lardner
		17	Presilla dau. of Thomas & Elizabeth Orton
		20	Thomas son of William & Mary Packer
		23	Sarah Peters a foundling
		30	Elizabeth Peters a foundling
	February*	3	Katherine dau. of Elias & Katherine Russell
1681	March	25	William son of William & Mary Cox
		27	Alexander son of Alexander & Hanna Caster
	April	3	Mary dau. of Thomas & Debora Salter
		13	Susana dau. of Samuell & Katherine Smyth
		17	Johanna dau. of John & Ann Starkey
		17	Randolph son of Randolph & Susan Vodrey
	May	8	Hester dau. of Ralph & Mary Palmer
		22	Ann dau. of Henry & Elizabeth Cremer
	June	1	William son of Thomas & Bridget Phips
		16	Simond son of Simond & Ann Lynch
	July	15	Samvell son of Samuell & Elizabeth Black
	August	21	Samuell son of Philip & Mercy Stubbs
	September	8	James son of George & . . . . Gray
		9	Ann dau. of William & Leah Holiday
		18	Bartholomew son of Bartholomew & Sarah Pigot
	October	7	Elizabeth dau. of George & Hellen Achmotie
		16	Benjamin son of Benjamin & Mary Thorowgood
		16	Thomas son of Thomas & Ann Spence
		19	William son of William & Rachel Wonham
	November	18	Samuell son of William & Jane Knight
		20	Richard son of Richard & Elizabeth Shaw
	December	4	ffairfax Burden
		18	Ambros and William sons of Robert & Elizabeth Rowland
		18	Sarah dau. of Robert & Rachel Paget
	January	1	Thomas son of Thomas & Elizabeth Lardner

* The Register from Feb. 3, 1680-81 to Oct. 14, 1708, is subscribed "Will. Beueridge, D.D., Parson."

Years.	Month.	Day.	Names.
1681	January	1	Duce dau. of John & Elizabeth Parrot
		4	Thomas son of Paul & Martha Person
		26	Ann dau. of John & Elizabeth Hayard
		28	Elizabeth dau. of Charles & Mary Lane
		29	Perceval son of John & Susan Potts
	February	19	Edward son of George & Susan Clarke
		19	Mary dau. of John & Sarah ffilewood
		25	Sarah dau. of William & Alice Langmore
	March	2	Joseph son of Ralph & Elizabeth Smyth
		5	ffrancis son of ffrancis & Mary Sims
		17	John son of John & Sarah Blunt
		18	Susanna dau. of John & Sarah Thomas
		21	John son of Elias & Katherine Russell
1682	April	2	Mary dau. of Thomas & Elizabeth Willcox
		5	Charles son of Charles & Katharine Domvill
		8	Thomas son of Thomas & Elizabeth Orton
		26	Elizabeth dau. of Samuell & Ann Guinn
		30	Ann dau. of Thomas & Ann Darlestone
	May	14	Mary dau. of Richard & Ann Mariot
		16	John son of Abraham & Jane Hemeingway
		21	Christopher son of Alexander & Hanah Caster
		21	Simion son of Samuell & Katherine Smyth
	June	5	Elizabeth Curtis
		11	Ann dau. of Randolph & Susan Vodry
		27	Thomas son of Thomas & Johana Hanson
	July	11	Thomas son of Samuell & Elizabeth Black
		12	ffrances dau. of ffrancis & Philip Chase
		22	Ann dau. of Nicholas & Ann Swingler
	August	1	Mary dau. of Philip & Mercy Stubbs
		3	John son of Thomas & Mary Phips
		20	Ann dau. of John & Elizabeth Graves
	September	14	Mary dau. of Benjamin & Mary Thorowgood
		24	Ralph son of Ralph & Mary Palmer
		24	Elizabeth dau. of William & Hanna Tigh
	October	1	Elizabeth dau. of John & Ann Starkey
		7	Mary dau. of Thomas & Ann Spence
		27	Susana dau. of John & Sarah Cockeram
	November	5	Theophiles son of Simond & Anne Linch
		9	Gabriall, son of William & Rachel Wonham
	December	3	Linford son of Thomas & Elizabeth Larner
		9	Mary dau. of Edward & Jone Howard
		10	John son of John & Mary Loyd
		24	Ann dau. of John & Elizabeth Parrot
		26	Elizab' dau. of Robert & Elizabeth Rowland
		29	Charles son of James & Debora Vtburt & also Debora, their dau' twins
	January	12	Thomas son of Thomas & Ann King
		18	Elizabeth dau. of Paul & Martha Person
	February	9	Hester dau. of Richard & Hester Bartlett
		23	Jonathan son of Thomas & Elizabeth Egerlie
		25	Mary Crawley, aged 16 years*
		25	Thomas Crawley, aged 13 years
		25	Sarah Giles servant to Mr Nicholas Dawes
	March	4	Katherine dau. of John & Susan Potts
		4	Susana dau. of William & Mary Paget

* The number of adult baptisms in the years following up to 1699 is remarkable.

Years.	Month.	Day.	Names.
1682	March	9	Ann dau. of George & Hellena Achmoutie *alias* Acmoody
		18	Elisha son of John & Phillippa ffrancis
1683	April	1	Susanna dau. of George & Susanna Clarke
		26	Abraham son of Abraham & Jane Hemingway
		27	John son of Andrew & Bridget Yates
	May	31	Roger son of John & Sarah ffilewood
	June	5	William son of William & Jane Knight
		24	Richard
	July	8	Stephen son of Samuell & Katherine Smyth
	August	1	Jacob son of Philip & Marcy Stubbs
		5	William son of John & Sarah Wiburne
		11	William son of Charles & Katherine Domvill
		16	Thomas son of Thomas & Elizabeth Willcox
	September	20	Elizabeth dau. of Thomas & . . . . Chamberlin
		30	Thomas son of Thomas & Elizabeth Newton
	October	11	Sarah dau. of Ralph & Elizabeth Smyth
		28	Mary dau. of Thomas & Elizabeth Lardner
		28	Isaac son of Richard & Elizabeth Shaw
	November	4	Ann dau. of William & Alice Langmore
		4	Henry son of Will. Newball
		4	Humphry son of Richard & Martha Wareing
		7	John Cooke, a Blackamoore*
		7	Elizabeth dau. of Benjam. & Mary Thorowgood
		18	Sarah dau. of John & Ann Starkey
		18	Rebecca dau. of Henry & Rebecca Murry
	December	2	Cave son of Simond & Ann Linch
		16	Sarah dau. of John & Elizabeth Parrot
		16	Rebecca dau. of Joseph & Sarah Willmott
		18	Mary dau. of Charles & Mary Lane
	January	6	Elizabeth dau. of Thomas & Martha Hunsdon
		13	Thomas son of Paul & Martha Person
		16	Herbotle the Son of William Luckins, Baronet, and Mary his wife†
		18	Thomas son of Richard & Hester Lewis
		27	Anthony Edgehill, aged about 18 years
		29	Elizabeth dau. of William & Mary Brookeman
	February	1	Joseph son of James & Debora Vtburt
		10	Rebecca Charlton at Womans estate
		19	Sigismond son of Thomas & Bridget Phips
		29	John son of John & Levine Gentry, born 14 Feb.ʸ
	March	2	Elizabeth dau. of John & Elizabeth Cooke
		9	Mary Cole, aged about 16 years
		9	Elizabeth dau. of Thomas & An Spence
		16	George son of George & Susan Clarke
1684	April	1	John son of Thomas & Debora Salter
		22	Robert son of John & Elizabeth Hayward
		27	Elizabeth dau. of John & Susan Potts
	May	2	Thomas Peters
		4	Martha dau. of Edward & Jone Howard
		11	William son of John & Mary Lloyd
		11	Benjamin son of William & Ann Langhton

* Numerous entries of Blacks and Negroes will be found in this Register.

† Sir William Luckyn, Bart., was son of Sir Capel Lucking, Bart., of Messing Hall, Essex, created a Baronet June 2, 1660, by Mary, eldest daughter of Sir Harbottle Grimston, Speaker of the House of Commons. He married at St. Peter's, Cornhill (see Marriages *post*), on December 1, 1681, Mary, dau. of Mr. Alderman Sherrington, of that Parish. This "Herbotle," his son and successor, died unmarried in 1736.

Yeare.	Month.	Day.	Names.
1684	June	1	Thomas son of Abraham & Jane Hemingway
	May	18	Thomas son of Rich^d & Mart. Drafgate
	June	8	Mynn dau. of ffrancis & Elizabeth Kirby
		8	Mathew son of William & Rachel Wonham
		15	Hugh son of Lewis & Jane Willson
		15	Elizabeth dau. of John & Sarah ffilewood
		22	William son of Andrew & Bridget Yates
		29	Mary dau. of Richard & Elizabeth Harcourt
	July	6	John son of Richard & Joyce Miller
		27	Jacobus son of Edward & Martha Pitts
	August	10	Philippia dau. of William & Philippia Chase
		16	Bridged dau. of Richard & Hester Bartlett
		31	John son of Philip & Mary ffincher
	September	2	Susana dau. of Oliver & Susana Andrews
		7	Martha dau. of Richard & Ann Mariot
		21	Thomas son of Randolph & Susan Vodrey
	November	1	Thomas Oldham, aged 21 years
		2	Elizabeth Dobson a maryed woman, about 30 years of age
		21	Henry son of James & Mary Latham
		23	John son of John & Mary Drury
	December	7	Mary dau. of John & Mary ffern
		14	John son of John & Ann Starkey
		21	Richard Clement, aged about 22 years
		25	Samuel Byard, aged about 3 years
		26	Beathel dau. of Barmby & Elizabeth Weberd, aged 9 years
		26	Elizabeth dau. of Barmby & Elizabeth Weberd, aged 2 years
	January	4	Goodlife dau. of Henry & Rebecca Murry
		5	Samuell son of Thomas & Elizabeth Lardner
		6	Elizabeth dau. of Thomas & Hannah Leach
		18	Henry Tony, a Negro about 20 years of age
		18	Elizabeth . . . . a maried woman
		20	John son of Henry & Bridget Palmer
		25	William son of William & Elizabeth Hardy
	February	1	James son of James & Martha Branch
		13	Thomas son of William & Lea Holyday
		13	Mary dau. of William & Mary Paget
	March	4	Nathaniel son of Samuell & Elizabeth Clarke
		8	Sarah dau. of Thomas & Elizabeth ffreeman
		8	James son of James & Debora Vtburt
		8	James son of Ralph & Mary Palmer
		15	William son of Joseph & Ann Arey
		15	Walter son of ffrancis & Elizabeth Kerby
1685	April	6	John son of John & Hannah Parrot
		8	Maria dau. of Benjamin & Mary Thorowgood
	May	10	Jane Black, aged about 20 years
	July	5	Martha dau. of John & Susan Pott
		12	Hannah dau. of Thomas & Debora Salter
		12	Mary dau. of John & Sarah Wiburne
		21	Elizabeth dau. of John & Elizabeth Howard
		26	Katherine dau. of Coling & Sarah Bendy
			Mary dau. of Thomas & Elizabeth Couse
	August	9	William son of John & Sarah ffilewood
		16	Jane dau. of Abraham & Jane Hemingway
		21	Woodward son of Henry & Ann Rosser
	September	8	Dulsebella dau. of Bartholomew & Sarah Pigot
		10	Elizabeth dau. of Simond & Ann Linch
		20	Elizabeth dau. of Thomas & Elizabeth Willcox

Years.	Month.	Day.	Names.
1685	September	27	Richard son of Richard & Elizabeth Parrot
		27	Elizabeth dau. of Thomas & Judeth Paine
	October	1	Sarah dau. of William & Mary Brookman
		8	Heritage son of Heritage & Susana Hartford
		25	Lenard son of Lenard & Mary Short
		28	Grace Rose of the parish of S^t . . . . about 20 years old
	December	1	Dorithy dau. of Richard & Martha Wareing
		6	Mary dau. of John & Margaret Price
	January	11	John son of John & Susanna Wareing
		14	John son of Randolph & Susan Vodry
		17	Elizabeth dau. of Thomas & Elizabeth Lardner
		28	Barbara dau. of Thomas & Martha Hunsdowne
	February	7	An' Arrold a maried woman
		7	An dau. of William & Ann Layton
		7	Martha Nuttle, a maid about 20 years of age
		16	John son of John & Ann Starkey
		16	Rebecca dau. of Oliver & Susanna Andrews
	March	11	Ann dau. of John & Mary ffern
		13	James son of George & Hannah Smyth
		14	Elizabeth dau. of Thomas & Mary Sweeting
		21	John son of John & Auise Gwilliam
		21	John son of John & Ann Dauson
1686		28	Barbary Blunt, aged about 16 years
	April	13	Rebecca Coventry, aged about 18 years
		18	William son of Charles & Katherine Domvill
		20	James son of Joseph & ffrances Goodale
		25	Mary dau. of William & Alice Pepys
	May	17	Mary dau. of William & Alice Longmore
		23	John son of Richard & Elizabeth Shaw
		28	Mary Hull
		28	Leah Lovell
		30	Elizabeth dau. of Samuell & Elizabeth Clarke
	June	6	Susanna Winkle, aged about 17 years
		13	Marjon Winckles, aged 13 years
		13	John Winckles, aged 8 years
		13	Ann Winckle, aged 6 years
		20	Thomas Bristow, aged 13 years
	July	4	Elizabeth dau. of John & Elizabeth Parrot
		11	Henry and John twins sons of Samvell & Ann Bothick
		16	Mary dau. of William & Elizabeth Hardy
		25	James son of James & Mary Smyth
		25	Hannah dau. of Charles & Mary Lane
		27	Stephen son of Henry & Mary Hartford
	August	10	Elizabeth dau. of Samvell & Elizabeth Black
		29	Henry son of Henry & Ann Rosser
	September	2	Elizabeth dau. of John & Augnes Carter
		7	ffrances dau. of John & Susan Pott
		26	William son of Thomas & Elizabeth ffreeman
		26	Jane dau. of William & Mary Brookeman
	October	7	Elizabeth dau. of William & Philipa Chase
		10	Peter son of Paul & Martha Person
	November	14	Elizabeth dau. of George & Susan Clarke
		14	Henry son of Henry & Ann Sanders
	December	16	Charles son of Charles & Ann Chappell
	January	9	Katherine Adams, aged about 18 years
		9	Vrsilla dau. of John & Vrsilla Tompson
		14	John son of Simond & Anne Linch

Years.	Month.	Day.	Names.
1686	January	23	Edward son of Edward & Jone Howard
		30	Elizabeth dau. of Joseph & Mary Barker
	February	17	Hannah dau. of Thomas & Hannah Leach
		18	Mary dau. of John & Elizabeth Cookes
		20	Richard son of Richard & Ann Marjot
	March	1	James son of Richard & Hester Bartlet
		10	Elizabeth dau. of Calverly & Dorithy Bewicke
		13	Thomas son of Thomas & Judeth Paine
		13	Elizabeth Good, aged about 20 years
		13	Martha dau. of James & Martha Branch
1687	April	7	Nathanel son of John & Lavine Gentry born March 19
	May	1	Philip, son of Joseph & ffrances Goodale
		8	Amey dau. of John & Amey Guillim
		16	Ann dau. of John & Katherine Blizard
	June	8	Robert son of George & Hannah Smyth
		12	James son of John & Sarah ffilewood
		15	Ann dau. of Rich^d & Martha Drafgate
		18	Jane dau. of Ralph & Mary Palmer
	July	10	James son of Thomas & Bridget Phips
		27	Jane dau. of William & Bridget Gardner
	Sep.	1	Susanna dau. of Abraham & Jane Hemingway
		17	Mary dau. of Nicholas & Mary Exton
	Nov.	4	Anne dau. of James & Debora Vtburd
		13	Charles son of Lewis & Jane Willson
		13	Susan dau. of Gilburt & Hannah Lacy
		20	Katharine dau. of Richard & Mary Ilive
		20	Sarah dau. of Walter & Ann Lane
		24	Benjamin son of John & Susanna Pott
		30	John son of John & Elizabeth Cooper Linen draper
	Jan.	1	Josua Browning, aged 21 years
		3	Benjamin son of Thomas & Ann Alford
		15	Samuel son of John & Eliz: Ingle
		29	Jane dau. of George & Susanna Clarke
		29	Rachel Wetherly, aged 21 years
		30	Elizabeth dau. of John & Mary fferne
	February	2	Anne dau. of William & Alice Langmore
	March	13	John son of Heritage Hartford
		22	Moses son of Edward & Rebecca Page
1688	April	8	Mary dau. of Edward & Elizabeth Burton
		26	Christopher son of Thomas & Elizabeth Lardner
	May	6	Elizabeth Wetherly, aged 18 years
		17	Mary dau. of William & Ann Layton
		21	Thomas son of John & Elizabeth Cooke
	June	6	John son of Thomas & Han' Leech
		17	John son of John & Sarah Tureby
		17	Joseph son of Joseph & Mary Barker
		17	Elizabeth dau. of John & Joan'a Butler
		24	Ann, a Black, aged about 20 years
	July	1	Thomas son of Thomas & Martha Hunsdon
		15	James son of James & Hanah Serjant
		16	Edmund son of John & ffrances Gardner
		16	John son of William & Philipa Chase
	August	2	Jane dau. of John & Elizabeth Parrat
		12	Mary dau. of Philip & Mary Plimshaw
		12	Ann dau. of Thomas & Elizabeth Willcox
		12	Ann dau. of William & Mary Pagget
	October	14	Henry son of Richard & Mary Cordwent

Years.	Month.	Day.	Names.
1688	October	18	Jane dau. of Calverley & Dorithy Bewicke
		19	Sarah dau. of Abraham & Jane Hemeingway
	November	4	Elizabeth dau. of Joseph & ffrances Goodale
		4	Elizabeth Chiptis, a person of years
	December	3	William son of William & Bridget Gardiner
		6	Charles son of Charles & Mary Lane
		9	William son of John & Susana Pepys
		31	ffolk son of Henry & Ann Rosser
	January	1	Mary dau. of John & Mary Loyd
		10	John son of Rich^d & Martha Drafgate
		27	Elizabeth dau. of James & Martha Branch
	February	13	John son of Thomas & Ann Alford
		15	William son of John & Mary Rodes
	March	10	Richard son of Thomas & Judeth Paine
1689		31	Elizabeth dau. of John & Sarah fflewood
	April	27	George son of George & Susan Clarke
		27	Sarah Peters, a foundling
		28	Mary dau. of Richard & Mary Ilive
	May	2	William son of John & Susan Pott
		2	James son of George & Hannah Smyth
		29	John son of John & Agnes Carter
		29	Richard son of John & Johan'a Butler
		30	William son of Thomas & Elizabeth Larner
	July	21	John son of Daniel & Mary Medows
	August	4	Mary dau. of James & Elizabeth Ashton
		20	Benjamin son of John & Sarah Parker
	September	8	Samuell son of Philip & Mercy Stubbs
		15	Nathaniell son of Joseph & Susan Taylor
		22	Richard son of Richard & Katharine Wing
		26	George son of Thomas & Alice Simco
		29	Sarah dau. of Richard & Sarah Young
	October	15	Anna Maria dau. of John & Elizabeth Cooper
		10	Elizabeth dau. of John & Elizabeth Cookes
	November	5	Lancelot son of Lancelot & Jane Skinner
		16	John son of George & Mary Betts
	December	3	John son of John & Ann Eales
		22	Ann dau. of John & Barbury Sparkes
	January	5	Joseph Hanson, aged about 20 years
		14	Robert son of Calverly Bewick & Dorothy his wife
		21	Elizabeth dau. of Robert ffowler & Elizabeth his wife
	Feb.	16	Lydia dau. of Thomas Daffin & Mary his wife, aged 18 years
		27	Elizabeth dau. of Richard Cordwent & Mary his wife
		28	Mary dau. of Thomas & Elizabeth Haughton
1690	March	25	Elizabeth dau. of John Lloyd & Mary his wife
		30	Henry son of Henry & Mary Hartford
		30	Thomas son of William & Anne Tirrell *alias* Turtle
	April	6	Anne dau. of John & Anne ffreeman
		12	Ellen dau. of John & Mary ffern
		17	Margaret dau. of Thomas & Bridget Phipps
		20	Anne daughter of Richard & Elizabeth Parrott, was received into the Church, but baptized the second day
		24	Lewis son of William & Mary Wood
		25	Hannah dau. of John & Mary Porter, aged about 20 years, from St Giles Cripplegate
	May	16	Richard Peeters found in Leaden Hall market
		31	Elizabeth Peeters found upon Mr Parrots stall, haberdacer in leaden Hall streete

Years.	Month.	Day.	Names.
1690	June	3	Ann Rosser dau. of Henery & Ann his wife, Barber in Grace Church Street
		5	Cathrine dau. of Abraham Brand & Dulcibella his wife
	.	24	Mary Peeters found in Peeters Aley
		24	Elizabeth Peeters found in Leaden Hall market
	July	6	Isaac Butler son of John & Marcy his wife
		12	Joshua Smallman son of John & Mary his wife
		13	Hanna Sergent dau. of James & Hanna his wife
		13	Elizabeth Hunsdon, dau. of Thomas & Elizabeth his wife
	August	1	Hanna Fillewood dau. of John & Sara his wife
		21	Alexander son of Alexander & Mary Parratt
		31	William Mead son of George & Mary Nelson
	September	7	Elizabeth dau. of Thomas & Elizabeth Rea
	October	7	Elizabeth dau. of John & Mary Rodes
	November	8	Jane dau. of Lancelot & Jane Skinner
		16	David son of Robert & Susanna Brook
		23	Elizabeth dau. of John & Anne Appleyard
	December	11	Elizabeth dau. of John & Elizabeth Cooper
		21	Anne dau. of John & Anne Eales
		25	Mary Barker aged about 23, of the parish of St Edmund Lumbard Str.
	January	8	Richard son of George & Elizabeth Burnham
		11	Daniel son of Henry & Anne Sanders
		22	Barbara dau. of Calverly & Dorothy Bewick
	February	5	William son of John & Elizabeth Cookes
		15	Alice Sturges of St Botolphs Bishopsgate, aged about 22 years
		15	Thomas son of Edward & Rebecca Robinson
		26	Judeth taken up in Bishopsgate street
	March	1	Joseph son of Joseph & Mary Barker
		1	Philidelphia dau. of Crane & Katherine Complin
		8	Anne Weatherall of St Botolph, Bishopsgate, aged about 18 years
		14	Sarah dau. of Thomas Wallis of Stepny
1691		31	Hannah dau. of Hannah Smith widow of George Smith, lately decd
	April	5	Mary dau. of John & ffrances Gardiner
		16	Charles son of John & Susanna Pott
		16	Anne dau. of William & Priscilla Grove
		19	Elizabeth dau. of James & Elizabeth Smith
		26	Sarah dau. of John & Anne ffreeman
		28	Margaret dau. of John & Mary Lloyd
	May	3	Elizabeth dau. of Abraham & Jane Hemingway
		26	Samuel taken up in St Peters Alley
	June	10	Sarah dau. of William & Bridget Gardiner, Merchant
		13	Peter taken up in Corbits Court
	July	10	Hester taken up in Corbits Court
		15	Jonathan son of John & Eliz. Ingle
	August	2	Robert son of Robert & Elizabeth ffowler, Hosier
		4	James son of Thomas & Anne Alford, Vintner
		12	Thomas son of Thomas & Debora Salter, Linnen Draper
		21	Elizabeth dau. of Thomas & Alice Simcoe, Upholdster
		25	James & Elizabeth Children of Henry & Anne Rosser, Barber
	September	3	John son of William & Mary Wood
		4	John son of John & Sarah Atkins
	October	11	Mary dau. of John & Sarah Parker

Years.	Month.	Day.	Names.
1691	November	7	Martha ffitzwilliams, aged 87 years
		8	Sarah dau. of Nathan & Sarah Cordell
		29	Mary dau. of John & Barbara Sparkes
	December	5	Martin Sarch, aged 16 or 17 years
		5	William son of Richard & Alice Partridge
		9	John son of Thomas & Bridgett Phipps
		21	Elizabeth, a foundling
	January	17	Thomas son of William & Mary Brookeman
		17	Robert son of Robert & Susan Brooke
		17	William son of Leonard & Mary Short
		24	Susanna dau. of John & Anne Appleyard, Grocer
	February	14	Sarah Robinson, aged about 20
		16	Susanna dau. of John & Elisabeth Cookes
		18	Samuel son of John & Elizabeth Cooper, Linnen Draper
		25	William son of Lancelot & Jane Skinner, Cheesemonger
		25	John son of Humphrey & Mary Overton, Upholder
		28	John son of Henry & Anne Sanders, porter
	March	3	Margaret dau. of John & Anne Pricklove, Distiller
		19	Ursula dau. of Daniel & Mary Hewlin, Baker
1692	April	6	Joseph Isintree, a Black aged 17 years
		10	Simon son of Henry & Mary Hartford, Pewterer
		16	Abraham (being the second son of that name) son of Abraham & Jane Hemingway
	May	22	Edward son of John & Sarah Mould, Leather Gilder
		27	John son of John Crofts, Upholster, & Mary his wife
	July	14	Judeth dau. of William Rowlandson & Judeth his wife
		15	Bithiah Knight an adult person, aged about 22 years
		15	Susanna dau. of John Pott & Susanna his wife
		22	Thomas son of Calverley Bewick, Grocer, & Dorothy his wife
	August	23	Philip son of Philip ffincher, Ironmonger, & Mary his wife
	September	4	Elizabeth dau. of Robert Brooman, Cordwainer, & Elizab' his wife
		5	Eliza. dau. of Richard & Martha Drafgate
	October	18	Hannah dau. of Richard Woolley, Clerk, & Elizabeth his wife
		17	Mary ffarthing of St Mary White Chappell, aged about 27 years
	November	4	William son of Thomas Brown, Callender, & Martha his wife
		10	John son of John Lloyd, perfumer, & Mary his wife
		17	William son of William Clarke, Victualler or Cooke, & Anne his wife
		20	John son of John Mirfin, Butcher, & Rebecca his wife
	December	4	William son of John Parker, Waxchandler, & Sarah his wife
		4	Mary dau. of James Branch, Poulterer, & Martha his wife
		5	Sarah an Infant taken up in Corbits Court
		5	William taken up in the same Court
		18	Mary dau. of Joseph Barker, Innholder, & Mary his wife
		15	Diana dau. of Henry Rosser, Barber, & Anne his wife
		21	Mary dau. of Robert ffowler, Hosier, & Elizabeth his wife
		26	Mary dau. of William Higgs, a Lodger, & Catherine his wife
	January	8	Edward son of Robert Cage, ffishmonger, & Jane his wife
		29	ffrancis Swain, aged 34 years
	February	5	Daniel Anderson, aged 24 years
		5	Anne Anderson, aged 20 years

Yeare.	Month.	Day.	Names.
1692	February	5	Mary Anderson aged 17 years
	March	4	John son of William Vanlute, Merch^t, & Sarah his wife
		4	John son of John Purchass, Poulterer, & Penelope his wife
		18	Elizabeth dau. of Humphry Overton, Upholdster, & Mary his wife
		19	Richard son of John Sparks, Stocking Weaver, & Barbara his wife
1693		26	Thomas son of Robert Brooke, Victualler, & Susanna his wife
		26	Anne dau. of Richard Arnold, ffruiterer, & Anne his wife
		80	Jane dau. of John Cooper, Linendrap^r, & Elizabeth his wife
	April	18	Katherine dau. of Lancelott Skinner (& Jane his wife), Cheesemong^r
		18	Rebecca dau. of Roger Chapman (& Elizabeth his wife), Packer
		18	Richard & Anthony twins sons of Richard Moy (& Mary his wife), Leatherseller
		22	Hannah dau. of Joseph Smith & Anne his wife
		30	Thomas son of Thomas Warham (& Mary his wife), Cooke
	May	8	Anne dau. of William Grove (& Priscilla his wife), a Porter
		21	Parthena Robinson aged near 17 yeares, a stranger
		21	Mary dau. of Thomas Andrews, Butcher, & Mary his wife
		23	James & George sons of James Bowie & Mary his wife, Lodgers
		28	Anne dau. of George Burnham, porter, & Elizabeth his wife
		28	Sarah dau. of Thomas Pain, Upholdster, & Judith his wife
	June	8	Robert son of John Beard, Gent., & Katherine his wife
		17	Mary dau. of William Chase, Haberdasher of small wares, & Philip his wife
		23	Elizabeth dau. of John Cole (& Mary his wife), Victualler
	July	6	Joseph son of Calverly Bewick, Gro', & Dorothy his wife
		11	Mary dau. of Thomas Alford, Vintner, & Anne his wife
		31	Eleanor dau. of Thomas Phipps, Linnendraper, & Bridget his wife
	Aug.	8	Katherine dau. of John Crofts, Upholdster, & Mary his wife
	September	2	William son of William Rowlanson (& Judith his wife), a Tapster at the Spread Eagle Inn, Received into the Church October 1st
		3	Rachell Maiden of St Clements Danes, aged 19 years
		19	Theodosia, dau. of William Tilly (& Theodosia his wife), Cabinet Maker
		21	Richard son of Richard Pateridge (& Alice his wife), Brasier
	October	6	Charles son of William Wood (& Mary his wife), Surgeon
		22	Sarah dau. of Richard Stockhall (& Sarah his wife), Cooke
		26	James son of John Lloyd (& Mary his wife), Perfumer
	November	12	Richard son of William Clarke (& Anne his wife), Cooke
		20	Mary dau. of John Mirfin (& Rebecca his wife), Butcher
	December	24	Elizabeth dau. of Richard Taylor (& Agnes his wife), porter
	January	21	Elizabeth Ward, aged about 25 years
		21	Catherine dau. of William Watson & Elizabeth his wife
		23	Hugh taken up in Leadenhall Street

Years.	Month.	Day.	Names.
1693	February	1	Mary dau. of Humphry Overton (& Mary his wife), Upholder
		4	Zachariah Morgan, aged about 27 years
		14	George son of George Pedley & Susanna his wife
	March	4	Catherine dau. of John Sculthorp & Elizabeth his wife, Barber
		6	Jane dau. of John Pott & Susanna his wife
		15	Robert son of Robert ffowler (& Elizabeth his wife), Hosier
1694		29	Elizabeth dau. of Philip ffincher, Ironmonger, & Mary his wife
	April	18	Roseanna Johnson a Negro
	May	13	Edward son of John Mould, Leather gilder, & Sarah his wife
		27	Elizabeth Holmes of St Vedast's, *alias* ffosters, aged about 20 years
		29	William son of Thomas Smith, Butcher, & Sarah his wife
	June	4	Anne Charnock of St Mary White Chappell, aged about 40 years
		2	Edward son of John Sparkes, Stockin weaver
		8	Elizabeth dau. of Thomas Warham, Cooke, & Mary his wife
		29	Joan Young, of St Paul Shadwell, aged 21 years
	July	2	Roger son of Roger Chapman, Packer, & Elizabeth his wife
		4	Edmund son of Thomas Alford, Vintner, & Anne his wife
	August	21	Calverly Bewick son of Calverly Bewick, Grocer, & Dorothy his wife
	September	3	Susanna dau. of Nathaniel Cam (& ffrances his wife), Cook
		30	Daniel son of Daniel ffordham, Clothworker, & Catherine his wife
	October	1	Benjamin son of John Clements, ffishmonger, & Susanna his wife
		14	Sarah dau. of Edward Timson, Butcher, & Mary his wife
		22	Rachell dau. of Thomas Marshall & Elizabeth his wife, of St Mary Whitechappell, aged 6 years
	November	4	John Ketteridge of St Botolph Bishopsgate, aged about 19 years
		6	John son of Lancelot Skinner, Cheesemonger, & Jane his wife
		8	Thomas son of Thomas Andrews, Butcher, & Mary his wife
		11	Elizabeth dau. of Hen: Harford, Pewterer, & Mary his wife
		21	William son of William Brookman (& Mary his wife), a Poulterer
		27	Anne taken up in St Peters Alley
	December	1	Edward son of Edward Bull & Elenor his wife, a stranger
		6	Susanna dau. of Jacob Russel, Strong water man, & Elizabeth his wife
		25	Anne dau. of Thomas Nicholls & Mary his wife
		30	John Asby, a youth aged between 16 & 17 years
	January	1	Cyrus-Peters Collico servt to Lancelot Skinner, Cheesemonger, aged about 17 years A Black
		13	James son of James Branch, Poulterer, & Martha his wife
		14	Robert son of Robert Hart, Tobacconist, & Anne his wife

Years.	Month.	Day.	Names.
1694	January	15	Martha dau. of Thomas Paine, Upholdster, & Judith his wife
		20	Jane dau. of John Tilly, Cabinet maker, & Theodosia his wife
	February	21	Mary Smith of Isleworth, aged 20 years
		21	Elizabeth dau. of Alexander Parrott, Haberdasher of Hats, & Mary his wife
		24	Henry Marson of St Botolph Aldgate, aged 20 years
	March	10	Rebecca Billing of St Botolph Bishopsgate, aged 22 years
		17	Sarah dau. of Richard Arnold, fruiterer, & Sarah his wife
		19	Samuel son of Enoch Porter, ffactor, & Mary his wife
1695	April	28	John son of Benjamin Elford, Grocer, & Lydia his wife
			Anne dau. of John Lloyd, perfumer, & Mary his wife
	May	6	James son of William Wood, Surgeon, & Mary his wife
		26	John taken up in Weighouse yard in Cornhill
		29	Hannah Stafford of St Pauls Shadwell, aged 38 years
		22	Richard son of Richard Stockhall (& Sarah his wife), Cooke
		30	William son of John Cooper, Linnen Draper, & Elizabeth his wife
	June	23	Thomas son of Thomas Warham, Cooke, & Mary his wife
	July	4	Jeremiah son of Jeremiah Robins, Victualler, & Rebecca his wife
		22	Hannah Jones, aged near 17 years
	August	16	Sarah dau. of John Gibson, Linen draper, & Sarah his wife
		18	Jane dau. of Richard Willcox (& Mary his wife), Butcher
	September	5	William son of John Cookes, Linen draper, & Elizabeth his wife
		8	Sarah dau. of John Smart, ffishmonger, & Sarah his wife
		29	Thomas son of William Darlston, Writing Master, & Arabella his wife
	October	6	John son of Richard Taylor, Porter, & Agnes his wife
		17	Elianor dau. of John Sparks (& Barbara his wife), Stocking Wea'
		30	Thomas son of Robert ffowler, Hosier, & Elizabeth his wife
	November	7	Dorothy dau. of Calverly Bewick, Gro'
	December	12	Samuel son of Lancelot Skinner, Cheesemonger, & Jane his wife
		23	Peter son of Thomas Phipps, Linendraper, & Bridget his wife
		30	William son of Richard Parteridge, Brasier, & Alice his wife
	January	28	Mary dau. of Robert (& Mary) Garbrand, Linendraper
	February	2	Congnard son of John & Theodosia Tilly, Cabinet Maker
		25	Catherine dau. of William (& Catherine) Gardiner, Mercht
	March	12	Martha dau. of Philip (& Mary) ffincher, Ironmonger
1696		29	John son of John (& Elizabeth) Sculthorpe, Barber
	April	7	Sarah dau. of William (& Philippa) Chase, Haberdasher of small wares
		7	Mary dau. of Charles & Mary Carter Cooper
		19	Elizabeth dau. of John Mould (& Sarah his wife), Leather gild'
		26	John son of John Clements (& Susanna his wife) ffishmonger
		29	John son of Edward Short (& Jane his wife) Leatherseller

Years.	Month.	Day.	Names.
1696	April	29	Sarah dau. of Thomas Andrews (& Mary his wife), Butcher
	May	18	Katherine an Infant taken up in Sugar loafe Alley in Bishopsgate Street
	July	23	Enoch son of Enoch Porter (& Sarah his wife), a Porter
	October	12	Beverly son of Elisha Dod & Mary his wife, Lodgers
		15	William son of William Wyat (& Sarah his wife), Iron-mong^r
		21	William son of Robert Woodny (& Alice his wife), Haberdasher of Hats
		25	Mary dau. of ffrancis Higginbotham & Rebecca his wife, Lodgers at Robert Pagets, Victuall^r
	November	3	Sarah dau. of Henry & Elizab' Stopps, Lodgers
		8	Elizabeth dau. of Edward Bethel, Packer, & Sarah his wife
		19	John son of Thomas Warham (& Mary his wife), Cooke
		11	Jane dau. of Alexander Parrot (& Mary his wife), Haberdasher of Hats
		26	Thomas son of Richard Taylor (& Agnes his wife), Porter
		29	Mary dau. of Richard Stockall (& Sarah his wife), Cook
		29	Elizabeth dau. of Robert Hart
	December	3	James son of Nicholas Jarvis (& Mary his wife), Poulterer
		8	Samuell son of Christopher Coney (& Anne his wife), Victu :
	January	14	Anne dau. of Benj. Elford (& Lydia his wife), Grocer
		22	Henry son of John fford, Polterer, & Sarah his wife
		22	Alice dau. of Richard Parteridg, Brasier, & Alice his wife
		31	Mary dau. of John Snart, ffishmonger, & Mary his wife
	February	25	Thomas son of Robert ffowler, Hosier, & Elizabeth his wife
		28	Richard son of Richard Arnold, fruiter^r, & Sarah his wife
			Thomas son of Thomas Pain, Upholdster, & Judith his wife
	March	19	Mary dau. of John Cooper, Linendraper, & of Elizabeth his wife
		23	Elizabeth dau. of Thomas Alford, Vintner, & Anne his wife
1697	April	4	Daniel son of Daniell ffordham, a Lodger, & Katherine his wife
		4	Esther dau. of John Cooper, Victualler, & Anne his wife
		18	Benjamin son of William (& Mary) Brookman, Poulterer
		26	William son of Robert Julian, ffactor, & Elizabeth his wife
		27	John son of John (& Sarah) Gibson, Linnendraper
		29	Mary dau. of Ezekiell Shewin, Shoemaker, & Mary his wife
	May	25	Mary dau. of Richard Jenings, Drugster, & Judeth his wife
	June	13	Elizabeth dau. of John Adams, fflaxman, dec^d by Elizabeth dau. of Robert Gainesford, Cutler, born May 29
		27	Mary dau. of Thomas Smith, Butcher, & Mary his wife
	August	7	Mary dau. of Lancelott Skinner, Cheesemonger, & Jane his wife
		17	William son of John Lloyd, perfumer, & Mary his wife
		29	William son of John Sparks (& Barbara his wife), Stocking weaver
	September	24	William son of Rebecca Sheepherd, begotten (as she saith) by William Stevenson, a Scot, a Surgeon at Sea
		26	John son of William Kettle, pattern drawer, & Anne his wife

Years.	Month.	Day.	Names.
1697	October	7	Robert son of Robert (& Mary) Garbrand, Linendraper
		15	William son of Philip (& Mary) ffincher, Ironmonger
		19	Elizabeth dau. of Robert (& Alice) Woodney, Haberdasher of Hats
		7	Anne Hardiman, aged about 85 years
	November	28	Jane dau. of Edward Short (& Jane his wife), Leatherseller
	December	8	John son of John Cookes (& Elizabeth his wife), Linendraper
	February	20	John son of Atwood Charke (& Mary his wife), Shoemaker, a Lodger
		24	Anne dau. of Humphry Patty (& Mary his wife), Butcher, a Lodger
		27	John son of John fford (& Sarah his wife), Poulterer, Lodgers
		27	Anne dau. of Richard Stockhall, Cooke, & Sarah his wife
		28	William son of Thomas Petty (& Elizabeth his wife), Cook
1698	March	31	Anne dau. of Richard Partridge (& Alice his wife), Brasier
	April	3	Rachell dau. of John Sculthorp (& Elizabeth his wife), Barber
		18	Katherine dau. of Thomas Ayloffe,* Dr of Laws, & Susanna his wife, Lodgers at Mr Roycrofts in Leadenhall Street
	May	8	Mary dau. of John Cooper, Victualler, & Anne his wife
	June	5	Richard son of Robert Wolfe, Distiller, & Sarah his wife
		5	Daniel fforsoo, a Blackmore, aged about 20 years
		22	Rebecca dau. of Thomas Warham (& Mary his wife), Cook
		28	Richard son of Richard Jenings, Drugster, & Judith his wife
	July	5	John son of Robert Hart, Strong waterman, & Anne his wife
		6	William son of Nicholas Jarvis, Polterer, & Mary his wife
		20	William son of Will. Kempster, Packer, & Mary his wife
		29	Edward son of William Lowther, Vintner, & Mary his wife
	August	25	Mary dau. of Willia' Wyatt, Ironmonger, & Sara' his wife
	September	30	Rebecca dau. of William Elliott, porter, & Rebecca his wife
	November	12	Edward Stanton aged 16 years and Sarah Stanton his sister aged 20 years
		26	John Philips a blackmoor aged 15 years
		27	Isaac son of Isaac Cole, Victualler, formerly a Confectionr, & Mary his wife
	December	1	Thomas son of Thomas Dowsland, Butcher, & Mary his wife
		20	Margaret dau. of Robert & Mary Garbrand
		22	Edward son of John Cookes, Linendraper, & Elizabeth his wife
	January	1	John son of John Cooley, Poulterer, & Hannah his wife
	February	20	Richard Richardson aged 26 years John & Dorcas taken up in the street
		25	Hannah wife of Henry Watts of St Michael Queenhith, aged about 28 years

* Son of James Ayloffe, of Melbourn, in Cambridgeshire, by his second wife Elizabeth, dau. of Thomas Penyston, Esq., of Rochester, and grandson of Sir William Ayloffe, of Braxted Magna, created a Baronet Nov. 25, 1612.

Years.	Month.	Day.	Names.
1698	March	18	Joseph Bowman from St Botolphs Algate, aged 19 years
		20	Edward son of George Allen, Packer, & Katherine his wife
		20	William son of Richard Stockall (& Sarah his wife), Cook
1699	April	11	Susanna dau. of Edward Bettell, Packer, & Sarah his wife
		11	Lewis son of Lewis Quignard (& Elizabeth his wife), a tapster at the Spread Eagle Inn
		19	William son of William Kettle, a pattern Drawer, & Anne his wife
		27	Elizabeth dau. of Richard (& Judith) Jennings, Drugster
	May	17	Lydia a ffoundling dead
		19	Sarah dau. of Robert (& Alice) Woodney, Haberdasher of Hats
		28	Sarah dau. of William (& Anne) Matthews, Taylor
	June	5	Rebecca Hawkins, an adult person from St Bridgets parish
		5	Elizabeth Collins, an adult person from Peckham
		12	William son of Thomas (& Mary) Smith, Butcher
	July	2	John son of John Cooper, Victual^r, & Agnes his wife
		4	Elizabeth dau. of Nicholas Jarvis (& Mary his wife), Poulterer
		7	George son of John Gibson (& Sarah his wife), Linen-draper
		9	Mary dau. of Robert Hart (& Anne his wife), Tobacconist
		25	James son of Robert ffowler (& Elizabeth his wife), Hosier
		25	Anne dau. of Nathaniel Norris (& Anne his wife), ffishmong^r
	August	8	Catherine dau. of Peter Motteux & Priscilla his wife, Lodgers
		17	Edward son of John Sparks (& Barbara his wife), Stocking weaver
		20	Mary dau. of Thomas Warham (& Mary his wife), Cook
			Henry son of John & Elizab : Bainham, Barb^r
	September	6	Mary dau. of Richard Partridge (& Alice his wife), Brasier
		17	Mary dau. of Benjamin Conley (& Martha his wife), Victualler
		26	David son of Samuell Lloyd (& Mary his wife), Shoemaker
	October	1	Rebecca dau. of Thomas Pain (& Judith his wife), Upholdster
		21	Phœbe dau. of Robert Garbrand (& Mary his wife), Linen draper
		29	John son of William (& Rebecca) Elliot, Porter
	November	26	Joseph son of William (& Mary) Brookman, Poulterer
	December	24	Elizabeth dau. of Nicholas (& Elisabeth) Thomas, ffishmonger
		24	Rebekah dau. of Henry (& Mary) Pike, Mariner
	March	17	ffrancis son of ffrancis (& Agnes) Clifton, Baker
		17	Lydia dau. of Benjamin (& Lydia) Elford, Grocer
		19	the Child was received into the Church
		23	Mary dau. of Jacob & Deborah Spooner
1700	April	14	Alice dau. of Richard Stockall (& Sarah his wife), Cook
	May	2	Sarah dau. of John Sculthorpe, Barber, & Elizabeth his wife
		29	Edward son of Richard Taylor, Porter, & Agnes his wife
	June	2	John Aurling of Stepny, aged 28
		30	Anna-Catherina dau. of ffrancis & Elizabeth Scampton, Cutler

Years.	Month.	Day.	Names.
1700	July	7	Mary Hollings, of St Botolphs Algate, aged 12 years

Years.	Month.	Day.	Names.
1700	July	7	Mary Hollings, of St Botolphs Algate, aged 12 years
		7	Elizabeth dau. of Robert Brooke, Tapster, & Jane his wife
		17	Causabon son of George ffairclough M.D. & Martha his wife
		21	Robert son of John Cooper, Victualler, & Anne his wife
		21	Robert Boswell of St Andrews Holborn, aged 19 years
	August	25	Robert son of Nicholas Jarvis, Poulterer, & Mary his wife
		25	Susanna dau. of William Hollyday, Tallow Chandler, & Mary his wife
	September	5	Isabell Katherine dau. of Peter Motteux (& Priscilla his wife), an Officer at the Post house
		15	James son of John Sparkes (& Barbara his wife), Stocking weaver
	October	11	John son of Robert Woodny (& Alice his wife), Haberd: of Hats
		20	William son of William Matthews (& Anne his wife), Tayl^r
	November	14	Sarah dau. of John Lloyd (& Mary his wife), Perfumer
		17	Anna dau. of Thomas Griffin (& Catherine his wife), Pack^r
	December	15	Alexander son of Alexander Parrott (& Mary his wife), Haberd^r
		16	Susanna dau. of John Brush (& Mary his wife), Gunsmith
		22	Elizabeth dau. of Thomas Smith (& Mary his wife), Butcher
		27	Thomas son of Thomas Edwards (& Elizabeth his wife), Linendraper
	January	1	Jane dau. of John Roberts (& Jane his wife), Vintner
		11	Thomas Stephens, a negro, aged about 22 years
		16	Sarah dau. of William Kettle (& Anne his wife), Pattern drawer
	February	1	Ambrose son of Thomas Warham (& Mary his wife), Cook
	March	3	Mary dau. of Thomas Jones (& Mary his wife), Millener
1701	April	2	Jane dau. of Richard Moy (& Mary his wife), Leatherseller
		13	Elizabeth dau. of John Bainham (& Elizabeth his wife), Barber
		15	William a Child taken up
		24	Anne dau. of George Scot & Priscilla his wife, Lodgers
	June	1	Agnes dau. of ffrancis Clifton (& Agnes his wife), Baker
		1	Ruth dau. of Robert Hart (& Anne his wife), Tobacconist
		9	Phebe dau. of Robert Garbrand (& Mary his wife), Linendraper
	July	16	Gentry a Child taken up in Corbits Court
		17	Sarah dau. of John Pierce (& Elizabeth his wife), Barber
		17	Mary dau. of Samuell Willobey (& Mary his wife), Weaver from Spittle ffields
	August	24	Leonard son of Richard (& Agnes) Taylor, a Porter
	September	27	Henrietta dau. of Henry (& Mary) Pike, Marriner
		19	Jane dau. of Peter (& Priscilla) Motteux, Lodgers
		28	Martha dau. of John (& Elizabeth) Cowper, Linendraper
		29	ffrances dau. of Richard Chase
	October	15	Mary dau. of Robert (& Alice) Woodney, Haberdasher of Hats
		28	ffrancis Cross taken up in the parish
	November	3	Edward son of Edward (& Ellenor) Crocker, Lodgers
		23	John son of Richard & Mary Benington, Victualler

Years.	Month.	Day.	Names.
1701	November	28	John son of John & Elizabeth Contrell, Poulterer
	December	7	ffrances dau. of John (& Elizabeth) Cooper, Cook
		19	Samuel son of John (& Anne) Orton, Lodgers
		21	William son of Richard & Mary Stockall, Cook
	January	1	Henry son of ffrancis Scampton
		25	Maria a Black aged about 33 years
	February	11	Joyce dau. of William (& Anne) Kettle, Haberdasher of small wares
		16	Elizabeth dau. of Richard & Elizabeth Allum, Stocking weaver
		22	Anne dau. of Edward & Jane Day, Leatherseller
		25	Catherine dau. of Edward & Bridget Serle, Merchant
	March	13	Elizabeth dau. of John & Hanna Hilliard, Mariner
1702	April	5	Joseph & Elizabeth, twins, son & dau. of John & Grace Horsley
		7	Hannah dau. of John & Elizabeth Bainham, Barber
		7	Joseph Trahern, Mariner, aged 27 years
	May	5	Elizabeth dau. of Thomas & Mary Smith, Butcher
		25	Martha dau. of Thomas & Mary Jones, Milliner
	June	13	Anne dau. of Philip & Elizabeth Presbury, Barber
		20	Mary Quinney, aged 24 years
		20	Sarah Cole, aged 17 years
		30	Thomas son of John & Elizabeth Sculthrop, Barber
	July	28	Richard son of Robert & Mary Garbrand, Linnen draper
	August	10	William son of Richard & Elizabeth Chase, Haberdasher
		27	Sarah dau. of George & Elizabeth Hagne, Victualler
		27	ffrances dau. of ffrancis & Agnes Clifton, Baker
		23	Anne dau. of William & Mary Holyday Tallow, Chandler
		30	James son of Christopher & Mary Martin, Carpenter
	September	2	Nathanael son of Nathanael & Anne Norris, ffishmonger
		20	Mary dau. of Henry & Elizabeth Burridge, Butcher
		24	Robert son of Robert & Anne Hart, Tobacconist
	October	6	ffrances dau. of John Looker, Surgeon, & Anne his wife
		10	Susanna dau. of John Pierce, Barber, & Elizabeth his wife
		20	Henry son of Henry Pike, Mariner, & Mary his wife
	November	1	Hannah dau. of Emmanuel, Vincent, Butcher & Sarah his wife
		29	Robert son of Edward Coke, a lodger, & Elenor his wife
		30	Mary dau. of Richard Trenance, Victualler, & Mary his wife
	December	13	William son of William Ellet, Porter, & Rebeka his wife
		15	Mary dau. of Henry Smith, Mariner, & Mary his wife, from St Ethelberges parish, aged 4 years
		25	Catherine dau. of Thomas Griffin, Packer, & Catherine his wife
	January	1	Richard son of Richard Partridge, Brasier, & Alice his wife
		3	Elizabeth dau. of Richard Stockhall, Cook, & Sarah his wife
		22	Lydia a foundlin taken up in the street
	February	3	Robert son of Robert Woodney, Haberdasher of Hats, & Alice his wife
		20	Peter a foundling
		16	Anna Maria dau. of John & Mary Brush, Gunsmith
	March	7	Anne-Margaret dau. of Nicholas & Mary Jarvis, Poulterer
		9	Christian dau. of John Cantrill (& Elizabeth his wife), Poulterer
		21	Catherine dau. of Wentworth Dilk, Apothecary, & Mary his wife

Years.	Month.	Day.	Names.
1702	March	14	ffrancis son of ffrancis Scampton, Turner, & Elizabeth his wife
1703	April	21	Joseph son of John Purchass, Poulterer, & Penelope his wife
		23	Alice dau. of William Langmore, Upholdster, & Elizabeth his wife
		30	Martha dau. of Charles Norris (& Margaret his wife), Box maker
	June	14	Catherine a foundling taken up in
		20	Joseph son of Jacob Briggs & Dorothy his wife, Victualler
		27	Morley son of Robert & Rachell Matthews, Victualler
	July	28	Bridget dau. of Edward & Bridget Serle, Merchant
	August	3	Elizabeth dau. of John & Elizabeth Bainham
		8	Richard son of Richard & Margaret Benington, Victualler
		16	Mary dau. of John & Hannah Cowley, Poulterer
		29	Lætitia dau. of William & Anne Kettle, Haberdasher
		29	Alice dau. of Richard & Agnes Taylor, Porter
	September	2	ffrancis son of Matthew & Anne Joyner, Shoemaker
		2	Mary & Elizabeth twin daughters of John & Mary Martin
		9	Sibylla dau. of Thomas & Elizabeth Edwards, Linen draper
		2	John son of Richard & Elizabeth Chase, Haberdasher
	October	7	Judith dau. of Matthew & Mary-Anne Hebert, Mercer
		8	Alice a ffoundling taken up in
		14	ffrances dau. of James & Anne Biggs, Lodgers
		24*	John son of Emanuell & Sarah Vincent, Butcher, Lodgers
	November	5	John son of John & Elinor Naseby, Butcher, Lodgers
		7	Richard son of Henry & Elizabeth Burridge, Butcher
		14	Thomas son of Alexander & Hannah Crudge, Vintner
		18	Anna dau. of George & Elizabeth Haigh, Victualler
	December	9	Edward son of Robert & Mary Garbrand, Linnen draper
	January	23	Sarah dau. of Thomas & Mary Smith, Butcher
	February	1	Mary dau. of William & Mary Malden, Patten Maker
		18	Martha dau. of Richard & Martha Trenance, Victualler
		18	John son of Thomas & Magdelen Grant, Victualler
1704	April	13	Luke son of Martin James (& Elizabeth his wife), Gent., Lodgers
	May	22	Thomas son of Edward & Catherin Ellet, Barber
		24	Anne dau. of William & Mary Bull, ffishmonger
	June	4	Charles son of John & Elizabeth Cantrell, Poulterer
		4	Rachell dau. of John & Mary Day
		30	Robert son of Robert & Martha Porter
	July	6	Benjamin son of Nicholas & Elizabeth Thomas, ffishmonger
		21	Anne dau. of Robert & Alice Woodney, Haberdasher of Hats
		30	Jane dau. of William & Susanna Simons, a Butcher
		31	Morley son of Thomas & Martha Unwin, a Grocer
	August	13	Joseph son of Richard & Agnes Taylor, a Porter
		20	George & Anne Twins son & dau. of John & Sarah Snart, an Officer at one of the Counters
	September	3	Richard son of Richard son of Richard & Sarah Stockhall, Victuʳ
		14	John son of John & Mary Woodley
	October	15	Mary dau. of George & Mary Tudsbury
	November	21	Elizabeth dau. of Richard & Elizabeth Chace, Haberdasher

* The Register from October 24, 1704, to March 16, 1722, is subscribed "John Waugh, D.D., Parson." He was Bishop of Carlisle, and was buried here on Nov. 3, 1734. (See Burials, *post.*)

Years.	Month.	Day.	Names.
1704	November	26	George son of William & Anne Matthew
		27	Bridgett dau. of Elizabeth & John Waugh D.D., & Rector of St Peters, Cornhill, Born Nov. 16
		28	William son of William & Eliz. Langmore, Upholster
	December	31	Robert son of John & Elizabeth Sculthrope, Barber
	January	3	Elizabeth Peters
		30	Rebekah dau. of John & Mary Evans, a Stranger
	February	4	Thomas son of William & Anne Kettel, Haberdasher
		19	Elizabeth dau. of Christopher & Mary Martin
1705	March	25	Elizabeth dau. of John & Elizabeth West
	April	1	Elizabeth dau. of John & Mary Day
		2	Sarah Dodman, aged 27 years
		15	Charles son of Thomas & Mary Smith
		26	John son of Edward & Jane Day
	May	18	Sarah dau. of Walter & Hannah Adamson, Gentl.
		20	John son of William & Mary Bull, Fishmonger
	July	13	John son of John & Hannah Riseing
		28	James son of Benjamin & Mary Phillips, Barber
	August	13	John son of John & Eliz. Bainham, Barber
	September	2	John son of Charles & Ann Dumvile
		2	Katherine dau. of Richard & Sarah Stockall, Cook
		18	Richard son of John & Elizabeth Frampton, Linen draper
		30	Samuel son of Francis & Agnes Clifton
	October	7	Patience dau. of Richard & Agnes Taylor
		7	Anne dau. of John & Susanna Adee, Free poulterer
		16	William son of Thomas & Katherine Griffin, packer
		24	Richard son of Richard & Elizabeth Chase, Tobacconist
	November	11	William son of Richard & Elizabeth Cowdry, Feltmaker
		11	Charles son of John & Elizabeth Haigh
		20	Alice dau. of William & Elizabeth Langmore, Upholster
		23	John son of John & Anne Gore, Apothecary
		28	Alder son of John & Elizabeth Cantrell, poulterer
		30	Hannah dau. of Alexander & Hannah Crudge, Vintner
1706	April	8	Mary dau. of Thomas & Magdalen Grant
		11	Richard son of Nicholas & Mary Gervice
		14	Edward son of John & Frances Nasby
		18	Hannah dau. of Robert & Alice Woodney
		18	Mary Cotten, aged about 21 years
	May	8	John son of William & Sarah Hare
	June	6	Sarah dau. of Richard & Alice Partridge, Brasier
		6	Jane dau. of William & Mary Molden, patten-maker
		11	Martha dau. of Richard & Anne Mount, Tayler
	August	3	Hanna dau. of Christopher & Mary Martin
	September	4	Katherine dau. of Richard & Isabel Waylett
		22	Samuel son of Francis & Agnes Clifton
	October	8	Isaac son of Henry & Hannah Sharpe
		9	Elizabeth dau. of John & Anne Gore
		13	Richard son of Richard & Mary Stockall
	November	5	Mary dau. of Richard & Elizabeth Chase
		10	Mary dau. of Charles & Anne Domvile
		21	George son of William & Elizabeth Langmore
	December	5	Elizabeth dau. of Zephaniah & Sarah Page
	January	2	Martin son of Thomas & Martha Unwin
		12	Ruth dau. of Robert & Anne Hart
	February	6	Anne dau. of William & Catherine Barton
		9	Edward son of John & Jane Swallow
		20	Elizabeth dau. of William & Anne Kettle

Years.	Month.	Day.	Names.
1707	May	4	Ursula dau. of William & Elizabeth Martin
	July	9	Samuel son of Robert & Alice Woodney, Haberdasher
		15	John son of John & Susanna Adee
	August	12	Henry & Philip sons of Henry & Hannah Sharpe
		12	Thomas son of John & Elizabeth Bainham, Barber
		28	Elizabeth dau. of Thomas & Katherine Griffin
	September	2	Martha dau. of John & Mary Day
	October	12	Matthew son of Matthew & Anne Heber
	November	11	Anne dau. of Henry & Elizabeth Ford, Barber
		21	Elizabeth dau. of John & Elizabeth Gore, Apothecary
	December	14	Edward son of Edward & Bridgett Searle, Merchant
		23	Sarah dau. of Thomas & Sarah Oland
	February	2	John son of John & Frances Nesby
	March	7	Anne dau. of John & Margarett Parsons
		20	Anne dau. of Charles & Anne Donvile
		30	Lancelot son of Thomas & Martha Unwin, Groser
1708*	April	4	George son of Richard & Sarah Stockell
		11	Sarah dau. of Michael & Jane Gregory
	May	9	Elizabeth dau. of Samuel & Susanna Christie
		16	William son of Roger & Rebeckah Walter
	June	6	Elizabeth dau. of John & Elizabeth Cantrill
	July	6	William son of Zephaniah & Sarah Page
		16	George son of Richard & Elizabeth Chase
	October	2	Richard son of Richard & Isabel Waylet
	December	17	Margarett dau. of Anthony & Anne Ferris
		23	Frances dau. of Thomas & Frances Warham
		26	Elizabeth dau. of Daniel & Elizabeth Smith
	January	11	Thomas son of Thomas & Catherine Griffin
		26	William son of William & Catherine Barton
	February	2	Thomas son of Robert & Alice Woodney
		27	Mary dau. of Charles & Mary Dauling
	March	11	Dennis Justus Beck son of Rachell & Justus Beck
		19	Mary dau. of Edward & Bridget Searle
		22	Jane Peters a Foundling
1709	April	5	John son of William & Elizabeth Langmore
		17	Elizabeth dau. of Charles & Anne Donvil
		19	William son of William & Susanna Simons, Butcher
		21	Thomas son of John & Francis Nesby
		28	Richard son of Anthony & Mary Wybird, poulterer
	May	8	James son of John & Elizabeth Buchanan, Haberdasher of Small Wares
	June	14	John son of Charles & Sarah Hoyle, Leather-Seller
		17	Samuel son of Henry & Hannah Sharpe, Brazier
	July	8	James son of Richard & Elizabeth Chase
		19	Howard son of Zephaniah & Sarah Page, Distiller
		24	Richard son of John & Susanna Edee
	September	14	John son of Christopher & Mary Imber, Shoemaker
		30	Sarah dau. of Moses & Sarah Robins, Confectioner
	November	10	William son of John & Elizabeth Bainham, Barber
		18	James son of William & Anne Kettle
		18	Elizabeth dau. of Edward & Mary Mitchell
		20	Eden dau. of Michael & Jane Gregory, Barber
		27	Mary dau. of John & Elizabeth Cantrill
	December	11	John son of John & Elizabeth Reeves
			Robert son of Henry & Elizabeth Forde

* Sic.

Years.	Month.	Day.	Names.
1709	December	28	John son of Samuel & Susanna Cristie, Turner
	January	12	John son of James & Sarah Harriman, Lodger
	January	20	Sarah dau. of Wᵐ & Elizabeth Westbrook
		29	George son of Jacob & Margaret Hayes
	February	15	Sarah Peters a Foundlin
1710	March	26	James son of Benjamin & Elizab. Taylor
	April	2	Ann dau. of Daniel & Elizabeth Murfin
		10	Ann dau. of John & Ann Looker
		10	George & Anne Peters, two foundlings
		23	John son of Richard & Sarah Stockall, Cook
		30	Mary dau. of Roger & Rebecka Walter
	May	16	John son of John & Hannah Rising
		21	Thomas son of John & Margarett Parsons
	June	80	Susanna Jones an Adult of Sᵗ Dunstans Stepney
	August	5	Joyce dau. of John & Elizabeth Buchanan, Haberdasher
		7	Mary dau. of Anthony & Mary Wybird, poulterer
		20	Johanna dau. of Edward & Jane Day, Victualler
		25	Robert son of Thomas & Frances Warham, Cook
	September	9	Charles son of Richard & Elizabeth Chase
	October	29	Pagget son of Thomas & Susanna Salisbury
		30	Sarah dau. of John & Sarah Crook, Butcher
	November	9	Abraham, Isaac & Jacob Peters, three Foundlings
		26	Elizabeth dau. of Edward & Mary Mitchell
	December	11	Sarah dau. of Michael & Jane Gregory, Barber
		22	Slayfield son of John & Mary Marsh, Barber
	February	9	Mary dau. of Charles & Mary Chapman
		25	Elizabeth dau. of Thomas & Elizabeth Kelly
1711	April	8	Dorothy dau. of Benjamin & Elizabeth Taylor
		4	Susanna dau. of John & Elizabeth Potts, Oyleman
		17	Mary dau. of Robert & Elizabeth Nicholl
	July	18	Sarah dau. of John and Rising (sic)
		18	John son of Robert & Rebecca Walter
		21	John son of John & Mary Goodwin
	August	5	John son of John & Anne Matthews, Linnen drapʳ
		9	Catherine dau. of Justus & Rachell Beck
		18	Elizabeth dau. of John & Ann Looker, Surgeon
		20	Matthias son of Thomas & Martha Unwin, Groser
		21	Johannah dau. of John & Elizabeth Bainham
	September	16	John son of John & Sarah Crook, Lodger
		19	Samuel son of Samuel & Bridgett Beachcroft, Upholsterer
	November	20	Rachel dau. of Richard & Frances Woolls, Lodger
		21	William son of Michael & Jane Gregory, Lodger
	December	2	Elizabeth dau. of William & Mary Costin, Glazier
		21	John son of William & Susannah Wood, Lodger
	January	3	Howard son of Zephania & Sarah Page, distiller
		10	Benjamin son of John & Ann Gore, Apothecary
	February	6	Elizabeth dau. of Miles & Eliz. Barnes, Linendraper
		6	James son of John & Elizabeth Buchanan, Haberdasher
		24	Elizabeth dau. of John & Elizabeth Thompson, of the parish of Sᵗ Mary Breading Canterbury
		28	Mary dau. of John & Cather: Templeman
	March	23	George son of Edward & Jane Day, Victualler
1712	April	21	John son of John & Elizabeth Potts, Oylman
	June	12	George son of Jacob & Margarett Hayes
	July	10	Sarah dau. of Thomas & Sarah Stringer
	August	8	George son of Richard & Sarah Stockall
		10	Rebecca dau. of Roger & Rebecca Walter

Years.	Month.	Day.	Names.
1712	August	31	Elizabeth dau. of Robt & Eliz. Nicholl
	September	12	Anne dau. of Richd & Elizabeth Chase
	October	8	John Dailing of St Maries Bedford, aged 15 years
	November	11	Martha dau. of Thomas & Martha Unwin
	December	6	Jacob George son of Justus & Rachel Beck
		27	Robert son of Samuel & Bridget Beachcroft
	January	11	Elizabeth dau. of Edwd & Mary Mitchell
		13	John son of Thomas & Catherine Griffin
	March	24	Robert son of John & Elizabeth Potts
1713	May	8	Mary dau. of Thomas & Eliz. Hunsdon
		21	Sarah dau. of Charles & Sarah Hoyle
	July	16	Anne dau. of Matthias & Anne Gainsb{rh}
		14*	Richard son of Richd & Bridget Knight
		13	Frances dau. of Richard & Eliz. Chase
	September	27	Richard son of John & Jane Wittington, Lodger
	October	21	Joseph son of Roger & Rebecca Walter
		26	Henry son of Joseph & Mary Newdick
	November	2	Joseph son of Samuel & Bridgett Beucroft
	March	1	Hanna Fairbrother dau. of Thomas & Judith Fairbrother
		4	Benjamin son of Benjamin & Eliz. Taylor
		6	John Peters, a parish child
		11	Henry son of John & Mary Grimmett
1714	April	1	Thomas son of Roger & Susanna Wighthart
		4	Susanna dau. of Charles & Sarah Hoyle
		29	Robert son of Matthias & Ann Gainsborough
	May	11	Elizabeth dau. of John & Eliz. Pott
	July	1	Mary dau. of Tho. & Catherine Griffin
	August	5	Hanna dau. of Samuel & Hanna Whighthead
		22	Elizabeth dau. of John & Eliz. Bainham
			Johanna Peters, Foundling
		23	James son of Joseph & Martha Hewes
	September	5	Thomas son of Thomas & Dorithy Norris
		16	John son of William & Elizabeth Westbrook
		19	Richard son of Richard & Elizabeth Smith
	October	14	Mary dau. of Joseph & Mary Newdick
		22	Mary wife of James Acres, Aged 86 years, of St Pauls Shadwell
		28	Elizabeth dau. of Samuel & Brigett Beachcroft
	November	3	Mary Knight dau. of Richd & Briget Knight
	January	16	Elizabeth dau. of Robt & Eliz. Langdale
		30	Thomas son of Edward & Mary Michel
	February	11	Elizabeth Peters, a Foundling
		25*	John son of Thomas & Martha Unwin
		15	Robert son of Robt & Mar. Fitzhugh
	March	18	Edward Moor, aged 15 years
1715	May	10	Jane dau. of John & Eliz. Pott, Oylman
		12	Sophia dau. of Justus & Rachell Beck
		15	Jane dau. of Thomas & Judith Fairbrother
	July	28	Anne dau. of Thos & Eliz. Hunsdon
	August	19	George & Anne Peters, Foundlings
	September	9	Elizabeth dau. of Joseph & Anne Walker
		23	George Peters, Foundling
	October	2	John son of Thomas & Frances Wais
		28	Elizabeth Peters, Foundling
	November	6	Robt son of Thomas & Dorothy Lewin

* Sic.

Years.	Month.	Day.	Names.
1715	December	9	Mary dau. of Roger & Rebecka Walter
		10	. . . . Peters, Foundling
	January	23	John Living of Chersey in Surry
		26	Susanna dau. of Matthias & Ann Gainborow
	January	31	Catherine dau. of Thomas & Cath. Sharrett
	February	5	Richard son of Richard & Mary Sparks
	March	8	William son of W^m & Eliz. Westbrook, Merch^t
1716	May	11	George son of John & Eliz. Pott, Oylman
	June	26	George Marratt, a Black ab^t 7 years old
		29	William Knight son of Rich^d & Briget Knight
	August	8	Frederick son of Justus & Rachel Beck
		26	Henry son of Henry & Frances Burton, Lodger
		27	Barbara dau. of Thomas & Eliz. Hunsdon, Fishm^r
	September	6	James son of James & Grace Jervis, poulterer
		12	Benjamin Peters, a Foundling
		30	Thomas son of Thomas & Judith Fairbrother, Vict^r
	October	7	William son of Robt & Eliz. Langdale, Barber
		28	William son of Francis & Eliz. Francis, Lodger
		29	Thomas Alcock son of John & Margarett Colling
	November	4	Margarett Evens, a parish child
		5	Anne dau. of Miles & Eliz. Barnes, Chinaman
		20	Thomas son of Robert & Martha Fitzhugh
	December	7	Mary Dun, An Adult of 14 years of Age
		27	James son of James & Magdalin Nash, Lodger
	February	8	Jacob Peters, a Foundling
		19	Mary dau. of Thomas & Mary Cartwright
		24	Elenor dau. of Rich^d & Mary Margeson
	March	12	John son of Joseph & Anne Walker, Lodg^r
		21	John son of Roger & Rebecka Waters, Cook
1717	April	5	Martha dau. of Joseph & Martha Windham, Linendraper
		11	Mary dau. of Mathew & Anne Gainsborough
		12	Bridgett dau. of Samuel & Bridget Beachcroft
		19	William son of Rich^d & Mary Sparks, Lodger
	May	5	John son of Thomas & Dorothy Morris, Fishm^r
		8	William son of William & Eliz. Westbrook
		21	Martha dau. of Jos. & Mary Newdick
		24	Anne Perters (sic), a Foundling
	June	27	Mary dau. of Robt & Eliz. Nicols
		29	Thomas Peters, a Foundling
	August	19	Samuel son of Thomas & Katherine Griffin
		20	Nathaniel & Edward sons of Edward & Mary Mayber, Norich Factor
		20	John Peters, a Foundling
	September	5	Anne dau. of Thomas & Anne Fowler
		10	Henrietta dau. of Sr Justus & Dame Rachiel Beck, Merchant
		24	William son of John & Anne Mascall, Lodger
	October	6	William son of William & Margaret Gorden, Victualler
		6	Mary dau. of George & Jane Laythyn
		20	Stockall son of Charles & Mary Bayly
		28	Phebe dau. of John & Rebecka Pannell
		30	William son of Robert & Martha Fitzhugh
	December	5	Edward son of John & Elizabeth Pott
		17	Charles son of Charles & Sarah Hoyle
		27	Thomas Peters, a Foundling
	January	13	Grace dau. of James & Grace Jervis
	February	26	Mary dau. of Joseph & Martha Windham

Years.	Month.	Day.	Names.
1717	March	15	Mary dau. of George & Mary Bourne
1718	April	1	Thomas son of Thomas & Catherine Sharett
		27	Anne dau. of Edward & Mary Mitchell
	May	10	Thomas son of Thomas & Eliz. Hunsden
		11	William son of Joseph & Allice Vincent
		21	Elizabeth dau. of William & Eliz. Westbrooke
		25	Hermon son of Hermon & Hannah Mackcleene
	June	1	Anna Maria dau. of Luke & Mary Davis
		13	William son of Nath. & Mary Gladman
		29	Thomas son of Thomas & Judith Fairbrother
	July	20	Thomas son of Thomas & Anne Fowler
	August	4	Matthias son of Matthias & Anne Gainsborough
	September	8	Margaret Parne of Crookhorn in Somersetshire
		11	Elizabeth dau. of George & Mary Bourne
		26	Robert son of Robert & Elizabeth Nichols
		29	Elizabeth dau. of Thomas & Eliz. Jackson
	November	4	Rebecka dau. of John & Rebecka Pannell
		5	Miles son of Miles & Elizabeth Barnes
		11	Charlotte dau. of Sr Justus & Dame Rachel Beck
		18	William Story, an Adult 28 years old
		19	Richard son of Charles & Sarah Hoyle
	December	9	Mary dau. of Robert & Marth Fitzhugh
		19	Mary dau. of Edward & Mary Mayber
		28	William Peters, a Foundling
	January	2	Anne dau. of John & Elizabeth Pott
		14	John son of Sander & Anne Davis
		28	Sarah dau. of Benjamin & Eliz. Taylor
	February	22	James son of James & Eliz. Branch, Poulterer
1719	March	29	Wm son of Thomas & Dorothy Norris, Fishmonger
		29	Anne dau. of Ford & Anne Beecham, Victualer
	April	12	Joseph son of Joseph & Eliz. Barber
		16	Easter dau. of Roger & Rebecca Walter, Cook
		26	Wm son of William & Mary Bubb, Fishmonger
	May	4	Thomas son of Clarke & Anne Barnardiston, L. draper
	July	8	Charles son of Hermon & Hannah Mackleen
		26	Eliz. dau. of Wm & Izabella Coker
		29	John son of George & Mary Wegge
	August	24	Moye son of Robert & Eliz. Nichols, Leathersellr
		30	Joseph & Benjamin sons of Joseph & Eliz. Crossly
	September	13	Alice dau. of Robt & Eliz. Langdale, Barber
		16	Willoughby son of Willouby & Anne Smith, Mercer
		27	Robert son of Robt & Anne Bonskell, Victualer
	October	11	Ralph son of Thomas & Catherine Sharrett, Barber
		18	Martha dau. of John & Martha Forde, poulterer
	December	1	Joseph son of Jos. & Mary Newdick, Colourer
		3	Frances dau. of Matth. & Anne Gainsborough
		10	Rebecka dau. of John & Reb. Pannell, Haberd.
		21	Mary dau. of James & Grace Jervis, poulterer
	January	1	. . . . dau. of John & Eliz. Pott, Oyleman
	March	1	William son of Wm & Rebecca Gower, Haberd.
		8	Ford son of Ford & Anne Beacham, Inholder
		8	John son of John & Patience Morris
		18	Abraham son of Thomas & Anne Fowler, Groser
1720	April	6	Elizabeth dau. of Wm & Mary Hayward
		10	John son of John & Anne Olden, Victuler
		10	Thomas son of Joseph & Eliz. Barber, Fruiterer
		10	John son of George & Jane Lathem

Years.	Month.	Day.	Names.
1720	April	17	Richard son of Roger & Rebecka Walters, Cook
		24	Anne & Mary twins dauˢ of John & Anne Maskall
	July	7	James Peters, a Foundling
		19	Anna Maria dau. of Clark & Ann Barnardiston
	August	14	Anne dau. of Wᵐ & Mary Bubb, Fishmonger
		19	Anne dau. of John & Eliz. Hill, merchant
		28	Mary dau. of John & Mary Wilson
		31	Anne dau. of Robᵗ & Eliz. Nichols, Leatherseller
	September	8	Miles son of Wollowby & Anne Smith, Mercer
		30	Edmond son of Joseph & Allice Vincent, Lodger
	October	6	Jane dau. of Hermon & Hannah Macklean
		14	Lucy Culling dau. of Thomas & Anne
	November	9	Mathew son of Sʳ Justus & Dame Rachel Beck
		17	James Peters, a Foundling
	December	4	Edward Peters, a Foundling
	January	29	John son of Charles & Hannah Duncombe
		31	Martha dau. of John & Elizabeth Pott, Oyleman
	February	5	James son of Thomas & Rebecka Kimmis
		5	Samuel son of Wᵐ & Mary Hayward, Merchant
		9	James son of Nathaniel & Mary Gladman
		24	Mary Peters, a Foundling
	March	5	George son of George & Jane Laythem
		6	Frances dau. of Wᵐ & Rebecka Gower, Haberd.
		10	Elizabeth dau. of Wᵐ & Anne Gibson, Victuler
		22	Edmond son of Zephania & Mary Page, Distiller
1721		27	Jane dau. of Forde & Anne Becham, Victuler
	April	15	Mary dau. of Wᵐ & Eliz. Westbrooke, merchant
		23	Mary dau. of Wᵐ & Isabella Caker
		23	Elizabeth* Joseph & Elizabeth Barber
		28	Mary dau. of John & Mary Stanly, Haberd.
		30	Thomas son of Joseph & Elizabeth Crosly
	June	27	Robert son of John & Anne Olden
	July	12	Mary dau. of Thomas & Anne Fowler, Grocer
		14	John son of John & Olive Clifton
		30	Anne dau. of Wᵐ & Anne Blundell, poulterer
	August	5	Anne dau. of John & Anne Maskall
		6	Cornelius son of George & Sarah More
		13	Elizabeth dau. of Henry & Grace Quintry
	September	3	Robert son of Thomas & Dorothy Lewin, Fishmʳ
		5	Anthony son of Robert & Eliz. Nicholls, Leathersʳ
		5	Elizabeth dau. of Richᵈ & Eliz. Boyce, Bay*
	October	17	Harry son of John & Patience Morris, Inholder
	November	5	Jane dau. of John & Mary Wilson
		13	John son of John & Mary Finch, Ironmongʳ
		19	William son of Wᵐ & Eliz. Tomkinson, Butcher
	December	6	William son of Wᵐ & Mary Langford, Barber
	January	9	Elizabeth dau. of James & Anne Coulter
		29	Elizabeth Maria dau. of Jos. & Eliz. Roadaway
	February	4	Thomas son of Wᵐ & Mary Bubb, Fishmonger
		11	John son of Thomas & Eliz. Gasey, Victuler
		14	Frances dau. of John & Eliz. Pott, Oyleman
		23	John son of Thomas & Jane Hine, parish Clerk
	March	16	John son of Hermon & Hanna Macklean
		16	Frances dau. of James & Grace Jarvis
1722	April	1	Rebecka dau. of Jos. & Eliz. Barber

* Sic.

Years.	Month.	Day.	Names.
1722	April	12	Catherine dau. of Edward & Mary Maber
	May	10	Mary & Eliz. dauˢ of Tho. & Rebecca Kimmis
	July	12	Nath. Cross, an Adult aged abᵗ 21 years
	August	9	Eliz. dau. of John & Susanna Franks
		10	Eliz. dau. of Tho. & Anne Fowler
		12	Eliz. dau. of Wᵐ & Eliz. Tomkinson
		19	Samuel son of Charles & Hanna Doncombe
		23	Charles son of Nathˡˡ & Mary Gladman
		24	Joseph son of Joseph & Mary Newdick
	September	14	Robert son of Robᵗ & Eliz. Nicholls
	October	21	Hanna dau. of John & Mary Wilson
	November	2	Mary dau. of John & Mary Finch
		4	Samuel son of John & Ann Mascall
	December	20	Richᵈ son of Richᵈ & Anne Lund
		21	James son of James & Anne Colter
	February	7	William son of Wᵐ & Isabella Coker
	March	1	William son [of] Richᵈ & Eliz. Boyce
		3	Eliz. dau. of Edwᵈ & Mary Mitchel, Grinder
		16	Hen. son of Wᵐ & Mary Bubb, Fishmonger
		24*	Anne dau. of Jer. & Eliz. Arrowsmith, Butchʳ
1723		29	Mary dau. of Wᵐ & Mary Langdale, Barber
	April	7	Nath. son of Tho. & Dorothy Lewin, Fishmonger
		10	Earle son of Jo. & Mary Stanly, Haberdasher
		11	Jos. son of Jos. & Eliz. Barber, Fruiterer
	July	18	Sarah dau. of John & Anne Ingham, Lawyer
		19	Sarah dau. of James & Grace Jervis, Poulterer
	September	1	John son of Richᵈ & Mary Coney, Cobler
		22	Jos. son of Wᵐ & Mary Hayward, Merchant
	October	19	Anne dau. of Jo. & Eliz. Manship, Linendrapʳ
	November	9	Edwᵈ son of Jo. & Eliz. Wayles
		24	Hen. son of Henry & Susan Boyce, Baker
	December	12	Nath. son of Wᵐ & Rebecka Gower, Haberdʳ
		12	Tho. son of Tho. & Eliz. Gasey, Victualer
	January	26	Ann dau. of Tho. & Rebecka of* Kimist
	February	7	Tho. son of Tho. & Anne Fowler, Grocer
	March	1	Eliz. dau. of Jo. & Anne Mascall, Salesman
1724	April	6	Martha dau. of Jonathⁿ & Hester Flude, Grocer
		17	Anne dau. of Michˡ & Eliz. Tompson, L. draper
	May	4	. . . . dau. of Jo. & Mary Stanly, Haberdʳ
		10	James son of Jos. & Eliz. Barber, Fruiterer
		24	Sarah dau. of Robᵗ & Mary Mellowes, Barber
	June	14	Tho. son of Tho. & Henrietta Morson, Lin. draper
		24	Mary dau. of Wᵐ & Mary Cam, Threadman
	July	10	Mary dau. of Wᵐ & Mary Langford, Barber
	August	16	Mary & Anne, twins, dauˢ of Dan. & Eliz. Davies
		16	Wᵐ son of Charles & Margᵗ Eastwood
		23	Wᵐ son of Robᵗ & Frances Stebbing, Lin. draper
		30	Tho. son of Ford & Anne Becham, Victuallʳ
	September	4	Geo. son of Nath. & Mary Gladman, Trunkmaker
		12	Wᵐ son of Jo. & Susan Franks, Vintner
		18	Peter son of Peter & Amy Burrell, Merchant
		18	Charles son of Charles & Hannah Duncombe
	October	26	Anne & Rachel dauˢ of Benjamin & Hannah Ware
	November	4	Anne dau. of John & Mary Finch, Ironmonger

* The Register from March 24, 1722-23, to March 23, 1726-27, is subscribed "Jo. Carliol, Parson Commendat."   † Sic.

Years.	Month.	Day.	Names.
1724	November	22	Jerm. son of Jerm. & Eliz. Arrowsmith, Butcher
		23	Rich^d son of Robt & Eliz. Nichols, Leather seller
	December	15	Eliz. dau. of W^m & Anne Blundell, poulterer
		27	Mary Feather, an Adult ab^t 38 years of age
		81	Matthew son of Jo. & Eliz. Pott, Oylman
	January	17	Mary dau. of Charl. & Sarah Bayley
		24	Jo. son of Jo. & Mary Wilson, Cobler
	February	12	Jo. son of Hermon & Hannah Macklecan, Cabinet m^r
	March	5	Eliz. Mariah dau. of Jo. & Eliz. Manship, Lin. d^{pr}
		6	Peter son of Eliz. Wilson, a single woman
		10	Jane Peter, a Foundling
1725		28	Tho. son of Tho. & Mary March
		28	Jos. son of Jo. & Anne Mascal, Salesman
		28	Eliz. dau. of Tho. & Catherine Hanlee
	April	2	Anne dau. of James & Grace Jervis, poulterer
		11	Sarah dau. of Francis & Sarah Bull
	May	2	Eliz. dau. of Robt & Martha Powell
		8	John son of Thos & Rebecca Cutler, Lodgers
		9	Anne dau. of Joseph & Eliz. Barber, Fruiterer
	June	8	Eliz. Peters, a Foundling
		25	Tho. son of Jo. & Eliz. Parker, Lin. draper
	July	25	Hannah dau. of Edwd & Mary Michel
	August	5	Robt son of Robt & Farances Stebbing, Lin. dr.
		11	Tho. son of Tho. & Martha Erston
		18	Jo. son of W^m & Rebecka Gower, Hab-dasher
		22	Tho. son of Tho. & Rebecka Kimist, porter
		80	W^m son of Rich^d & Susanna Price, Lodgers
		31	Godf. son of Godf. & Eliz. Curry, Lodgers
	September	1	Anna Maria Peters, a Foundling
		5	Sam. son of W^m & Eliz. Tompkinson, Butcher
		12	Martha & Elioner twins dau^s of Robt & M. Mellows
		20	Henrietta dau. of Jo. & Mary Stanly, H.dasher
	October	3	Mary dau. of Benj. & Marg^t Hughes, Butcher
		24	Mary dau. of W^m & Mary Bubb, Fishmonger
		7	Sarah dau. of Henry & Susanna Boyce, Baker
	November	9	Robt Peters, a Foundlin
	December	15	Thom^s son of Isaac & Mary Goodwin, Lodgers
	January	8	Wm Finch son of of Jno & Mary Finch, Ironmonger
		9	John son of John & Susanna Franks, Vintner
		9	Moses son of Jno & Mary Willson, Cobler
		30	John son of John & Mary Goodwin
		31	Mary Peters, a Foundlin
	March	1	W^m son of Robt & Elizth Nichols, Leather seller
		6	W^m son of Ford & Anne Beacham, Victualler
		13	Griffith son of Rich^d & Mary Coney, Cobler
		12	Maria Elizabetha dau. of John & Martha Higgate, Curate of this Parish
		20	Mary dau. of Charles & Hannah Duncomb
1726	May	22	Hannah dau. of Joseph & Elizth Barber
	June	19	Henry son of Thos & Henrietta Morgon, Linen draper
	July	10	John son of Thos & Elizth Gasey
		17	Mary dau. of Morrice & Susanna Cartee
		20	Thos son of Robt & Frances Stebbin
		29	Jno Bull son of Francis & Sarah Bull
	August	15	Charles Solendine son of Henry & Susanna Boyce, Baker
	September	5	Joseph Jackson, a parish Child
	August	9	Elizth Tomkinson dau. of Willm & Elizabeth Tomkinson

Years.	Month.	Day.	Names.
1726	October	4	Anne Peters, a parish Child
	December	17	Richard Watts Stephenson son of Richard & Mary Stephenson, Cheesemonger
		19	Rose dau. of Thomas & Joanna Thompson, Calender
		22	Elizabeth dau. of John & Elizabeth Parker, Linendraper
		25	Joseph son of W^m & Mary Cam, Thread-man
	January	2	James Peters, a parish Child
		11	Robert son of Jno & Susan Franks, Vintner
		26	Henry son of Harman & Hannah Macklecan, Looking glass seller
	February	3	Dorothy dau. of Joseph & Mary Barnes, Hatter
		13	Eliz. Holland dau. of John & Barbara Holland, Leather seller
	March	2	Lydia dau. of John & Anne Ingham, Lawyer
		23	Willm son of John & Mary Finch, Ironmonger
		24*	Frances dau. of W^m & Jane Elliot, poulterer
1727	April	14	Samuel son of W^m & Rebecca Gower
	May	14	Jno son of W^m & Sarah Blundell, Bacon man
		25	Thomas son of Thos & Rebecca Cuttler, Lodgers
	June	1	Martha dau. of Jno & Martha Higgate
		11	Mary dau. of Joseph & Eliz. Barber, Fruiterer
	July	12	Thos son of Jno & Mary Henry, Lodgers
		21	Anne Caroline dau. of George & Anne Connell, Apothecary
		30	Rebecka dau. of Thos & Rebecka Kimist, porter
	August	4	Mary dau. of Robt & Frances Stebbin, Lin: drap.
	September	6	Kezia dau. of James & Grace Jarvis, Polterer
	October	1	Richard son of Rich^d & Mary Coney, Cobler
		22	Joseph Gasey son of Thos & Eliz. Gasey, Victualler
		24	Theophilus & Margaret Peters, Foundlins
	November	19	Eliz^th dau. of Benj. & Marg^t Hughs, Lodgers
	December	1	James Peters, a Foundlin
	January	7	Jno son of John & Mary Gregory, Lodgers
		14	Mary dau. of John & Mary Willson, Lodgers
		15	Mary dau. of John & Susan Franks, Vintner
	February	3	Hercules Peters, a Foundlin
		6	Sarah dau. of Rich^d & Eliz^th Boys, privately bapt.
		13	Eliz^th dau. of Jno & Eliz^th Nelson, Distiller
		16	Jno son of Joseph & Mary Barnes, Hatter
	March	8	Jno Wood, a Foundlin born in the Street
		17	Thos son of Charles & Hannah Duncombe, Cutler
		17	Mary dau. of Charles & Marg^t Eastwood
1728	April	8	Barbara dau. of Jno & Barbara Holland, Leatherseller
		14	Sarah dau. of Francis & Sarah Bull
	May	13	Richd Newman, a Child born in ye Street
		13	Jno Tomkinson son of W^m & Eliz^th†
		21	Rich^d son of Thomas & Joanna Thompson, Calender
	June	23	Joseph son of Joseph & Eliz^th Barber, Fruiterer
		23	William son of W^m & Mary Cam Threadman
		23	Carolina dau. of Rich^d & Anne Lunn
	July	2	John Peters, a Foundlin
		23	Richard son of Robert & Frances Stebbin, Linendraper
	August	19	Benjamin son of Benj. & Mary Workman, Lodgers
		28	Jno son of Jno & Rebecca Colby, Surgeon, privately bapt^d
	September	1	Anne dau. of Peter & Mary Martin, Lodgers

* The Register from March 24, 1726-27, to Dec. 30, 1729, is subscribed " Jo. Carliol, Parson ;" and from Dec. 30, 1729, to Feb. 21, 1730-31, " Jo. Carliol."

† Sic.

Years.	Month.	Day.	Names.
1728	September	4	Mary Peters, a Foundlin
		7	Jn° son of Jn° & Martha Higgate, privately bapt^d
		8	W^m son of W^m & Anne Blundell, Poulterer
		12	George Phenney son of George & Anne Connell, Apothecary
		18	Elizth dau. of W^m & Rebecca Gower, Hab.dasher
	November	4	Jeremiah son of W^m & Dorothy Bentley, Tea-man
		8	Jn° son of Jn° & Mary Gregory, Lodgers
		13	Robt Peters, a Foundlin
		17	Judeth dau. of Harman & Hannah Macklecan, Looking glass seller
		27	Mary Peters, a Foundlin
		29	Mary dau. of Jn° & Mary Finch, Ironmonger
	December	4	James son of James & Mary Glascock, Strangers at the Bull Inn
	January	16	Rachel Peters, a Foundlin
		22	Elizth dau. of Thos & Elizth Gasey, Victualler
	February	9	Anne dau. of Thos & Anne Farrer, Haberdasher
	March	2	Jane dau. of Thos & Rebecca Kimist, a Porter
		6	Henry Batten, servant to Mrs Bently, Pastry Cook, Aged 23 years
		11	Anne dau. of John & Anne Ingham, Lawyer
1729		30	Anne dau. of Francis & Sarah Bull, Glasier
	April	3	Elizth dau. of Thos & Rebecca Cutler, Lodgers
		22	Anne dau. of Robt & Elizth Nichols, Leather sell^r
	May	25	W^m son of George & Marg^t Flower, Lodgers
		29	Richard son of Rich^d & Martha Davies, Packer
	June	7	Sarah Peters, a Foundlin
		10	James son of Robt & Frances Stebbing, Linendr.
		10	John son of John & Mary Henry, Lodgers
		15	James son of Thos & Sarah Austin, Vintner
		16	Zillah dau. of James & Grace Jarvis, Poulterer
	July	20	Hannah dau. of Joseph & Elizabeth Barber, Fruiterer
		27	Jn° son of Jn° & Mary Tayler, Grocer
		29	Walter Peters, a Foundlin
		29	Peter Monneret, a natural Child
	August	7	Thos son of Jn° & Susan Franks, Vintner
		13	Mary dau. of Abraham & Anne Ellis, Lodgers
	September	27	Henry & Walter West, twins, sons of one of our Pensioners
	November	3	Richd Peters, a Foundling
		6	Jervoice son of Jn° & Mary Finch, Ironmonger
		17	Samuel son of Jn° & Rebecca Colby, Surgeon
		29	Walter Peters, a Foundlin
	December	11	W^m son of W^m & Dorothy Bentley, Tea-man
		30	Rebecca dau. of W^m & Rebecca Gower, Haberdasher
		30	Henry son of Geo. & Anne Connell, Apothecary
	January	11	Rich^d son of Jn° & Elizth Angell, Pastry Cook
		25	W^m son of Jn° & Eliz^{rh} Nellson, Distiller
	February	10	Charles Page, son of a poor woman who fell in labour in the Street
	March	2	Thos son of Thos & Joanna Thompson, Calender
		18	Sarah Curtiss, born of a poor woman taken in Labour in the Street
		22	Jn° son of Jn° & Rachel Salmon, Victualler
1730	April	30	Susanna dau. of Joseph & Mary Philby, Lodgers
	May	8	Mary Greenwood, born of a poor woman taken in labour in the Street
		10	Mary dau. of Jn° & Mary Wilson, Lodgers

Years.	Month.	Day.	Names.
1730	June	7	Jnº son of Thoˢ & Margaret Hutchinson, Butcher
		21	Thoˢ son of Benjamin & Margaret Hughes, Butcher
		21	Philip son of Thoˢ & Sarah Austin, Vintner
		25	Susanna dau. of Robᵗ & Elizᵗʰ Nichols, Leatherseller
	July	2	Esther dau. of Charles & Mary Trefry, Apothecary
		7	Jnº son of Jnº & Dorothy Hickling, Butcher
		14	Frances dau. of Robᵗ & Frances Stebbing, Linen draper
		28	Anne Peters, a Foundling
	September	5	Mary Peters, a Foundling
		5	Frances dau. of Francis & Rachel Oldfield, Strangers
		20	Jnº son of Jnº & Jane Grimes, Butcher
		20	Joseph son of Joseph & Elizᵗʰ Barber, Fruiterer
	October	8	Anne dau. of Jnº & Anne Barlyman, Lodgers
		22	Jnº son of Wᵐ & Ann Blundell, Poulterer
	December	1	Robᵗ Peters, a Foundling
		13	Elizᵗʰ dau. of Wᵐ & Dorcas Turner, Lodgers
		20	Susannah dau. of Jnº & Elizᵗʰ Angell, Pastry Cook
		24	Mary Anne dau. of Walter & Mary Vane, Merchᵗ
		30	Rebecca Peters, a Foundling
	January	1	Dorothy dau. of Wᵐ & Dorothy Bentley, Tea merchᵗ
	February	7	Ann dau. of Wᵐ & Mary Cam, Threadman
		21	Elizᵗʰ dau. of Wᵐ & Elizᵗʰ Ellet, Butcher
	March	1*	Martha Jarvis dau. of James & Grace Jarvis, Poulterer
		22	Jacob son of Jnº & Susan Franks, Vintner
1731	April	4	Joseph son of Joshua & Martha Wood, Lodgers
	May	31	Robᵗ son of Jonathan & Sarah Vautier, Lodgrˢ
	June	3	Joseph son of Mary & Joseph Philby, Lodgers
	July	8	Edward son of Jnº & Elizᵗʰ Parker, Linen drapʳ
	August	1	Jnº son of Jerim. & Elizᵗʰ Arrowsmith, Butcher
		6	Elizᵗʰ dau. of Geo. & Mary Macadam, Barber
		8	Sarah dau. of Jnº & Elizᵗʰ Nelson, Distiller
		8	James son of James & Mary Crispin Hillyard
		12	Wᵐ son of Jnº & Mary Woodley
		12	Lydia Peters, a Foundling
		24	Jane Young, a natural child
	September	24	Robᵗ son of Wᵐ & Rebecca Gower, Haberdasher
	October	14	Mary dau. of Henry & Deborah Adams, Lodgers
		18	Joseph son of Joseph & Mary Blagdon, Ironmonger
		29	Richard son of Richᵈ & Elizᵗʰ Boys, Factor
	November	4	Joseph son of Thoˢ & Anne Fowler, Grocer
		11	Wᵐ son of Jnº & Ann Ingham, Attorney
		14	Harman son of Harman & Hannah Macklecan
	December	23	Mary dau. of Thoˢ & Elizᵗʰ Gasey, Victualler
		27	Susanna dau. of Jnº & Jane Grimes, Butcher
	February	3	Willᵐ son of Jnº & Dorothy Hickling, Butcher
	March	16	Charles son of Jnº & Rebecca Colby, Surgeon
1732	April	13	Jnº son of Robᵗ & Frances Stebbin, Linendrapʳ
		25	Godfry Woodward son of Walter & Mary Vane, Merchᵗ
	May	8	Mary dau. of Geo. & Mary Sibley
	June	4	Thoˢ son of Wᵐ & Dorcas Turner, Shoe maker
	July	5	Wᵐ son of Thoˢ & Joanna Thompson, a Calender
		11	Benjamin son of Benj. & Margᵗ Hughes, a Butcher
	September	3	James son of Josiah & Mary Wood, Lodgers
		14	Samˡˡ son of Wᵐ & Ann Brown, Shoemaker

* The Register from March 1, 1730-31, to Feb. 27, 1736-37, is subscribed " John Higgate,
M.A., Curate ;" " John Higgate, M.A. ;" and " John Higgate, Curate."

Years.	Month.	Day.	Names.
1732	September	17	Ann dau. of Jnº & Elizth Angell, Pastry Cook
	October	7	Draper son of Jnº & Susan Franks, Vintner
		23	Jnº Roe, a Parish Child
		24	W^m* son of Peter† Burrell, Esqr, & Amy Burrell his wife
		26	Joseph son of W^m & Dorothy Bentley, Tea M^t
		27	Joseph son of Joseph & Mary Blagdon, Ironmonger
	December	3	Anne dau. of Jnº & Elizth Nelson
	January	9	Jnº Barber, priv. bapt^d
		21	Thoˢ son of Jnº & Elizth Lucey, Butcher
		28	Jnº son of Jnº & Ann Chittoe, Butcher
	February	28	Elizth dau. of Jnº & Marg^t Phillips, Cabinet seller
1733	April	1	Elizth dau. of Jonas & Martha Firth, Inn-holder
		5	Thoˢ son of Robt & Frances Stebbin, Linendrap^r
		10	Hester Keys, a Pensioners Child
		19	Isaac Peters, a Foundlin
	May	15	Jnº son of Jnº & Susanna Lawrence, Lodgers
	June	18	Jane dau. of Jane & Jnº Grimes, Butcher
	July	16	Thoˢ son of Jnº & Dorothy Hickling, Butcher
		22	Jane dau. of Charles & Mary Eastwood, Tayler
	August	5	Jnº son of Henry & Marg^t Russell, Lodger
		12	Sarah dau. of Christopher & Priscilla Abbot, Green Grocer
		23	Mary dau. of Joseph & Mary Blagdon, Ironmonger
	October	7	W^m son of Jnº & Elizth Angell, Cook
	November	1	Ann dau. of W^m & Dorothy Bentley, Tea M^t
	December	4	Valentine son of Susan Franks, widow & Vintner
		9	Sarah, dau. of Thoˢ & Sarah Austin, Vintner
		18	W^m son of Jnº & Elizth Hare, Lodgers
		30	Alice dau. of W^m & Eleanor Eames, Victualler
	January	13	Geo. son of Geo. & Ann Chapman, Butcher
		30	James Peters, a Foundlin
	February	5	Elizth Peters, a Foundlin
		11	Mary dau. of James Crispin Hillyard, Lodger
	March	3	Elizth dau. of Charles & Elizth Wood, Victaller
		4	Titus son of Robt & Frances Stebbin, Linen draper
		8	Ann dau. of Joseph & Elizth Meadows, Baker
1734	April	9	Joseph son of Mary & Joseph Philby, Butcher
	May	5	Willm son of Robt & Mary Stephenson, Fishmong^r
	July	10	Sarah dau. of Joseph & Mary Blagdon, Ironmong^r
		13	Benj. Baldwin, from the Workhouse
		21	Ann dau. of Jnº & Elizth Nelson, Bacon-seller
		24	Josiah son of W^m & Ann Browne, Shoe-maker
	September	22	Sarah dau. of Thoˢ & Mary Hunt, Butcher
		22	Marg^t dau. of Benj. & Marg^t Hughs, Butcher
	October	8	Jnº son of Jnº & Ann Moor, Polter
		29	W^m son of Rich^d & Elizth Boys, Factor
	November	19	Patty dau. of W^m & Rebecca Gower, Haberdasher
	December	8	W^m son of Henry & Marg^t Russell, Lodgers
		15	Mary dau. of W^m & Ellen Emmes, Victualler
	January	6	Jnº son of Jnº & Elizth Lucey, Butcher

* He was third son of Peter Burrell, Esq., afterwards LL.D. and Chancellor to the Bishop of Worcester; F.R.S.; M.P. for Haslemere 1768-1774; a Director of the South Sea Company; appointed a Commissioner of Excise 1774. He married in 1773 Sophia, daughter and coheir of Sir Charles Raymond, of Valentine House, co. Essex, Bart., and was grandfather of the present Sir Walter Wyndham Burrell, Bart., M.P.

† Peter Burrell, Esq., was of Beckenham in Kent; Sheriff of that County 1722; M.P. for Haslemere 1727-1747 Died April 16, 1756. Amy, his wife, was eldest daughter of Hugh Raymond, Esq., of Saling Hall, Essex, and Langley in Beckenham. She survived him, and was living in 1778.

Years.	Month.	Day.	Names.
1784	January	9	Sarah dau. of W^m & Dorcas Turner, Shoemaker
		12	Jn° son of W^m & Mary Camm, Threadman
		29	Walter son of Walter & Mary Vane, Merch^t
	February	16	Timothy son of Thos & Jane Walker, Barber
	March	13	Thos son of Jn° & Eliz^th Angel, Cook
1735	April	3	Cook Stebbin, priv. bapt^d
		27	Francis son of Francis & Sarah Bull, Glazier
		27	Mary dau. of Geo. & Mary Chapman, Butcher
	June	8	Eliz^th dau. of Josiah & Mary Bazire, Butcher
		12	Jn° son of Joseph & Mary Philby, Butcher
	August	14	Jn° Blagdon, privately bapt^d
		13	Sarah Evelyn dau. of William Glanville* Esqr, & Bridget his wife, was born & bapt^d Sept ye 9th 1735
		22	Richard-Harry-Cotter was born & bapt^d Sept. 16 1735
	September	26	Mary dau. of Matt^w Gilpin & Mary Pot, a natural Child
		30	Hannah Barber, privately bapt^d
	October	19	Ann Maria dau. of Thos & Mary Metcalf, Lodgers
	December	8	Sam^ll Peters, a Foundlin
	January	4	Eliz^th dau. of Charles & Ann Morgan, Lodgers
		25	Jn° son of Jn° & Eliz^th Nelson, Bacon man
	February	24	Stephen son of David & Sarah Kirby, Lodgers
		29	Willm Christopher son of W^m & Eliz^th Meadows, Lodg^rs
1736	March	31	Cæsar son of W^m & Mary Lycett, Lodgers
	June	6	Eliz^th dau. of George & Mary Chapman, Butcher
	July	16	Ann dau. of Charles & Jane Boehm, Merch^t
	August	16	Sarah & Mary dau^rs of Joseph & Mary Blagdon
		22	Eliz^th Julian dau. of Jn° & Eliz^th Lucey, Butcher
	September	2	Jn° son of Jn° & Dorothy Hickling, Butcher
	October	8	Jn° Pool son of Henry & Margaret Russell, Lodgers
		13	Dorothy dau. of Joseph & Dorothy Truelove, Upholder
		28	Seymour son of Seymour & Eliz^th Hussey, Packer
		31	Sarah dau. of Benjamin & Marg^t Hughes, Butcher
	November	28	Mary dau. of Joseph & Mary Philby, Butcher
		28	Thos & Mary Hunt, Butcher
	December	8	Eliz^th dau. of Robt & Eliz^th Warham, Cook
		12	Hannah dau. of Joseph & Eliz^th Barber, Fruiterer
		27	Mary dau. of Mary & Dorcas Turner, Shoemaker
	February	7	Eliz^th dau. of Robt & Mary James, Clerk at ye India house
		27	W^m son of W^m & Ellen Emmes, Victualler
	March	13†	Eliz^th dau. of Joseph & Eliz^th Farry, Lodgers
		18	Harman son of George & Hannah Neal, Tayler.
1737	April	19	Jane dau. of James & Elizabeth Sylvester
		23	Sarah dau. of George & Eliz^th Townsend
		24	Joanna dau. of John & Elizabeth Nelson
		28	John son of Josiah & Mary Bazire
	June	3	Samuel son of Matthias & Hannah Huntley
		6	Isabella dau. of Thomas & Jane Lewin
	July	9	John son of Thomas & Eliz^th Cotton, Barber
	September	3	Elizabeth dau. of Joseph & Mary Blagdon

* William Glanville was fifth son of George Evelyn, of Nutfield, by Frances his wife, daughter of Andrew Bromhall, of Stoke Newington. He was baptized at Nutfield December 14, 1686; assumed the name of Glanville upon his marriage with Frances, daughter and heir of William Glanville, of Saint Clere, Ightham. Buried at Godstone October 2, 1766. Bridget, his second wife, was second dau. of Hugh Raymond, Esq., of Saling, co. Essex, and sister of Amy, the wife of Peter Burrell, Esq. (See *ante* October 24, 1732.)

† The Register from March 13, 1736-37, to Aug. 19, 1744, is subscribed "Richd Thomas, M.A., Curate," and "Richd Thomas, Curate."

Yeare.	Month.	Day.	Names.
1737	September	25	Philip son of William & Elizabeth Meadows
	October	3	John son of Edward & Anne Sparkes
		21	Thomas son of Robert & Elizabeth Warham
	November	7	Anne dau. of Thoˢ & Elizʰ Charlesley
		20	Thomas son of Thomas & Mary Hunt
	December	11	Anne dau. of Joseph & Mary Philby
		31	Humphrey son of Robert & Frances Stebbing
	January	25	John son of Jnᵒ & Mary Dolling
	February	25	Elizabeth dau. of Thoˢ & Elizabeth Crouch
	March	5	Robert son of Robert & Susannah Stevenson
		6	Charles Cæsar, a Black
1738	April	6	William son of William & Catherine West
		10	Margaret dau. of William & Dorcas Turner
		29	George son of George & Hannah Nail
	May	19	John son of Seymour & Elizʰ Hussey
	June	25	Charles son of Charles & Mary Airs
	July	16	Charles son of John & Elizabeth Nelson
		25	David son of David & Sarah Kirbey
	August	5	Sarah dau. of Thomas & Elizabeth Cotton
		20	Sarah dau. of Joseph & Elizabeth Barber
		27	John son of John & Jane Grimes
	September	10	Mary dau. of John & Mary Andrews
		14	Dorothy dau. of Thomas & Jane Lewin
	October	2	Mary dau. of Thomas & Harriott Long
			. . . . Son of William & Mary Lycett
	November	2	Mary dau. of George & Elizabeth Townsend
		7	Charles son of William & Jane Rogers
		14	Peter Peters, a foundling
		18	John son of Joseph & Mary Blagdon
		20	John son of John & Dorothy Hickling
	December	25	Elizabeth dau. of Robert & Anne Neighbour
		25	John son of John & Dorothy Dingly, aged 5 years
	February	23	Mabell dau. of Joseph & Margaret Keys
1739	April	3	Benjamin son of Joseph & Mary Philby
		23	John son of John & Anne Long
	May	29	Sarah Carey dau. of Charles & Mary Aires
	June	26	Hannah dau. of George & Hannah Naile
		27	Sarah dau. of Joseph & Mary Brazier
	July	19	Mary dau. of Robert & Mary James
		21	Richard son of Richard & Ann Foster
		27	Mary dau. of Robert & Elizabeth Warham
		29	Mary dau. of Aaron & Mary Newbolt
	August	9	Ruth dau. of John & Elizabeth Hare
		15	Mary Merrott dau. of Joseph & Sarah Hemming
		26	John son of Robert & Susannah Stevenson
		28	Sarah dau. of Robert & Frances Stebbing
	October	7	John son of John & Catharine Stearns
		10	Anne dau. of Joseph & Elizabeth Barber
		16	Mary dau. of William & Mary Munt
		25	Anne dau. of Jnᵒ & Anne Angell
	December	23	Sarah dau. of George & Catherine Luff
	January	4	Elizabeth dau. of Thomas & Elizabeth Cotton
		[Sic]	Abraham son of
		17	Elizabeth dau. of Jnᵒ & Jane Grimes
		30	Anne dau. of Joseph & Mary Blagdon
	February	11	Elizabeth Peters, a foundling
		11	Charity Peters, a foundling

Years.	Month.	Day.	Names.
1739	March	6	Dorothy dau. of Thomas & Jane Lewin
		6	Stuart Banford, pensioner
		9	James son of Jn⁰ & Elizabeth Nelson
1740	April	5	Benjamin Baldwin, pensioner
		6	Henry son of Henry & Sarah Brooks
		13	Robert son of Thoˢ & Mary Hunt
		13	Anne dau. of Thoˢ & Elizᵗʰ Babington
		28	Sarah Farrington, pensioner
		28	James Peters, a foundling
		30	Susannah dau. of Thoˢ & Elizᵗʰ Babington
	May	11	John son of John & Mary Andrews
	June	12	Elizabeth dau. of William & Elizʰ Meadows
	July	13	Thomas son of Thoˢ & Elizʰ Crouch
	August	9	Elizabeth dau. of George & Hannah Nail
		14	Elizabeth dau. of John & Elizʰ Hare
	September	18	Mary dau. of Henry & Mary Cliff
	October	12	John son of John & Mary Jones
	November	28	John son of Charles & Mary Aires
	December	11	John son of George & Elizᵗʰ Turner
		22	Josiah son of Joseph & Mary Bazier
	January	15	James son of Robert & Elizʰ Warham
		15	Sarah dau. of Joseph & Mary Philby
		16	Anna Maria dau. of Jn⁰ & Anne Angell
	March	6	Anne dau. of James & . . . . Coulter
		12	Robert son of Robert & Susannah Stevenson
1741	April	30	Joseph son of Joseph & Mary Blagdon
	June	14	George son of David & Sarah Kirby
	July	12	Henry Nelson son of Jn⁰ & Elizʰ Nelson
		31	Jeremiah son of Samuel & Sarah Warwick
	August	3	Anne dau. of John & Elizabeth Hare
		8	Sarah dau. of Thoˢ & Elizʰ Cotton
		15	Elizabeth dau. of Matthias & Hannah Huntley
		16	William son of Henry & Sarah Brooks
	September	10	Anne dau. of Thoˢ & Jane Lewin
		20	Mary dau. of George & Catherine Luff
		21	Harriot dau. of Thoˢ & Harriott Long
	October	12	Joseph son of Joseph & Sarah Heming
		26	Thomas son of Joseph & Margaret Key
	November	3	Mary dau. of John & Mary Jones
		9	George son of George & Hannah Nail
		15	Mary dau. of Thoˢ & Elizʰ Crouch
		26	Anne dau. of John & Mary Andrews
	December	18	Anne dau. of John & Jane Grimes
	February	24	Andrew son of George & Elizabeth Townsend
	March	22	Joseph son of George & Elizᵗʰ Turner
1742		28	. . . . son of Thoˢ & Mary Hunt
	April	9	Priscilla dau. of Arthur & Priscilla Perkins
	June	12	Jeffrey son of Robert & Elizʰ Warham
		13	Grace dau. of Charles & Mary Ayres
	July	4	Jeremiah son of Robᵗ & Elizʰ Arrowsmith
		5	Thomas son of William & Anne Cramond
		22	Anne dau. of Joseph & Mary Bazier
		23	Richarda dau. of Charles & Jane Boehm
	August	6	Mary dau. of John & Lois Gibson
		8	Deborah dau. of Thoˢ & Rachel Broughton
		26	Mary dau. of Joseph & Mary Blagdon
		27	William son of Jeremiah & Martha Burton

Years.	Month.	Day.	Names.
1742	October	3	Elizabeth dau. of Tho⁸ & Eliz. Crouch
		11	Bithiah dau. of George & Eliz^h Sherwin
		28	Mary dau. of Jn° & Eliz^th Palmer
		29	Mary dau. of Jn° & . . . . Irish
	December	13	Edmund son of Jn° & Catherine Stearns
		19	Thomas Johnson son of Tho⁸ & Jane Lewin
		27	Rachel dau. of Jn° & Mary Jones
		29	John son of John & Margaret Marriott
		31	Elizabeth dau. of Matthias & Hannah Huntley
	February	5	Thomas son of Robert & Mary Stevens
	March	8	Frances dau. of Thomas & Harriott Long
		10	Anne dau. of Jacob & Anne Binks
1743	May	6	Beeston son of Roger & Jane Drake
		13	Elizabeth dau. of William & Eliz^h Rogers
	July	1	Richard son of Rich^d & Anne Shakeshaft
		9	Conrade son of . . . . Brown
		27	Rich^d son of Tho⁸ & Rachel Broughton
		31	George son of George & Eliz^h Turner
	August	17	Anne dau. of Tho⁸ & Anne Davies
		18	Anne dau. of Rich^d & Anne Tod
		31	Robert son of Robt & Eliz^h Arrowsmith
	September	25	Edward son of John & Mary Andrews
	October	17	Mary dau. of Charles & Mary Aires
	November	4	George son of George & Eliz^h Sherwin
		5	Arthur son of Arthur & Priscilla Perkins
	December	18	Rachel dau. of Phillip & Anne Hall
		29	John son of John & Eliz^h Windsor
	January	6	John son of Joseph & Sarah Heming
		23	Frances dau. of Robert & Eliz^h Warham
	February	3	Thomas son of Rich^d & Eliz^h Wright
		21	Susannah dau. of W^m & Eliz^h Wright
1744	April	12	John son of George & Hannah Nail
		24	Mary dau. of Thomas & Jane Lewin
	May	10	Elizabeth dau. of W^m & Catharine Par
	June	28	Mary dau. of Thomas & Mary Parrot
		28	John son of John & Mary Jones
	July	6	John son of Rich^d & Anne Shakeshaft
		12	Mary dau. of Robert & Mary Stevens
		26	Daniel son of Daniel & Jane Cork
	August	5	Thomas son of Tho⁸ & Elizabeth Crouch
		15	William son of George & Eliz^h Turner
		19	Elizabeth dau. of Christopher & Sarah Asquith
		27*	Elizabeth dau. of Jacob & Anne Binks
	October	27	Mary Peters, a Foundling
	November	2	Mary dau. of Willm & Anne Cramond
		2	Charles son of Charles & Mary Aires
		25	Betty dau. of John & Mary Andrews
		26	Anne dau. of Robert & Mary James
	December	2	John son of Robt & Elizabeth Arrowsmith
		16	William son of Willm & Edy Hankes
	February	26	Elizabeth dau. of Thomas & Anne Davies
	March	20	Ambrose son of Robt & Elizabeth Warham
1745	May	5	Josiah son of Joseph & Mary Bazire
		13	Anne dau. of James & Anne Wilsford
		28	Arabella dau. of Tho⁸ & Harriott Long

* The Register from August 27, 1744, to August 29, 1747, is subscribed " R. Wynne, Curate."

Years.	Month.	Day.	Names.
1745	June	18	Anne-Jemima dau. of Francis & . . . . Wroughton
		28	William son of Willm & Anne White
	August	11	John son of Thomas & Elizabeth Crouch
		11	George son of Rich^d & Anne Shakeshaft
		22	Elizabeth dau. of John & Eliz. Turner
		30	Mary dau. of Kezer & Mary Yoell
	September	3	John son of John & Cath^{ne} Silvester
		8	Sarah dau. of . . . . Sarah Potter
		10	Thomas son of Jacob & Anne Binks
		10	Samuel son of John & Jane Grimes
		22	Jonathan son of Jonathan & Anne Hall
	October	5	Rebecca dau. of Robt & Mary Stevens
		11	Eleanor dau. of Peter & Dorothy Robertson
	December	3	Mary dau. of Christopher & Sarah Asquith
		11	Sarah dau. of George & Mary Mansfield
		29	Jane dau. of Charles Boehm, Esq., & Jane his wife
	January	15	Mary dau. of Rich^d & Mary Wright
		19	William son of Thomas & Mary Hunt
	February	16	Joseph son of Robt & Susanna Stevenson
1746	April	8	Anne dau. of Thos & Ann Davy
		30	William son of John & Mary Jones
	May	6	Elizabeth dau. of Eliz. & Thomas Parvis
		6	Martha dau. of William & Ann Cram'ond
		20	Mary dau. of Daniel & Jane Corke
	June	14	Sarah dau. of Jane & Thos Broughton
		25	Alexander Henry son of Robt & Susan Leroux
		29	Thomas son of Thos & Elizabeth Page
	July	13	Robert son of Willm & Elizabeth Gledhill
		31	Sibella dau. of George & Hannah Nail
	August	10	Thomas son of Thos & Eliz. Arrowsmith
		16	John son of Willm & Christiana Benn
		25	James son of Arthur & Priscilla Perkins
	September	7	Anne dau. of Rich^d & Anne Shakeshaft
		19	John son of John & Elizabeth Todd
		30	Mary dau. of Willm & Anne Wood
	October	9	Sarah dau. of John Lawley & Anne Gibbs, illeg^{te}
		10	Margaret dau. of Willm & Elizabeth Rogers
		12	Robert son of Willm & Susannah Cottle
	November	2	Susannah dau. of Thos & Elizabeth Crouch
		16	John son of William & Anne Henley
	December	4	Anne dau. of John & Anne Flower, Suffolk
		17	William Pennant son of Thomas & Harriott Long
		21	Catherine dau. of Robert & Elizabeth Warham, privately
	January	18	Sarah dau. of Thos & Charlotte Laverick
	February	6	Eliza dau. of Peter & Eliz. Mixer, privately. Received into the Church Feb. 12
	March	5	Jacob son of Jacob & Anne Binks
1747	April	9	John son of George & . . . . Turner, Butcher
	June	23	John son of Thos. & Anne Davis
	July	1	Thos son of Samuel & Hannah Parry
		14	John son of Thos & Anne Walshaw
	August	9	Elizabeth dau. of . . . . Cannon, privately
		29	Thomas son of Willm & Anne White
	September	27*	Joseph son of Samuel & Anne Peachy

* The Register from September 27, 1747, to April 12, 1765, is subscribed " William Shakleford, Curate," " Willm Shackleford, M.A., Curate."

Years.	Month.	Day.	Names.
1747	October	1	John son of George & Hannah Nail
		21	John son of Daniel & Jane Cork
		27	Sarah dau. of William & Martha Jordan
	November	11	John son of John & Hannah Chivers
	December	7	John Harris Page son of Thomas Page
		25	John & Sarah son & dau. of Joseph & Mary Basier
		27	Anne dau. of W^m & Susannah Cottel
	January	10	John son of Richard & Rachel Burrows
		25	Robert son of William & Anne Wood
		31	Elizabeth dau. of William & Eliz. Gladhill
	February	14	Thomas son of Thomas & Sharlott Laverick
		22	Thomas son . . . . Sweetland
	March	20	Emila dau. of William & Eliz^th Gladman
		24	Thomas son of George & Eliz^th Turner, Butcher
1748	April	2	David . . . .
	May	22	Precila Stevens dau. of Robert & Mary Stevens
		24	Anne Pemberton, Traveller
		24	John son of Richard & Anne Tod
	June	12	John Asquith son of Christopher & Sarah
	July	1	Price son of John & Mary Jones
		8	William Hank son of William & Edy Hank
		14	Jonathan son of Jacob & Anne Binks
	August	1	Charles son of Thomas & Catherine Cooper
		25	Henry son of Charles & Mary Aires
	September	23	Elizabeth dau. of Robert & Elizabeth Wareham
	October	9	. . . . son of Thomas & Elizabeth Crouch
		11	John son of Thomas & Harriott Long
	November	2	Phillip son of John & Hannah Cheivers
		20	Samuel son of Samuel & Anne Peachy
	December	1	Anne dau. of Thomas & Anne Walshaw
	January	7	Thomas son of Thomas & Elizabeth Page
		10	Sarah Mapham dau. of Joseph & Sarah
	March	10	Isaac son of Robert & Martha Hunter. Born 26 Feb.
1749	April	12	William son of Thomas & . . . . Walker
		25	Anne Horrod, aged 13 years
		27	Jane dau. of W^m & Christiana Benn
	May	1	Elizabeth Jeffres, aged 23 years
	June	12	George son of George & Eliz^h Turner, Butcher
		20	Ann dau. of W^m & Sarah Rouggles
	July	20	William son of Thomas & Catherine Cooper
	August	13	Elizabeth dau. of Clement & Elizabeth Lazell
		27	Elizabeth dau. of Joseph & Elizab^th Clerk
	October	8	Susannah dau. of Willm & Susannah Cottle
		27	Thomas son of Daniel & Frances Grendon
	November	21	Ann dau. of Thomas & Elizabeth Crouch
	October	28*	Robert son of Thomas & Charlotte Laverick
	December	5	Ann dau. of William & Ann White
		22	Elizab^th dau. of Nicholas & Olave Farmborow
	January	6	Elizabeth Savannah, a Black, ab^t 17
		29	Sophia dau. of Thomas & Harriott Long
	February	1	Jane dau. of John & Hannah Chivers
		12	George son of Jacob & Ann Binks
	March	3	Eliz^th dau. of Willm & Catherine Pyndar
		4	Ann dau. of John & Ann Procter
		6	Thos Freeman son of Thos & Eliz^th Page

* Sic.

Years.	Month.	Day.	Names.
1749	March	9	Johanna dau. of Joseph & Sarah Mapham
		14	Ann dau. of Edwd & Alice Crouch
1750	April	14	Elizth dau. of Thos & Mary Gurnell
	August	24	Elizth dau. of John & Sarah Page
	September	20	Ann dau. of George & Elizth Turner
		23	Elizth Sarah dau. of Thomas & . . . . Walker
	October	21	Ann dau. of Thomas & Elizth Crouch
	November	11	Clement son of Clem^t & Elizth Lazell
	December	23	Hannah dau. of John & Hannah Chivers
	January	24	John son of John & Sarah Page
		27	Frances dau. of Nicholas & Olave Farmborow
	February	17	Mary dau. of Willm & Susan^h Cottle
	March	8	Henrietta-Maria dau. of Robert & Elizabeth Dorrell, aged 2 years
		24	Jane dau. of Willm & Martha Jordan
1751		29	Susannah dau. of John & Ann Pott
		30	Elizth dau. of W^m & Sarah Rougles
	August	25	Ann dau. of W^m & Christiana Benn
		28	Jane dau. of W^m & Ann White
	September	3	James-Charles son of Jonathan & Elizabeth Collins
		11	Catherine dau. of William & Catherine Pyndar
		16	Sarah dau. of W^m & Sarah Dawson
		22	Elizth dau. of W^m & Elizth Wilson
	October	8	Martha dau. of George & Eliz. Turner
		6	Edwd son of Edwd & Mary Tailsworth
		21	Elizth dau. of Thos & Elizth Page
	November	26	Jane-Chander dau. of Rich^d & Mary Mantle
	December	5	Sophiah dau. of Thos & Harriott Long
		23	Susannah dau. of Saml & Ann Peachy
1752	January	1	Edward son of Edwd & Elizth Manning
	February	5	George son of Geo. & Mary Mansfield
		14	Mary dau. of Thos & Mary Gurnell
	March	1	Rich^d son of John & Sarah Page
		1	Willm son of Josiah & Mary Bazier
		23	Hannah dau. of Jacob & Ann Binks
	July	2	Ann dau. of John & Hannah Chivers
		8	Thomas son of Thos & Ann Preston
		9	Robina dau. of Timothy & Ann Cicilian
		26	Ann dau. of Man^l-Francis & Ann Silva
	August	2	Willm son of W^m & Susannah Cottle
		12	John son of John & Ann Pott
		29	Mary dau. of Robert & Susannah Stephenson
	September	20	Mary dau. of John & Mary Jones
	October	2	Hannah dau. of Geo. & Hannah Mico
		17	Mary dau. of Edwd & Mary Tailsworth
		26	John son of Geo. & Elizth Turner
1753	January	4	Susannah dau. of James & Frances Cland
	February	22	Elizth dau. of Willm & Cath^{ne} Pyndar
	March	17	Mary Parson dau. of Peter & Martha Bostock
	April	12	Mary James, aged 21
	May	15	Ann dau. of Samuel & Mary Perry
		24	Ann dau. of Rich^d & Sarah Lawrence
		27	Jane dau. of Xtopher & Sarah Asquish
	June	9	Hannah dau. of Jacob & Ann Binckes
		10	Elizth dau. of W^m & Elizth Bunduck
	July	10	. . . . dau. of Geo. & Mary Mansfield
		20	Ann dau. of John & Hanna Chivers

Years.	Month.	Day.	Names.
1753	August	2	Robt-Higgs son of Robt & Elizth Mott
		2	John son of Robt & Elizth Wareham
	September	9	William son of John & Ann Pott
		30	Mary dau. of John & Mary Capper
	October	15	Mary dau. of W^m & Sarah Dawson
	November	25	George son of Charles & Mary Lemon
	December	2	Lawrence son of Cha. & Sarah l'aissiere
		2	Elizth dau. of Edward & Mary Page
1754	January	27	Thomas son of Thos & Jane Malden
		29	John Peter, a foundling
		29	George [son] of Thos & Elizth Page
	February	15	Samuel [son] of Rich^d & Mary Ward
	March	24	Susannah dau. of Thos & Mary Gurnell
	May	19	George son of Francis & Phyllis Craycraft
		19	Sarah dau. of Jacob & Hannah Gordon
		28	Phœbe dau. of Charles & Hester Holdsworth
	June	9	William son of Jonathan & Elizth Collins
		19	Joseph-Williams son of Rich^d & Sarah Lawrence
	August	16	William son of Thomas & Sarah Maynard
		20	Richard son of Rich^d & Ann Shakeshaft
		29	Ann Yate dau. of John & Dorothy Elizth Whiteside
	September	28	Samuel son of Samuel & Mary Perry
	October	5	Edward son of Edward & Elizabeth Jorden
		13	Jane dau. of John & Elizabeth Potter
		27	Elizabeth dau. of James & Elizth Coles
	November	3	Jemima dau. of Charles & Mary Lemon
	December	25	John [son] of John & Judith Hands
1755	January	22	William son of W^m & Sarah Dawson
	February	9	John-Brailsforth son of W^m & Elizth Bonduck
	March	8	Willm son of W^m & Elizth Wallis
	April	2	Reginald son of Willm & Catherine Pyndar
	May	12	Mary dau. of George & Mary Mansfield
		25	Thomas son of Xtopher & Sarah Asquish
	June	13	William son of Joseph & Mary Dalmeida
	July	13	Mary dau. of Thomas & Elizth Page
	September	2	Thomas son of Edward & Mary Page
		8	William son of John & Ann Pott
		21	Sarah dau. of Robert & Mary Erwing
	October	4	Sarah dau. of John & Sarah Cuttell
		16	Richard son of Rich^d & Ann Bullen
		20	Philip-Payne son of Thos & Sarah Maynard
	November	10	Susannah supposed dau. of Thomas Card & Susannah Warner
	December	10	Robert son of Robt & Elizth Warham
		10	John Thomas son of Thos & Ann Hughes
		28	Mary dau. of James & Elizth Coles
1756	January	30	Arabella dau. of Willm & Sarah Dawson
		31	John son of Rich^d & Sarah Stevens
	February	11	Sarah dau. of Edward & Mary Wix
	March	8	Thomas son of Thos & Mary Gurnell
	April	17	Elizth dau. of John & Elizth Jarvis
	July	12	Giles son of Samuel & Elizth Dean, born June 27, 1749
	August	2	James son of James & Jane Loyd
		4	Daniel [son] of Jacob & Ann Binks
		5	Mary dau. of Danl & Frances Greudon
		12	Jane dau. of W^m & Mary White
	September	5	Susannah dau. of Jacob & Hannah Gordon

Years.	Month.	Day.	Names.
1756	September	13	Johanna dau. of W^m & Cath^{ne} Pyndar
		23	Sarah dau. of Rich^d & Sarah Lawrence
	October	17	Amelia dau. of Giles & Mary Cooper
		17	Willm son of Thos & Elizth Page
	November	8	Joseph son of Thos & Jemima Philips
		14	Thomas son of John & Martha Lucy
1757	January	9	Robert son of Robert & Susan^h Stephenson
		16	John son of W^m & Elizth Bonduck
	February	3	Robert son of John & Ann Pott
		20	Robert son of Robt & Elizth Mott
	March	8	John son of John & Sarah Cuttel
		17	Elizabeth Maria dau. of Robt & Marg: Mandeville
		25	Jemima dau. of Charles & Mary Lemon
	April	3	John son of Joseph & Susan Barber
		17	Thomas son of Robert & Elizabth Warham
	May	10	Edward Halled son of W^m & Susan^h Jephcoat
		15	W^m son of Willm & Ann Baement
	June	23	Thomas son of Josiah & Mary Bazire
	July	30	Mary dau. of John & Elizabeth Jarvis
	August	4	John son of John & Mary Beech
	October	24	Sarah dau. of Willm & Elizth Wallis
	November	7	Sarah dau. of John & Sarah Page
		10	Robert son of George & Mary Manfield
	December	4	John son of John & Rose Lewis
		12	James son of James & Marg^t Higginbotham
		18	Thomas son of Thomas & Elizabeth Hilton
		18	Henry son of Thomas & . . . . Hardy
1758	February	5	Elizabeth dau. of Edward & Mary Wix
		8	George son of Samuel & Ann Perry
		10	Jemima dau. of Thomas & Jemima Philips
		17	James Peter son of Timothy & Betteris Seaman
	March	7	Ann Elizth dau. of John & Elizth Legros
		27	Charles son of William & Elizabeth Hall
	April	23	Ann dau. of Robert & Ann Brown
		30	Nathaniel son of Giles & Mary Cooper
	May	4	Elizabeth dau. of Robert & Marg^t Mandeville
		16	Sarah dau. of Michael & Ann Pace
		22	Ann dau. of Thomas & Mary Gurnell
	June	24	Ann dau. of Edward & Rebecca Laurence
		25	Elizth dau. of Robt & Susannah Stephenson
		26	Jane dau. of Thos & Elizth Hosking
	July	17	Richard son of Richard & Sarah Lawrence
		26	Robert son of Thomas & Sarah Maynard
	September	2	Noah son of Noah & Susannah Le Crass
		24	John son of John & Martha Lucy
	October	15	Thomas son of Thos & Elizth Pitman
		17	Ann dau. of William & Ann Bement
	November	19	Elizth dau. of John & Elizth Jarvis
1759	February	19	Mary dau. of Josiah & Mary Bazire
	March	25	James son of John & Elizth Legross
	April	2	Susannah dau. of George & Elizth Fennilow
		5	Mary dau. of Charles & Mary Lemon
		11	Henry son of Wm Jeffery & Elizth Cely
	May	25	Martin Patrick Blake son of Robert & Margaret Mandeville
	June	24	Sarah dau. of George & Mary Mansfield
	July	22	Alexander Charles son of Robert & Elizabeth Warham
		26	Robert son of Robert & Jane Brown

Years.	Month.	Day.	Names.
1759	August	2	William son of Robert & Elizth Motte
		8	Edward son of W^m & Susan^h Jephcoat
	September	2	Martha dau. of Edward & Mary Wix
		2	Ann dau. of Jacob & Hannah Gordon
		16	Ann Theodosia dau. of Luke & Susannah Merton
	October	8	Mary Ann dau. of John & Sarah Cuttell
		21	Mary dau. of William & Mary Mansfield
		30	William son of Edward & Rebecca Laurence
	November	21	Thomas son of Bicknell & Rebecca Coney
	December	9	Jane dau. of Thoma' & Elizabeth Pitman
1760	January	13	Thomas son of William & Ann Bement
	February	3	Mary dau. of John & Ann Cox
		9	Thomas son of Peter & Mary Sheldon
		21	Mary dau. of John & Martha Lucy
	March	9	Joseph son of Joseph & Elizth Orpwood
		23	Robert son of John & Elizth Jarvis
		23	Jane dau. of Thomas & Elizth Hilton
	April	12	William son of W^m & Mary Hickling
	July	13	William son of Thomas & Mary Gurney
	September	22	Robert Dennis son of Robt & Marg^t Mandeville
		29	Willm Jeffery son of Wm Jeff^y & Elizth Sealy
	October	14	Ann dau. of Michael & Ann Pace
	November	28	Elizabeth dau. of Willm & Elizabeth Angel
		28	Rebecca dau. of Bicknell & Rebecca Coney
	December	18	Mary Sarah dau. of Wm Mitchel & Martha Sale
		21	John son of Robert & Jane Brown
1761	January	9	Mary Rous dau. of Jane & Hannah Powell
		12	John son of John & Elizabeth Legross
	February	20	Thomas John son of John & Ann Garey
	March	8	Frances dau. of Thomas & Elizth Pitman
		26	Elizth Smalley dau. of Willm & Elizth Wallis
	June	21	Willm son of Willm & Jane Jones
	July	3	Mary dau. of Samuel & Mary Hodgson
		5	George son of George & Elizabeth Fennilow
		24	Sarah dau. of Jelf & Elizth Lamb
		26	Margaret dau. of John & Mary Childrey
	April*	26	Mary Ann dau. of John & Elizabeth Jarvis
	September	21	Mary Thomas, a Black, aged about 30
	October	11	Mary dau. of Thomas & Mary Hanson
		12	Rachel dau. of Willm & Elizabeth Smithers
	November	29	Richard son of Richard & Elizth Marks
	December	6	William son of Thos & Elizth Hilton
1762	January	3	Elizth Holt son of Luke & Susannah Murton
		7	John son of John & Mary Page
		10	Robert son of Robert & Sarah Lawrence
		31	Charles son of Samuel & Ann Perry
	February	·22	Henry son of William & Sarah Dawson
	March	11	Anna Maria dau. of W^m & Mary Mansfield
		20	Francis son of John & Elizabeth Legros
		24	John son of Richard & Mary East
	April	6	Mary dau. of Joseph & Elizabeth Orpwood
	May	16	Robert son of Willm & Mary Hickling
		19	Joseph Ellis son of Willm & Elizabeth Sely
		23	Edward son of Edward & Mary Wix
		30	William son of Robert & Jane Browne

* Sic.

Years.	Month.	Day.	Names.
1762	June	18	Joseph son of William & Jane Jones
	July	4	Thomas son of John & Martha Lucy
		4	Richard son of Thomas & Dorothy Besley
	August	1	Jn° son of Jn° & Eliz. Jarvis
	October	28	Elizth dau. of Samuel & Mary Hodgson
	November	10	Elizth dau. of Jelf & Elizth Lamb
		21	Sarah dau. of John & Sarah Peacock
	December	21	William & Dorothy son & dau. of Willm & Dorothy Thornton
1763	January	16	Thomas son of John & Mary Christian
	February	3	Elizabeth dau. of W^m & Elizabeth Smithers
		20	Mary dau. of Charles & Mary Townsend
		24	Robert son of Robert & Elizth Mott
	March	22	Sophia dau. of Joseph & Hannah Powell
		27	Elizabeth dau. of Francis & Mary Kensall
	April	6	Sophia Susannah dau. of John & Mary Symonds
		12	John son of William & Elizabeth Angel
	May	8	Thomas son of Thomas & Mary Hanson
		15	Paul son of Paul & Catherine Aylett
	June	26	Mary dau. of Willm & Mary Hickling
	July	24	Thomas son of Thomas & Mary Gurnell
	September	5	John Lernoult son of Joseph & Elizabeth Vaux
		19	Kent an Indian Black about 18 years old
	October	2	Ann dau. of Joseph & Ann Rigacci
		12	Elizabeth dau. of David & Elizabeth Court
		16	John son of John & Catherine Foster
	November	13	John son of John & Mary Childrey
		13	Thomas son of John & Sarah Nelson
	December	2	John son of Richard & Sarah Board
1764	January	15	Michael son of Robert & Jane Brown
		22	Mary Ann dau. of Richard & Elizabeth Porter
		24	Sarah dau. of Thomas & Dorothy Beezley
	February	5	Mary dau. of Thomas & Mary Tyrrel
		21	John son of Richard & Sarah Lawrence
		23	Ann dau. of George & Susannah Evans
		27	Sarah dau. of Thomas & Elizabeth Hilton
	March	11	Mary-Bliss-Atkins dau. of Jonathan & Martha Pinkney
		11	Martha dau. of John & Martha Lucy
		15	Jane dau. of James & Lydia Pickett
	April	21	Samuel son of John & Elizabeth Jarvis
	May	6	Margaret dau. of James & Margaret . . . .
		10	John Henry son of John & Sarah Peacock
	June	9	Ann dau. of James & Ann Townsend
		12	John Day son of Francis & Mary Kensall
	July	1	Susannah dau. of Luke & Susannah Murton
		22	Mary dau. of Rich^d & Elizabeth Marks
	August	16	Robert son of Willm & Elizabeth Smithers
	September	10	Mary dau. of Bloss & Sarah Branwhite
		16	Daniel son of Thos & Sarah Walker
	October	7	Willm son of Willm & Elizth Angel
		8	Thomas-Goodman son of David & Elizth Court
	November	4	William son of Edward & Mary Wix
		12	Jonathan son of Bicknell & Ann Coney
		20	James-Thos son of Thomas & Sarah Nicholson
		22	Daniel son of Daniel & Mary Spurgeon
	December	2	Dorothy dau. of Willm & Mary Hickling
		3	Sophia dau. of Willm & Sarah Dawson

Years.	Month.	Day.	Names.
1764	December	11	Joseph son of George & Mary Ann Mercer
		27	Catherine dau. of John & Cath^ine Woods
			Richard son of Rich^d & Sarah Board was born Oct. 16 1764 & bapt^d as certified by ye Godfathers & Godmothers. Thos Woods, Curate, 5 July 1786
1765	January	5	John son of Joseph & Eliz^th Greatrex
		10	Jane,* Daughter of the Most Noble John Duke of Atholl, and Charlotte his Dutchess, And
			George, son of James Farqurson† Esqr and the Right Honble Emelia Lady Sinclair his wife, were baptiz^d at his Graces house in South Audley Street, within the Parish of St George Hanover Square, this tenth day of January One Thousand seven hundred and Sixty five, by me John Thomas, D.D., Domestick Chaplain to his Grace and Rector of this Parish
		20	Sarah dau. of Willm & Jane Rutland
		20	Elizabeth dau. of Joseph & Rachel Roberts
	February	24	Rebecca-Graham dau. of Thos & Mary Hanson
	March	17	Philadelphia, dau. of James & Ann Palmer
	April	12	Joseph son of Joseph & Elizabeth Vaux
		2‡	Edward son of Willm & Dorothy Thornton
		28	Sally dau. of Joseph & Hannah Powel
	May	19	Ann dau. of John & Sarah Nelson
	June	20	John-Jeffreys son of Wm-Jeffreys & Elizabeth Sely
	July	7	Elizabeth dau. of Thomas & Elizabeth Hilton
		21	Rebecca dau. of George & Susannah Evans
	August	4	John son of John & Ann Harrisen
		22	Ann-Whiteside dau. of Francis & Mary Kensal
	September	8	Mary dau. of John & Hester Smith
		18	Catherine Moss a Jamaica black woman ab^t 45
		25	Jane-Elizabeth dau. of Andrew & Martha Johnson
	October	1	William-Francis son of Richard & Sarah Board
		6	John son of Robert & Jane Brown
		28	Ann dau. of William & Elizabeth Angel
	November	12	James son of James & Lydia Pickett
		21	Thomas Villiers son of Thomas & Maria Theresa Lamb
	December	22	John son of John & Elizabeth Grimstone
1766	January	1	George son of John & Martha Lucy
	March	18	Jane dau. of Thomas & Sarah Nicholson
	April	6	Elizabeth dau. of Joseph & Elizabeth Greatrex
		27	Dorothy dau. of Charles & Mary Townsend
	May	25	Elizabeth dau. of John & Sarah Peacock
		27	Elizabeth Peters } Foundlings
		81	John Peters
	June	6	Bloss Branwhite son of Bloss & Sarah
		27	Elizabeth dau. of Joseph & Elizabeth Vaux
	July	13	Anna Maria dau. of James & Ann Palmer

* She was born Dec. 2, 1764, and married August 8, 1785, John Grossett Muirhead, Esq. Her father was John, third Duke of Atholl, who died Nov. 5, 1774; her mother was Charlotte, only surviving daughter of James second Duke of Atholl.

† Of Invercauld. He married Amelia, daughter of Lord George Murray, fifth son of John, first Duke of Atholl. She married firstly in 1750, John, eighth Lord Sinclair, who was attainted for his concern in the rebellion in 1715, and died in 1750.

‡ The Register from April 2, 1765, to May 28, 1772, is subscribed " E. Tinley, Curate ; " and from June 21, 1772, to December 4, 1774, " E. Tinley, Register."

Years.	Month.	Day.	Names.
1766	July	20	William son of Luke & Susannah Murton
		27	George son of John & Mary Childrey
		27	William son of Wm & Mary Hickling
	August	24	John Folgham son of William & Jane Rutland
	September	2	William son of Bicknell & Ann Coney was born
			This was omitted. E. Tinley, Curate
	October	15	Sihon son of Jno & Elizabeth Rofe. Adult
		16	Rebecca dau. of Henry & Eliz. Pyefinch
	November	16	Edward son of Wm & Dorothy Thornton
1767	January	4	Mary dau. of Thomas & Elizabeth Hilton
		31	Clementina dau. of John & Esther Smith
	February	8	Thomas son of Jno & Eliz. Cuthbert
	March	8	Joseph son of Joseph & Hannah Powell
	April	2	John son of John & Elizth Brown
		6	Mary dau. of James & Frances Westall
	May	5	Francis son of Francis & Mary Kensall
		6	James son of Anthony & Leonora Gilman
		17	Mary dau. of Robert & Jane Brown
		24	John son of John & Jane Dyster
	June	4	Ann dau. of Chas & Mary Townsend
		7	Elizabeth dau. of Francis & Eliz. Baker
		28	Elizabeth Martha dau. of George & Eliz. Anthony
	July	8	Rebecca dau. of Edwd & Mary Wix
		16	Wm son of Michael & Esther Eaton
	August	16	Sarah dau. of John & Ann Harrison
	September	2	Thos son of Thos & Hannah Brown
	October	16	William Sandall son of Wm & Eliz. Angell
		22	Samuel John son of Geo. & Eliz. Cooper
	November	1	Mary dau. of Richd & Mary Hatt
		5	Letitia Ann dau. of Wm Jeffreys & Eliz. Sely
		6	Robt Walpole son of Walpole & Margaret Chamberlayn
		24	Jno son of Jno & Lettice Wilson
	December	1	Ann dau. of Wm & Ann Lovegrove
		12	Samuel Francis, a Black
		12	Robert Hardwicke, a Black
		29	Thos son of Wm & Dorothy Thornton
1768	January	6	Alice Mary dau. of Joseph & Eliz. Greatrex
		10	Hannah Beckett dau. of John & Elizabeth Grimstone
		24	Hannah Smith dau. of James & Ann Palmer
	February	7	Rebecca dau. of Wm & Mary Hickling
		19	John son of Jno & Sarah Thompson
		24	Henry son of Henry & Eliz. Pyefinch
	March	9	Sarah dau. of Jno & Eliz. Brown
	April	17	James Hilton son of Thos & Eliz. Hilton
		20	Sally Bulmer dau. of Wm & Sarah Bulmer
	June	13	Adrian Lernoult son of Joseph & Eliz. Vaux
	July	2	Mary dau. of Ann —— & Herman Nail
		17	Ann dau. of Francis & Eliz. Baker
	August	3	Wm George son of Jno & Margaret Coleman
		15	Sally dau. of Jno & Sarah Peacock
		28	Sarah dau. of Bloss & Sarah Branwhite
	September	20	Edwd son of Michael & Margt Lacey
		26	Mary dau. of Edwd & Mary Bacon
	October	10	Thomas son of Thos & Sarah Grape
		12	Maria dau. of Jno & Christian Handy
		12	Jno son of Jno & Ann Letts
	November	6	Jas son of Jno & Susanna Grimes

Years.	Month.	Day.	Names.
1768	December	11	Edward son of Eliz. & Sam¹ Tugwell
		27	Johanna Leonora dau. of Anthony & Leonora Gilman
1769	January	1	John Jeremiah son of Jnᵒ & Anne Skinner
		15	Wᵐ George Small son of Jnᵒ & Mary Small
		22	Eliz. dau. of Wᵐ & Dorothy Thornton
	February	1	Wᵐ son of Francis & Mary Kensall
		12	Eliz. dau. of Wᵐ & Martha Nash
		19	Wᵐ son of Edwᵈ & Mary Wix
		26	Thoˢ son of Jnᵒ & Jane Dyster
	March	1	Robᵗ son of Robᵗ & Ann Ley
		5	Rebecca dau. of Jnᵒ & Ann Harrison
		21	Herbert son of Henry & Eliz. Pyefinch
		23	Jane Eliz. dau. of Jnᵒ & Eliz. Furman
	April	27	Jane Dorothy dau. of Wᵐ & Jane Holloway
		30	Robert son of Robert & Ann Tolley
	May	4	George son of George & Eliz. Anthony
		7	Michael son of Michael & Esther Eaton
		21	Joseph son of Joseph & Eliz. Greatrex
		28	Thoˢ son of Jnᵒ & Jane Dyster
	June	3	Catherine dau. of Wᵐ & Eliz. Angell
		14	Martha dau. of George Joseph & Mary Higginson
		18	James Thomas son of James Arthur & Jane Tuck
	July	2	Joseph son of Joseph & Hannah Powell
		23	Eliz. dau. of James & Ann Palmer
		30	George Wᵐ son of Anne & Herman Nail
		30	George son of George & Anne Urling
		31	Lucy dau. of Jnᵒ & Martha Lucy
	August	15	Wᵐ son of Jnᵒ & Mary Ackland
	September	3	Wᵐ son of Jnᵒ & Lettice Wilson
		10	Wᵐ son of Francis & Eliz. Baker
		13	James son of Thoˢ & Sarah Grape
		24	Margaret dau. of Jnᵒ & Eliz. Grimes
	October	4	Richard son of Richᵈ & Mary Hatt
		25	Ann dau. of Jnᵒ & Ann Letts
	November	1	Ann dau. of Jnᵒ & Jane Sharpless
		5	Joseph son of Jnᵒ & Esther Smith
		24	Henry son of Henry & Drusilla Penny
	December	17	Samuel son of Thoˢ & Eliz. Hilton
1770	January	8	Elizᵗʰ dau. of Edwᵈ & Mary Bacon
		14	Abraham son of Robᵗ & Jane Brown
		14	Thoˢ son of Robᵗ & Elizᵗʰ Mott
	February	20	Thoˢ son of Jnᵒ & Christian Hardy
	March	4	Francis son of Francis & Eliz. Thompson, Vintner
		11	Robᵗ son of Francis & Mary Kensall
		25	Mary dau. of Wᵐ & Mary Benn
	April	11	Mary dau. of Wᵐ & Sarah Thompson
	May	7	Susannah dau. of Sam¹ & Eliz. Bampton
		10	Thoˢ son of Wᵐ & Mary Cogan
		20	Mary dau. of Thoˢ & Hannah Rigal
	June	24	Miriam dau. of Jnᵒ & Mary Bailey
	July	1	Rachel dau. of Jnᵒ & Ann Harrison
		16	Joseph Henry son of Joseph & Eliz. Vaux
		15	Elizabeth dau. of Jnᵒ & Eliz. Furman
		17	William son of Wᵐ & Sarah Bulmer
	August	26	Anna Maria dau. of Wᵐ & Eliz. Angell
	September	2	Jonathan son of Chaˢ & Alice Garland
		2	Peggy dau. of Jnᵒ & Mary Childrey

Yeare.	Month.	Day.	Names.
1770	September	21	Tho⁸ Richard son of Tho⁸ & Sarah Grape
		23	Stephen Wright son of Jn° & Eliz. Grimstone
		30	Mary dau. of Bloss & Sarah Branwhite
		30	Olive dau. of Sam¹ & Elizabᵗʰ Tugwell
	October	5	Robᵗ son of Robᵗ & Ann Ley
		21	Grace dau. of Alpha & Grace Higgins
		21	Paul Tho⁸ son of Jn° & Jane Dyster
		24	Elizᵗʰ dau. of Herman & Ann Nail
		30	James Bishop, a Foundling
	December	1	Sarah dau. of Wᵐ & Ann Lovegrove
		16	Cha⁸ son of Jn° & Mary Ackland
		18	Harriet, dau. of Jn° & Rebecca Flude
		25	Dan¹ son of Dan¹ & Mary Spurgeon
		26	Amy dau. of Joseph & Elizᵗʰ Greatrex
1771	January	14	Susanna dau. of Richᵈ & Mary Hatt
		20	George son of Jn° & Sarah Blaksley
	February	3	George son of Tho⁸ & Eliz. Hilton
		10	Elizᵗʰ dau. of Ja⁸ Arthur & Jane Tuck
	March	3	Sam¹ son of Edwᵈ & Mary Wix
		17	John son of Jn° & Lettice Wilson
	April	14	Anna Maria dau. of Francis & Eliz. Baker
		14	Sarah dau. of Jn° & Ann Letts
		14	Gideon William son of Anthony & Leonora Gilman
	May	12	Urania dau. of Francis & Mary Kensall
		12	Henry son of Henry & Elizᵗʰ Loft
		14	Alexander son of George & Mary Bayly
	July	7	Tho⁸ son of Tho⁸ & Hannah Rigal
		7	Tho⁸ Caleb son of Joseph & Hannah Powell
	August	7	Wᵐ son of Jn° & Sarah Peacock
		15	Elizᵗʰ dau. of Henry & Drusilla Penny
		10	Mariana, dau. of Edwᵈ & Mary Tinley
	September	22	Elizᵗʰ dau. of Cha⁸ & Alice Garland
		29	Jane dau. of Tho⁸ & Mary Cotygarne
		29	Charles son of Cha⁸ & Mary Sweetenburg
	October	13	Richard & Sarah son & dau. of Michael & Esther Eaton, twins
	November	13	George son of Robᵗ & Ann Ley
		24	Hannah dau. of Ann & Herman Nail
		27	Mary dau. of Robᵗ & Mary Hulme
1772	January	24	Orlando son of Jn° Beverly & Eleanor Watts
	February	9	Wᵐ & Ann, son & dau. of George & Ann Urling, twins
	March	16	Sam¹ son of Richᵈ & Mary Hatt
		22	Sarah dau of Wᵐ & Sarah Thompson
	April	5	Samuel son of Sam¹ & Elizabeth Tugwell
		15	Mary Cæcilia dau. of Joseph & Elizᵗʰ Vaux
	May	10	George, son of Wᵐ & Eliz. Angell
		15	Elizᵗʰ dau. of Tho⁸ & Sarah Grape
		24	Jn° son of Francis & Elizᵗʰ Baker
		28	Elizᵗʰ dau. of Rowland & Frances Richardson
	June	21	Jn° son of Jn° & Ann Letts
		28	Mary Harrison, dau. of Jn° & Mary Ackland
	August	9	Junia Augusta dau. of Jasper & Hannah Lucas
	September	29	Mary dau. of Edward & Mary Tinley
	October	4	Joseph son of Francis & Elizᵗʰ Thompson, Vintner
		18	Mary dau. of Ja⁸ Arthur & Jane Tuck
	November	1	Elizᵗʰ dau. of Jn° & Elizᵗʰ Grimes
		15	Robᵗ son of Robᵗ & Jane Brown

Years.	Month.	Day.	Names.
1772	November	19	Francis son of Jnᵒ & Ann Nodin
1773	January	24	Jnᵒ Bailey, son of George & Mary Bailey
		28	Edwᵈ son of Jnᵒ & Catherine King
	March	13	Maria dau. of Jnᵒ Christian & Martha Hoffman
		18	Francis, son of Edwᵈ & Mary Bacon
		21	Martha dau. of Edwᵈ & Mary Wix
		26	Margaret dau. of Jaˢ & Ellen Brander
	April	4	Jnᵒ son of Anthony & Leonora Gilman
		20	Eliz. dau. of Jnᵒ & Eliz. Thomas
		25	Eliz. dau. of Robᵗ & Susanna Findlay
	May	2	Hetty dau. of Jnᵒ & Esther Smith
		4	Wᵐ Gilbert son of Wᵐ Gilbert & Sarah Matthews
		21	Sophia dau. of Joseph & Eliz. Vaux
	June	11	Herman son of Ann & Herman Nail
		20	Robert son of Robᵗ & Mary Hulme
		20	Caleb Edward son of Joseph & Hannah Powell
		23	Edwᵈ Sikes son of Edwᵈ & Ann Lowe
		23	Thomas son of Wᵐ & Ann Ball. Workhouse poor
	July	16	Jaˢ son of Jaˢ & Mary Woodmason, born June 20
	August	7	Harriet dau. of Michael & Esther Eaton
		22	Sarah dau. of Charles & Alice Garland
	September	10	Mary Ann dau. of Jnᵒ Beverly & Eleanor Watts
	October	17	Wᵐ son of Wᵐ & Mary Cogan
		18	Sarah Greatrex, dau. of Joseph & Sarah Greatrex. The Father was burᵈ 10 Sepᵗ
	November	25	Augustus son of Richard & Mary Hatt
	December	4	Jane dau. of Wᵐ & Eliz. Angell
		23	William son of Francis & Eliz. Thompson, Vintner
1774	January	14	Frances dau. of Rowland & Frances Richardson
		16	Mary dau. of Wᵐ & Jane Innes
		21	Nathanael Wright son of Jnᵒ & Sarah Blaksley
	February	6	Catherine Horton dau. of George & Ann Urling
		13	Helena dau. of Edward & Mary Tinley
	March	27	Thoˢ son of Danˡ Geeves & Sarah
	April	3	Sarah dau. of Thomas & Mary Wood
	May	8	Sarah Thomas dau. of Sarah & Thomas Loveday. The Father died Decʳ 20 last
		15	Sophia dau. of Francis & Elizabeth Baker
	June	5	Headley son of Jnᵒ & Mary Ackland
		5	Susanna dau. of Robᵗ & Susanna Findlay
		9	James Ryx son of Jnᵒ Christian & Martha Hoffman
		12	Peter William son of Peter & Ann Maber
		17	Martha dau. of Robert Cox & Mary Trapp
		19	Jnᵒ son of George & Mary Bayly
	July	8	Hannah dau. of John & Jennett Coutts
	August	28	Charles son of Wᵐ & Sarah Thompson, Calendar
	September	8	Francis son of Robᵗ & Catherine Wigram
		23	Mary dau. of James & Mary Magdalen Woodmason, born 28 Aug.
		26	Mary dau. of Wᵐ & Susanna Williams
	October	9	Jane dau. of Robert & Jane Brown
		18	Mary dau. of Thoˢ & Elizabeth Brown
		23	Martha Elizabeth, dau. of Jnᵒ & Sarah Price
		30	Thomas son of Thomas & Hannah Rigal
	November	20	Robert son of Robert & Mary Hulme
		29	Ann dau. of Wᵐ & Eliz. Stevens
	December	4	Martha dau. of Charles & Alice Garland

Weddings.

Years.	Month.	Day.	Names.
1673*	May	20	Benj. Poole of St Ann Aldersgate, & Anne Smith. Licence
	June	24	John Lowman of St Georges Southwark, & ffrances Knowles. Licence
		25	Osmund† Mordaunt son of John Lord Mordaunt of Fulham Midd^x and Mary Bulger of Lirgan n^r Goray in Ireland were married this day
	November	6	Willm Holiday of St Mary Magdalen & Leah King of St Peter Cornehill, London. Licence
	December	30	Christ^o Benardo Mitchell of Fanchurch Street London & Mary Slany of St Stephens Coleman Street. Licence
1675	August	5	Thomas Young of Hartly co. Kent & Ann Frankwell of Stoone in the same p'ish (sic). Licence
1676	May	16	Richard Roberts of St Peters Cornhill & Frances James of St Botolphs Bishopsgate extra. Licence
	July	15	Lawrence Wilsheir of Stepney co. Midd. & Jane Payne of St Mary Savoy co. Midd., widow. Licence
1677	March	17	Henry Uthwhat of St Margaret Westm^r & Elizabeth Fisher of Lambeth co. Surrey. Licence
1678	April	25	Henry Harington of St Peters Cornhill & Hannah Kingdome of the same parish. Licence
	May	20	Isaac Monly of St Mary Whitechapel & Mary Newland of Christ Church
	June	23	Benjamin Gravill of this parish, Bachelor, & Ann Lucas of St Butolph Bishopsgate London. Licence
	November	28	William Langford of St Andrews Holborn, Bachelor, & Elizabeth Purchase, maiden, of this parish. Licence
1681	May	12	William Ash of Paston co. Northampton, Bachelor, and Elizabeth Massinbird of the same place, widow. Lic.

* The Register from May 20, 1673, to May 4, 1704, is subscribed "Will. Beveridge, parson," "Will. Beveridge, D.D., parson."

† In respect to this entry there is preserved in the Register a letter from Sir John Page Wood, Bart., Rector of St. Peter's, dated 30 Nov., 1829, in which he says, "on minutely investigating the register of marriage of one Osmond Mordaunt with Mary Bulger, dated 1673, I am clearly of opinion that the said entry of marriage is a gross and clumsy forgery; my opinion is formed on the discrepancies which exist between the said entry and those of the same period before and after it. Its handwriting is evidently more modern than those near it; it is not entered like the others with a specification as to the ceremony's having been performed by the authority of Banns or Licence; the parchment it is written on is thinner in substance than the rest of the book, as if an erasure had been made. The entry is made at the bottom of the page and there is no signature thereon, either of Incumbent or Churchwarden, which occurs in every other page of that period." A pedigree is also given, drawn up by some member of the Heralds' College, by which it appears that Osmond Mordaunt, who was fourth son of John, created Lord Mordaunt of Ryegate, 10 July, 1559, was not more than eighteen years of age in 1677, and consequently would only have been fourteen at the time of this reputed marriage. In the Baptisms under date of 29 June, 1674, is this entry, "Peter, the son of Osmund and Mary." It is in a different handwriting to the other entries, is on the last line at the bottom of the page, and has evidently been inserted after the page had been signed Will: Beveridge, as one of the figures of the date crosses that signature, and in every other page a small space is left between the last entry and his signature. There can be no doubt but that both entries have been interpolated.

Year.	Month.	Day.	Names.
1681	December	1	Sir William Luckin* Baronet of Messinghall co. Essex & Mary Sherington of this parish. Licence
	February	23	Marmaduke Darell of Grays Inn co. Midd^x, Esq., & Mary Glascock of ffarneham co. Essex. Licence
1682	April	18	Thomas King & Ann Church
	June	1	Charles Whitaker of the par. of St John in Bedverdin co. Worcester, Bachelor, & Elizabeth Rogers of Chelmsford co. Essex. Licence
	July	2	ffra'cis Curby of this parish & Elizabeth Twelves of Linn Regis co. Norfolk. Licence

These weddings being omitted the Registring in their due places are here inserted for the benefit of those they may concern.

Year.	Month.	Day.	Names.
1679	September	12	John Wickins of St Saviours Southwark, Widower, & Mary Juson, Widow. Licence
1679	December	31	James Willson of St Peters poor London, Bachelor, & Mary Parker of the same parish, Maiden. Licence
1680	April	20	Samuel Wills of the parish of St John at Hackney, Bachelor, & Elizabeth Clarke of the same p'ish, widow, by Licence
1685	December	8	Daniel Antrobus of St Bartholomew the less, Bachelor, & Mary Hist of St Vedast London, Maiden. Licence
1688	July	22	John Roope, widower, & Anne Williams, Maiden, both of this p'ish. Licence
1695	January	9	John Gerrard of St Botolph's Bishopsgate, Bachelor Widower, & Mary Raynmorter of St Andrews Undershaft, Widow. Licence
1682	July	4	Thomas Gouldsmyth of Tudington co. Bedford, Bach^r, & Lidea Young of Pauls Walden co. Hartford. Licence
	October	25	Stephen Blackhead of St Solvares Southwark co. Surry & Elizabeth Lea of St Botolph Bishopsgate London. Licence
1683	October	17	Thomas Chappell of Walthamstow co. Essex, & Ann Clayton of the same place. Licence
	November	13	Robert Stiles of Lambeth co. Surry & Susanna Browne of St Peters Cornhill London. Licence
		18	John Weston & Elizabeth Stower both of St Peters Cornhill London. Licence
	December	2	Daniell Murfin of St Pulchers London & Hester Tapping of St Peters Cornhill London. Licence
	January	29	Thomas Willson Esqr of Lincolns Inn co. Midd^x & Elizabeth Colborne of St George Southwark co. Surry. Licence
1684	April	13	Nath'niel Derritt, of St Nicholas Coleabby & Jane Wood of St Sepulchers, widow
	June	8	John Heyling of St Martaines in ye feilds, Bacheler, and Sussan'a Sherman of the same parish. Licence
	August	5	Philip Browne vicar of Halstead Essex & Margarett Purchas of St Gregory London. Licence
	February	3	Anthony Hilder of Stepney, Bachelor, & Susan'a Greene of Christchurch London, maiden. Licence
	March	19	Henry Blackborrow of St Botolphs without Aldgate London, Bachelor, & Bridget Bonden of the same parish, maiden. Licence
1685	November	11	Henry Sanders of St Peters Cornhill London, Bachelor, & Ann Whetstone of the same parish, maiden. Licence

* See note *ante*, page 10.

Years.	Month.	Day.	Names.
1685	January	14	Thomas Pitts of St Martins Ludgate, Bachelor, & Ann Barloe of the same parish, maiden. Licence
	February	25	William James of St Clement Danes co. Middlesex & Sarah Church of St Georges Southworke co. Surry. Licence
1686	June	2	James Saywell of Wallingham co. Cambridge, Bachelor, & ffrances Gainesford of St Andrew Holburne. Licence
		30	James Donne of St Andrew Holburne, Bachelor, & Katharine Clarke of the foresaid parish. Licence
	July	16	Philip Brokesby of St Sepulcers, Wood^r, & Elizabeth ffowles of the City of Canterbury, widow. Licence
		21	Nicholas Harwood of St Margaret Lothbury, Bachelor, & Prisella Henn of St Peter Cornhill. Licence
	October	9	Thomas Tucker of St Lawrance Jury, Bachelor, & Hannah Eden of the parish aforesaid, maiden. Licence
		25	John Higgs of St Ethelburgh, Bachelor, & Mary Brett of St Bartholomew the Less, maiden. Licence
	November	29	Samvell Hutchins of Stamford river co. Essex, Bachelor, & Judith Stacy, maiden, of the same parish. Licence
		30	Nathanell Tompson of St Brides, Bachelor, & Sarah Waller of St Stephen Coleman Street, maiden. Licence
	January	4	William Jefferies of the par. of St Andrews Holburne, Wid^r, & Honora Sands of St Peters Cornhill, widow. Licence
		26	Samvell Newman of St Michel Cornhill, Bachelor, & Elizabeth Tillery of St Peters Cornhill. Licence
1687	March	30	James Smyth of St Peters Cornhill, Bachelor, & Elizth Wells of the same parish, maiden. Licence
	April	4	Richard Puckwell of East Grinsteed co. Sussex, Bachelor, & Sarah Tailer of the same parish, maiden. Licence
		2	Thomas Ray of St Peters Cornhill London, Bachelor, & Elizth Greene of Mepem co. Kent, maiden. Licence
		7	Thomas Dalton of St Mary Woolnoth, Bachelor, & Joyce Hall of St Peters Cornhill, widow. Licence
	May	16	Sr Edward Windham* Baronet of Orchard Windham co. Somerset & Katherine Leueson Gower of Trentham co. Stafford, maiden. Licence
	June	18	William Murford of St Michael Cornhill London, Bachelor, & Joyce Carter of this parish, maiden. Licence
	July	20	Patrick Curwen of St Michael Cornhill London, Bachelor, & Elizabeth Scott of the same parish, maiden. Licence
	October	17	Nathaniel Jarvis of St Dunstans in the East, Bachelor, & Hannah Church of St George Southworke, maiden. Lic.
		24	ffrancis Smyth of Abberton co. Essex, Bachelor, & Elizabeth Knapp of East Bergholt co. Suffolk, maiden. Licence
	November	17	John Loyd of this parish, Widower, & Mary Porter of the same, maiden. Licence
		22	William Lewis of Ross co. Hereford, Bachelor, & Sarah Barret of St Mary Le Bow London, maiden. Licence
	December	20	Hanbury Walthall of St Katherine Cree Church London, Bach^r, & Ann Hottoff of the same parish, Widow. Licence
	January	3	Emmanuel Hutson of St Olaves Southwark, Bachelor, and Elizabeth ffownes of Newington co. Middlesex, widow, p' Licence

* He third son of Sir William Wyndham, Bart., and father of Sir William Wyndham, Chancellor of Exchequer, temp. Q. Anne, buried at St. Decumans, co. Somerset, 29 June, 1695. She eldest daughter of Sir William Leveson Gower, of Trentham, Bart., by Lady Jane Granville, eldest daughter of John, Earl of Bath, buried at St. Decuman's, April 18, 1781.

Yeare.	Month.	Day.	Names.
1687	January	25	John Strother of St James Garlickhith, Bachelor, & Ann Loyd of the same parish, maiden. Licence
1688	May	2	Thomas Bateman of Gilsborough co. Northampton, Clerk & Bachelor, & Sarah Crook of the City of Oxford, maiden, p' Licence
	June	22	Anthony Parker of St Margaret Lothbury, Widower, & Hester More of Stepny, Widow. Licence
	August	2	Isaac Cornwell of St Margaret Loathbury, Bachelor, & Sarah Ragg of St Mary Islington, widow, co. Midd^x. Licence
		28	John Parker of St Peters Cornhill, Bachelor, & Sarah Crafts of St Margaret Loathbury, maiden. Licence
	September	6	Anthony Cossins of St Mary Aldermanbury, Bachelor, & Elizabeth Young of St Mary Abchurch. Licence
		18	John Cooke of Acton co. Midd. Esqr, and Elizabeth Hacket of North Crawly co. Buck, maiden. Licence
	October	6	George Capell of St Dunston in the East Bachelor, & Martha Cornwell of St Dunston in the East, spinster, Licence
	November	13	Richard Harison of St Bennet Gracechurch, Bachelor, & Ellzabeth Hampton of Blechinley co. Surrey, spinster, p' Licence
	December	15	John Lucas of St Dunstans in the East, Bachelor, & Judith Ayres of the same parish, Spinster. Licence
		20	William Wise of St Andrew Holborn, Bachelor, & Elizabeth Baker of St Bartholom Exchange, Spinster. Licence
	January	8	John Law of St Michael Cornhil, Bachelor, & Mary Cornish of St Mary Woollnorth, Spinster. Licence
	February	10	Oliver Morris of St Dunstans West, Widower, & Madiline Greene of St Peters Cornhill, widow. Licence
	March	5	Thomas Dyeson, of St Christophers London, & Elizabeth Cox of St Mary White Chappell, widow. Licence
		14	Joshua Taylor of St Martin in the feilds, Widower, & Grace Litleby of St Mary Whitechappell. Licence
1689	April	14	Robert Corbit of St Leonard Eastcheape, Bachelor, and Martha Lamb of St Giles Criplegate, Spinster. Licence
		23	John Vr . . . ge of St Mary Whitechaple, Bachelor, & Elizabeth Deacon, Spinster, of St Helens. Licence
		25	Francis Vickers of St Michael Cornhil, Bachelor, & Elizabeth Lamden of St Margaret Lothbury, Spinster. Licence
	May	5	Thomas ffowle of St Albain Woodstreete & Mary Nayler of the parish of Bread streete London, Spinster. Licence
		21	John Spencer of Sr Butolphs Bishopsgate, Bachelor, and Martha Nuttell of the same parish, Spinster. Licence
	June	8	Daniel Atkins of St Pauls Shadwell co. Middlesex & Jane Hyupp of St Martin Ironmonger lane London. Licence
		13	George Cupwell of Algate, widower, & Martha Vanham of St Mary Whitechappell, Widow. Licence
		18	Peter Fryer of St Martaine Vintrey, Bachelor, & Elizabeth Russell of St Peters Cornhill London, Spinster. Licence
	August	20	Zachary Wright of St Mary Whitechappell London, wid^r, & Mary Collington of the same parish, Widow Licence
	October	31	Jacob Powell of St Bartholomew the Great & Elizabeth Babington, of the parish of St Mary Whitechappell co. Middlesex, Spinster. Licence

Years.	Month.	Day.	Names.
1689	November	6	Edward Parrey of St Margaret Pattons, Bachelor, & Mary Alsop of St Bridget, Spinster. Licence
		26	Robert Johnson of Leatherhead co. Surrey & Elizabeth Lewin of the same place. Licence
	February	6	Jeremiah Waite of St Margaret New Fish street, widow^r & Debora Vtbert of St Katherine Creechurch, Widow of James Vtbert late of this parish. Licence
	March	4	Giles Powell of St Martins in the ffeilds, widow^r, & Dorothy Diggs of St Clement Danes, Widow. Licence
1690	June	10	Richard Partridge to Alice Longmore, both of St Peters Cornhill. Licence
	July	21	William Bayley of Hatfield Herts, & Frances Baker of St Peters Cornhill. Licence
		80	Thomas Dauies of St Sepulchers London to Paternelle Sandolle of St Bridgetts London. Licence
	August	31	John Hogg of St Nicholas Rochester co. Kent to Dorothy Robinson of St Peters Cornhill London. Licence
	September	2	Ichabod Tipping of St Mary Islington co. Midd^x to Mary Dix of the same parish. Licence
	October	28	Gerrard ffowke, widow^r, of St Martins in the Feilds, & Elizabeth Pottinger of Lambeth, Spinster. Licence
	February	14	Henry Briscoe, Bachelor, & Mary Stanley, maiden, both of St Swithin London. Licence
1691	July	16	Andrew Phillipps* of the Inner Temple, Esqr, & Elizabeth Oldfeild of Titsey in the County of Surrey, Maiden p' Licence
		21	John Kember of this parish & Susannah Rowland of St Botolph Bishopsgate. Licence
	October	15	William Nockells of St Botolph Bishopsgate, Widower, & Mary Redman of Stepny, Maiden. Licence
		22	Daniel Goldsmith, Bachelor, & Anne Read, Maiden, both of Hitchin co. Hartford. Licence
	December	10	George Cutbertson of Newcastle upon Tine & Jane Fenwick of St Giles in the Feilds, by Licence
		17	Benjamin Tiplady of St Leonard, Foster Lane, Bachelor, & Anne Wicks of St Sepulchres, by Licence
	January	12	Henry Tunstall of St Bartholomew the Great, Bach^r, & ffrances Richards of St Leonard Shoreditch, Maiden, by Licence
		26	John Cater of St Clements Eastcheap, Bach^r, & Mary Wessell of St Stephen Coleman Street, Spinst. Licence
1692	April	26	George Mason of St Martins Ludgate, Bach^r, and Katherine Standon of St Stephen Colman Street, Spinster. Licence
	June	2	George Barlow, Widower, & Jane Axtell, widow, both of the parish of St Mary Whitechappell. Licence
		15	Alexander Snape & Anne Marriott, both of this parish, by banns
		16	Richard ffarmer & Mary Gold, both of St Clement Danes, by Licence
	August	11	John Picard of St Giles without Cripplegate, Bach^r, and Christian Dod of St Faith, Widow, by Licence

* He son and heir of Fabian Phillipps of Leominster, co. Hereford. She eldest daughter of Sir Anthony Oldfield of Spalding, co. Lincoln, Bart., by Elizabeth, only daughter of Sir Edward Gresham of Titsey, Knt., baptized at Spalding 14 April, 1663, buried there 12 December 1724. She married to her second husband Maurice Johnson of Spalding, Esq., Barrister at Law.

Years.	Month.	Day.	Names.
1692	September	22	John Munrow of Rude Lane, Bach[r], & Margarite Mein of Stepny, Spinster, by Licence
	December	1	Philip Mills of S[t] Mary Islington & Mary Care of S[t] Bartholomew the less, spinster
	January	10	Robert Tristram of Sepulchres, Bach[r], & Mary Stowers, of S[t] Mary Summerset, Spinst, by licence
		31	John Yate of S[t] Mary Woolnoth London, Bach[r], & Margaret Watson of Derby, Spinst, by licence
	February	9	Nicholas Gillum of Brighthelmston in Sussex, Wid[r], & Hannah Usborn of this parish, Spinster. Licence
		23	Thomas Gall of Ipswich in Suffolk, Widower, and Katherine Burton of S[t] Bennet Grace Church, Spinster, by licence
1693	April	18	Daniel Smith of S[t] John Zachary London, Bach[r], & Anne Adams of the Town of Hartford, sp[r], by licence
		25	James Truelove of S[t] Nicholas Cole Abbey London, Bach[r], & Anne Mail of S[t] Andrew Holborn, Sp[r], by Licence
		23	John Howet of the parish of Sepulch', Bach[r], & Katherine ffrank of Botolph Aldersgate, Sp[r], by licence
		28	William Sedgewick of S[t] Olave Hartstreet & Susanna Phipps, Widow, of this parish, by licence
	June	29	Daniel Nickes of Stamford co. Lincoln, Bach[r], & Anne Sergeant of S[t] Andrew Undershaft Lond., Widow
	December	17	Thomas Bunch of S[t] Mary White Chappell, Wid[r], & Mary Taylor of S[t] George Southwark, sp[r], by licence
		26	Hopton Haynes, Gener. of S[t] Dunst. Stepney, & Hannah Sikes of the same parish, sp[r], by licence
	January	2	Thomas Vaughan of Greys Inn, Bach[r], & Mary Chapman of S[t] Giles in the ffeilds, sp[r], by licence
		7	John Mottram of S[t] Lawrence in City of Worcester, Bach[r], & Grace Southgate of S[t] Giles Cripplegate, sp[r], by licence
1694	April	7	Gabriel Pinke of S[t] Botolph Aldersgate, Bach[r], & Anne Clifford of the same parish, sp[r], by licence
		10	Richard Rogers of S[t] Giles Cripplegate, Wid[r], & ffrances Colt of S[t] Andrew Undersh., sp[r], by licence
		13	Thomas Burgh of Waltham Abby Essex, Bach[r], & Susanna Smith of Theydon Garnon in the same County, sp[r]
	May	1	Robert Wescott of S[t] Mary Wool Church, Bach[r], & Elizabeth Draper of this parish, sp[r], by licence
		29	Edward Hull of S[t] Dunstan, Bach[r], & Anne Clemenson of the same parish, sp[r], by licence
	June	3	James Smith Knight, Widower & Philadelphia Willson, sp[r], by licence
		24	Edward Rhett of Billerky co. Essex, Wid[r], & Anne Grocer of Walsham in the Willowes co. Suffolke, Maiden, by licence
	September	2	John Man of S[t] Stephen Colman Street, Bachelor, & Mary Whitehead of S[t] Olave Southwark, Maiden. Licence
	October	20	William Hardis of S[t] Sepulchres, Widower, & Mary Moulford of S[t] Hellens, Widow. Licence
		25	William Davies of Slimbridge co. Gloc[r], Bach[r], & Debora Davies of Sanderton, co. Bucks, Maiden. Licence
	December	13	John Wall of S[t] Catherine Cree Church, Bach[r], & Sarah Walling of the same parish, Maiden. Licence
	March	14	William Packer of this parish, Wid[r], & Margarite Browne of S[t] Botolph Aldgate, Widow. Licence

Years.	Month.	Day.	Names.
1695	March	28	James ffrench, of St. Clement Danes, Bach^r, & Rachell Lascow of St Botolphs Aldersgate, sp^r
	May	29	Richard Pierce of Sepulchres parish, Bach^r, & Martha Walker of the same parish, sp^r. Licence
		9	Edmund Taylor of St Mary Savoy, Bach^r, & Ann Mackworth of St Brides, sp^r. Licence
	July	4	Stephen Palmer of Beddington co. Surrey, Bach^r, & Eleanor Heath of the same parish, widow. Licence
	December	1	Walter Griffith of St Martins Outwich & Susanna Wright of St Ethelburga, widow. Licence
	January	9	John Gerrard & Mary Raynmorter
	February	25	Samuell Neal of St Bartholomew the less, Bach^r, & Sarah Stone of the same parish, sp^r. Licence
1696	May	28	Robert Julian of St Mildred Poultry, Bach^r, & Elizabeth Langmore of this parish, sp^r. Licence
	June	2	Gerrard Dannett of Elmbridge co. Worcester, Bach^r, & Elizabeth Caldwell of Ridgley co. Stafford, sp^r. Lic.
		29	Robert Bowcher of St Leonard Shoreditch, Bach^r, & Anne Sanders of this parish, widow. Licence
	December	21	Robert Parsons of St Botolphs Aldgate, Bach^r, & Hannah Holbule of the same parish. Licence
	January	24	William Kettle, Bach^r, & Anne Hall, sp^r, both of this parish. Licence
	March	18	Nicholas Ridley, Bach^r, & Elizabeth Turner, Widow, both of St Dunstan's Stepney. Licence
1697	April	8	George Gregory of St Botolphs Aldersgate, Bach^r, & Martha Cobb of St Anne Aldersgate, sp^r. Licence
		22	Thomas Parry, Bach^r, & Anne Wood, sp^r, both of St Olave Hart Street. Licence
	May	6	Thomas Hewett, Bach^r, & Elizabeth Bridges, both of St Olave Hart street. Licence
		25	Daniel Heley of Sepulchres, Wid^r, & Joanna Edwards of Andrews Holborn, sp^r. Licence
	June	3	John Gilham of Stoak co. Surry, Wid^r, & Jane Wharton of Guilford in the said County, Widow. Licence
	September	30	Daniel Ivings of St Botolphs Aldgate, Wid^r, & Honor Herbert of this parish, sp^r, by Banns
	October	2	William Plaxton, Bach^r, & Elizab' Briscoe, sp^r, both of St Mary Islington. Licence
	November	16	George Grout, Bach^r, of St Olaves Hartstreet, & Mary Aylife of Allhallowes Barking, Sp^r. Licence
	February	24	Charles Starmer of this parish, Bach^r, & Martha Heddy of the same parish, Sp^r. Licence
1698	April	24	William ffreeman of St Dunstans West & Elizab' Hawkins of this parish, by Banns
		25	Isaac Clowder of St Mary White Chappell & Mary Slaughter of this parish, by Banns
	June	2	John Jones of Edmunton in Middlesex, Bach^r, & Sarah Stone of this parish, Sp^r. Licence
	August	4	John Edwards of St Dunstan Stepney, Wid^r, & Elizabeth Chapman of the same parish, Widow. Licence
	September	5	ffrancis Violet of St Botolphs Bishopsgate & Jane Lloyd of this parish, by Banns
		15	John ffisher of St Gregory by St Pauls, Bach^r, & Amitia Owen of St Dunstans in the West, Sp^r. Licence
		20	Nathaniell Norris of St Botolph Aldgate, Bach^r, & Anne Dash of this parish, Widow. Licence

Year.	Month.	Day.	Names.
1698	October	8	Theodore Struper & Susanna Austin both of this parish, by Banns
		13	James Wareing of St Andrew Hubbard, Wid^r, & Dorothy Harding of St Dionis Back Church, Sp^r. Licence
	November	3	Thomas Sorrell of St Magdelin Bermonsey, Bach^r, & Sarah ffreeman of the same parish, Sp^r. Licence
	December	29	John Dudley of Darkin co. Surry, Bach^r, & Elizabeth Port of Banstead in the same co^J, Sp^r. Licence
	January	2	William Dawson of Swafham Norfolk, Bach^r, & Mary Porter of the same place, Sp^r. Licence
	February	2	John ffaller, Bach^r, & Mary Cousins, both of St Clement Danes. Licence
		2	Nicholas Thomas of this parish, Bach^r, & Elizabeth Gold of Allhallows Great, London. Licence
		4	Robert Ellis of St Martins in the ffields, Bach^r, & Alice Owen of St Clement Daines, Widow. Licence
		21	John Bennett of St Matthew ffryday street, Bach^r, & Elizabeth Thornburgh of St Botolphs Bishopsgate, Sp^r. Licence
1699	April	9	William Stowers, Bach^r, & Sarah Haines, sp^r, both of St Andrews Holborn. Licence
		26	Stephen Tanner, Bach^r, & Alice Adams, Sp^r, both of St Catherines nigh the Tower. Licence
	May	1	Richard Salloway, of St Pauls Shadwell, Wid^r, & Avis Miles of this parish, sp^r, by Banns
	April	30	Edward Wheeler of St Bennet ffink London, Bach^r, & Elizabeth Pritchard of St Botolph Aldgate, Sp^r. Lic.
	May	15	Charles Johnson of St Anne Westminster, Wid^r, & Mary Brograve in little Brittain, Widow. Licence
	June	15	William Church of St Olaves Southwark, Wid^r, & Rebecca Broome of St Lawrence Jewry. Licence
	July	31	John Meadowes of Westham co. Essex, Bach^r, & Anne Harvey of the same parish, Widow. Licence
	August	17	Thomas Richardson of St Botolph Bishopsgate, Bach^r, & Ursula ffrench of Cheshunt co. Hartford, sp^r. Licence
		24	George Willcocks, Bach^r, & Elizabeth Storer, Sp^r, both of St John at Hackney co. Midd^x, by Licence
		24	Thomas Railton & Isabella Corbreth, Sp^r, both of this parish, by Banns
	September	24	John Newman, Bach^r, & Anne Uran, Sp^r, both of this parish, by Banns
	October	12	Stephen Housell of St Dunstan's Stepney, Bach^r, & Sarah Welch of this parish, by Banns
		31	Richard Hornby, Bach^r, & Elisabeth Graham, Widow, both of this parish. Banns
	November	23	William Gray of St Mary Islington & Anne Baldwin of this parish, Sp^r. Banns
	January	8	Owen Jones of St Olaves Southwark, Wid^r, & Elisabeth ffoster of this parish, Widow. Banns
		23	ffrancis Martin of St Pauls Shadwell, Bach^r, & Anne Williams of this parish. Banns
	February	8	Daniell Southwicke of St Andrew Holborn, Bach^r, & Elisabeth Taylor of Lumbard Street, Sp^r. Licence
		11	John Buffer of St Giles Cripplegate, Bach^r, & Elisabeth ffish of St James Westminster, Sp^r, by Licence
		18	James Mareland of St Andrew Holborn, Bach^r, & Sarah Sanson of St Margarets Westminster, Sp^r. Licence

Year.	Month.	Day.	Names.
1699	February	13	John Watts, Bach^r, & Sarah Oliver, Sp^r, both of St Bridgets London. Licence
1700	April	2	William Holman of Hornchurch co. Essex, Bach^r, & Mary Page of this parish, Sp^r. Licence
		14	William Dixon of Lincolns Inn London, Bach^r, & Jane Thursby of Lumbard street London, sp^r. Licence
	May	14	Peter Price of St Botolphs Bishopsgate, Bach^r, & Susana Wormlayton, sp^r, of St Mary White Chappell. Lic.
	July	24	Charles Barker of St John Wapping, Wid^r, & Elizabeth Barker of Chesterfield co. Derby, Sp^r. Licence
	September	22	Henry Watkinson of St Vedast *al's* ffosters, Bach^r, & Mary Clarke of Alhall^s Barking, Spinster. Licence
	October	5	Richard Holt of Audley co. Stafford, Bach^r, & Elizabeth Bourne of St Catherine Cree-Church, sp^r. Licence
	September	16	John Lancaster of St Clement Danes, Bach^r, & Mary Johnson of this parish, Sp^r. Banns
	October	24	Thomas Osbourn of Nutimbur in Sussex, Bach^r, & Elizabeth Piggot of Horsted-Caynes in the same County, sp^r. by Licence
	November	5	Thomas Howson of St Edmund the King, Bach^r, & Jane Lambden of St Clement Danes, Sp^r. Licence
	December	2	Matthew Steel of Theydon Boys, Wid^r, & Malin White of Lamborn both in Essex, sp^r. Licence
		26	Christopher Smith of St Margarets New ffish street & Anne ffry in Tower liberty, sp^r. Licence
	January	23	William Usbourne, Bach^r, & Elizabeth Edwards, Sp^r, both of St Olaves Southwark. Licence
	February	27	Anthony Downing, Bach^r, & Anne Nevill, Sp^r, both of St Botolphs Bishopsgate. Licence
1701	April	22	Richard Newman of St Bennet Grace-Church, Bach^r, & Jane Spinage, Sp^r, of this parish. Licence
		29	Samuell Bourne of Epping Essex, Bach^r, & Sarah Edwards of St Olaves Southwark, Sp^r. Licence
	May	14	John Stallwood of St Mary Aldermanbury, Bach^r, & Mary Wood of St Botolphs Aldgate, Sp^r, by Licence
		2	Justus Beck of this parish, Bach^r, & Rachell dau. of Charles Chamberlain Esq., by Dr Beveridge Rector of this parish, in the Church of St Margarets Westminster, by Licence
	August	14	Charles Cornwell of St Botolphs Bishopsgate, Wid^r, & Susanna Rudd of this parish, Sp^r, by Banns
	November	10	Thomas Scot of St Vedast *al's* ffosters, Wid^r, & Anne Clarke of St Gregory's by St Pauls, Sp^r. Licence
		20	Nicholas Jones of Christ Church London, Bach^r, & Anne Raizon of St Bartholomew's Great, sp^r. Licence
	December	14	Anthony Dowdell of St John Wapping, Wid^r, & Sarah Jones of St Dunstans Stepney, Widow. Licence
		18	Henry fforster of St Goorge Southwark, Wid^r, & Elizabeth Paget of St Giles Cripplegate, Sp^r. Licence
	January	22	Herbert Rogers of St Margaret Westminster, Wid^r, & Sarah Gibbons of Christ Church London. Licence
		22	Stephen Watts of St Mary Aldermary, Wid^r, & Mary Bowman of St Botolphs Aldgate, Sp^r. Licence
		29	James Belchier of St Bridget London, Bach^r, & Hannah Cooke of Kingston in Surry, Sp^r. Licence
	February	5	Henry Kirby of ffulham, Bach^r, & Patience Ballinger of this parish. Banns

Years.	Month.	Day.	Names.

1701 February 16 Samuell Hardwick of St Dunstan's in the West, Wid^r, & Anne Langford of St Leonard Shorditch, sp^r. Licence

17 Abraham Bowers of St Nicholas Acons, Wid^r, & Margaret Pott of this parish, sp^r. Licence

March 3 Robert Pepys of St James Westminster, Bach^r, & Eldred Blackbey of Nutfield co. Surrey, Sp^r. Licence

1702 April 7 John Nasbey of this parish, Bach^r, & Elinore Bird of St Botolphs Bishopsgate, Sp^r. Licence

13 John Gumbleton of St Martins in the ffields, Wid^r, & Elizabeth Garrett of Portsmouth in Hampshire, Widow, by Licence

May 23 Daniel Harrisson of St Martins Ludgate, Bach^r, & Elizabeth Britton of St Dunstans Stepney, sp^r. Licence

June 11 William Bull of this parish, Bach^r, & Mary Oakley of Caterham in Surry, Sp^r, by Licence

September 3 Henry Anger of St Andrews Holborn, Wid^r, & Anne Jones, Widow. Licence

22 John Calcot of St Giles Cripplegate, Bach^r, & Anne Smith of St Andrew Wardrobe, sp^r

November 17 Thomas Bloss of Belsted in Suffolk, Wid^r, & Elisabeth Rouse of Baddingham in the same county, sp^r

December 22 Thomas Batison of the town of Bedford, Bach^r, & Elisabeth Paradine of the same town, sp^r

28 Thomas Scot of St Vedast in ffoster lane, Wid^r, & Mary Monger of St Andrews Holborn, Widow. Licence

31 John Gerrard of Stoke by Gilford in Surry, Wid^r, & Elisabeth Jelly of Wockin in the same County, sp^r

January 12 Nathanael Munings of Debnam in Suffolk, Bach^r, & Elizabeth Bennet of Alhallows the less, sp^r

February 2 John Starkey of St Leonards Eastcheap, Bach^r, & Elisabeth Giseland *alias* Gazeland of St Dunstans Stepney, Widow, by Licence

4 John Bacon of St Mary Rotherhith, Bach^r, & Mary Johnson of this p'ish, by Banns

20 Benjamin Thornton of Ashby De la Zouch co. Leicester, Wid^r, & Bithiah Williams of St Clement Danes, Widow. Licence

1703 April 1 Edward Parry of St Mary Mounthaw, Wid^r, & Mary Vaughan of St Bridget, Sp^r. Licence

15 Richard Burdet of St Swithins, Wid^r, & Sarah Harris of St Mary Aldermary, sp^r. Licence

22 Richard Trenance of this p'ish, Wid^r, & Martha Chessut of St James Westminster, sp^r

24 Edwin Wyat of Maidstone in Kent, Bach^r, & Elizabeth Hales of the same town, sp^r

May 6 Edward Cooper of St Mary Ab-Church London, Wid^r, & Mary Webb, St Catherines nigh the Tower, Widow. Licence

13 John Bartley of St Giles in the ffields, Bach^r, & Elizabeth Ketchmaid of St Clements Daines, Sp^r, by Licence

24 Joseph Clarke of St Catherine nigh the Tower, Bach^r, & Elizabet Jones of St Dunstans Stepney, Sp^r. Licence

June 6 Henry Wyley, Bach^r, & Anne Brewhouse, Sp^r, both of St Botolphs Bishopsgate, by Licence

July 1 Daniel ffield of St Stephen Coleman street, Bach^r, & Mary Askin of the same p'ish, Sp^r. Licence

Years.	Month.	Day.	Names.
1703	August	3	John Stoneham of St Mary Aldermary, Bach^r, & Mary Seely of St Mary Ab-Church, sp^r. Licence
		21	Daniel Spencer of St Clement Daines, Wid^r, & Christian Angell of St Paul Covent Garden, Widow. Licence
	October	5	Ezechiell Wood of St Peters Colchester, Bach^r, & Catherine Nicholls of the same parish. Licence
		19	Henry Stanley of Stifford in Essex, ... and Jane Norris of this parish, Sp^r. by Banns
	October	17	Edward Castle, Bach^r, & Jane Dorman, Sp^r, both of this parish, by Banns
	January	10	Giles Hall of St Hellens, ... & Mary Hilton of this parish, Widow, by Banns
	February	3	William ffarrer of the Inner Temple, Wid^r, & Elizabeth Cooke of St Margaretts Westminster, Widow. Licence
		17	William Burrowes of New Windsor in Berkshire, Wid^r, & Anne Payton of Abington in the same shire, sp^r, by Licence
		28	William Harwood of West Ham co. Essex, Bach^r, & Anne Bickmore of the same parish, Sp^r. Licence
1704	April	3	Henry Barclay of Alhallowes Barking, Bach^r, & Thomazine Bloome of the same p'ish, Widow. Licence
	May	3	Thomas Humphreys de Llanvechen in Mountgomeryshire, Clerk & Bach^r, & Anne Owen of St Margarets Westminster, Sp^r. Licence
		4	William Jewell of Sev'nock in Kent, Bach^r, & Margaret Burrow of Hartley in same County, sp^r. Licence
	July	17*	John Day of St Giles in the ffields, Bach^r, & Dorothy Earle of the same parish, sp^r. Licence
		22	Edmund Gibson† D.D. Rector of St Mary at Lambeth in the County of Surry, Batchelor, and Margaret Jones of the parish of St Martins in the ffields Westminster, spinster, by his Grace Thomas Lord Archbishop of Canterbury
	October	26	William Walker of Shoreham in Kent, Bach^r, & Hannah Porter also of Shoreham, sp^r. Licence
	November	23	Henry Philipps of Rotherhith co. Surry & Margaret Bennett of St Peter Cornhill, by Licence
		30	Thomas Rayner of St Catherine Creechurch London & Judith Gentry of Witham co. Essex, sp^r. Licence
1705	April	17	Thomas Smith of Deptford co. Kent & Catherine Cox of Greenwich in same county, sp^r. Licence
		19	John Nolborough of Colchester co. Essex & Mary Sharp of St Peters Cornhill London
	May	15	Robert Green of St Giles by Cripplegate London & Elizabeth Slaymaker of St Olave Hart Street London
	June	10	John Willis, Bach^r, & Hannah Hill, maid, both of this parish, by Banns
		27	William Acton of the Minoryes co. Middlesex & Martha Greene of the same parish. Licence
	July	10	John Nashby of St Peters Cornhill & Frances Hanson of St Catharine Creechurch London. Licence

* The Register from July 17, 1704, to July 14, 1714, is subscribed "John Waugh, Parson;" and from August 26, 1714, to November 25, 1722, "John Waugh, D.D., Parson."

† Son of Edmund and Jane Gibson; born at Knipe, in the parish of Bampton, co. Westmoreland, in 1669; held the living of Lambeth *in commendam* one year, being presented to it on Nov. 17, 1703; consecrated Bishop of Lincoln in 1715; translated to London May 4, 1723; died at Bath September 6, 1748, buried in churchyard of Fulham; Mural tablet to him in church there.

Yeare.	Month.	Day.	Names.
1705	July	24	John Harcum of this parish & Anne Noblett of St Mary Woolnoth London. Licence
	August	8	John Bussy of St Sepulchres London & Elizabeth Harrison of St James Clerkenwell. Licence
	October	23	Thomas Winwood of St Martins in Fields co. Midd^x & Sarah Pottinger of Lambeth co. Surry. Licence
	November	22	Matthew Woodward of St Ethelburga London & Anne Mollins of Alhollows Breadstreet London. Licence
	January	29	George Cole of Lambeth co. Surry & Margaret Puxty of Town Malling co. Kent. Licence
	March	19	John Hardy of St Pauls Shadwell co. Midd^x & Catharine Rous of St Salvator Southwark co. Surry. Licence
1706		29	John West of St Salvator Southwark co. Surrey & Sarah Valentine of the same parish. Licence
	April	25	William Fisher of St Mary Woolnoth London & Anne Cater of St Botolph Aldgate
		30	Joseph Hilder of St Edmund the King London & Frances Whitehead of the same parish. Licence
	May	2	John Carrier of St John Wapping co. Midd^x & Anne Stigans of Downes co. Kent. Licence
	June	6	Samuel Barcroft of St Margaretts Westminster & Jane Sherman of the same parish. Licence
	July	21	Edward Hook of St John Wapping co. Midd^x & Elizabeth Flight of the same parish
	September	1	John Graham of Sunbury co. Middlesex & Ruth Appelbey of St Stephen Coleman street London
		15	Thomas Oland of St Margarett New ffishstreet London & Sarah Filewood of St Peters Cornhill London
	November	14	George Wagstaffe of Lambeth co. Surrey & Alice Symons of the same parish
	December	19	William Marshall of Lambeth co. Surrey & Jane Dobbins of the same parish. Licence
		21	John Cooke of the Inner Temple London & Mary Lloyd of St Andrews Holborn London
	February	3	Joseph Hicks of Rochester co. Kent & Sarah Randall of the same. Licence
		23	William Barker of St Andrews Undershaft London & Judith Stroughton of the same parish
		24	John Lloyd of St James Westminster & Mary Burton of the same parish. Licence
1707	May	2	George Armstrong of St Andrews Holbourn co. Midd^x & Sarah Buck of the same parish. Licence
		29	Marke Tulley of St James Westminster co. Midd^x & Anne Parker of St Clement Danes in the same county, by Licence
	June	30	Edward Harrison of St James Clerkenwell co. Midd^x & Barbara Heath of the same parish. Licence
	August	4	Thomas Hudson of St Salvator Southwark co. Surry & Mary Blizard of Lambeth in same co^y. Licence
		10	Edmund Taylor of St Botolph Algate London & Mary Fortescue of St Mary White Chappell co. Midd^x. Lic.
	September	2	John Lidyeard of St Botolph Algate London & Elizabeth Hendrickson of St John Wapping co. Midd^x
		18	George Hastings of Stepney co. Midd^x & Jane Smith of the same parish
		30	Thomas Smyth of St Botolph Bishopsgate London & Mary Russell of Stepney co. Midd^x. Licence

Years.	Month.	Day.	Names.
1707	October	14	John Bunny of Hitcham co. Bucks & Sarah Law of Loughton co. Essex. Licence
		29	James Calcott of St Andrew Holbourn co. Midd^x & Mary Kempton of the same. Licence
	November	23	Joseph Pagett of St Brides London & Tabitha Forrest of the same parish. Licence
	December	10	George Balch of Bridgewater co. Somerset & Hannah Ludlow of Alhallows Barkin London. Licence
	January	13	James Worthington of St Pauls Covent Garden co. Midd^x & Frances Halstead of St Bridgetts *alias* Brides London. Licence
		22	Edward Simes of St Clements Dane co. Midd^x & Elizabeth Harris of St Andrews Holborne in same co^y. Licence
	February	17	Charles Chapman of St Botolph Bishopsgate London & Mary Everard of St Peters Cornhill London Licence
		17	Thomas Ball of Greenwich co. Kent & Gracia Evans of St Dionys Backchurch London. Licence
		17	Sr Bouchier Wrey* Baronett of Tavestock in the county of Devon and Diana Sparke of the same. Licence
	March	1	John Dalrimple of the parish of St James in the Fields co. Midd^x & Eleonor Campbell of St Margaretts Westminster in the same co^y. Licence
1708	April	6	Robert Nanson of St Margaretts Westminster co. Midd^x & Diana Rookes of the same parish. Licence
	June	9	Clement Lever of St Bridgetts *alias* Brides London & Elizabeth Seale of St Peters Cornhill London. Licence
		11	William Kenyon of Brinchley co. Kent & Elizabeth Lucas of St George Buttolph Lane London. Licence
		11	William Hill of St Giles in the Fields Midd^x & Anne Hucks of St Peters Cornhill London
	September	27	William Thompkins of St Botolphs Bishopsgate & Anne Matthews of St Peters Cornhill
	October	26	Richard Cooke of Stepney co. Midd^x & Jane Phiney of the said parish. Licence
	November	14	John Blinkhorne of St Andrew Holborn co. Midd^x & Jane Sexton of St Mary Woolchurch London. Licence
		25	Richard Langley of Wandsworth co. Surry & Joanna Bells of Stepney co. Midd^x. Licence
	February	15	Charles Bradford of Alhallows Barkin co. Midd. & Anne Seward of Aldgate in the same county. Licence
		24	Furnival Carlile of St John Wapping co. Midd^x & Elianora Henderickson of the same parish. Licence
		27	William Waterer of St Giles in the Fields co. Midd^x & Elizabeth Egleton of St Mary Whitechappel in the same co^y. Licence
	March	3	Webb Fleming of Alhallows the Great, London, & Elizabeth Jackson of St Michaels Cornhill London. Licence
		3	John Wilson of St Margaret's Westminster co. Midd^x & Sarah Thursby of Kensington in same Co^y. Licence
		8	William Leggatt of St Dunstans in the West London & Elizabeth Birch of St Clemens Dane co. Midd^x. Lic.
1709	May	2	James Reith of St Bridget *al's* Brides London & Christiana Middleton of Alverston co. Warwick. Licence

* He eldest son of Sir Bourchier Wrey, third Baronet, by Florence, daughter of Sir John Rolle, of Stevenstone, co. Devon, died 1726. She daughter of John Rolle, eldest son of Sir John Rolle, by Christian, daughter of the Earl of Aylesbury, widow of John Sparke, of the Friery, Plymouth, Esq.

Years.	Month.	Day.	Names.

1709 May 7 Thomas Wellings of Alveston co. Warwick & Elizabeth Hayley of St Botolph Aldgate London. Licence

12 Jeffery Fringe of Lambeth co. Surry & Frances Costin of St Buttolph Aldersgate London. Licence

June 23 Richard Shebbeare de Lyons Inn co. Midd^x & Mary Hooper of Salcomb co. Devon. Licence

October 22 Thomas Northey of the parish of St Nicolas Olive London and Debora Vanittern of St John Hackney in the county of Middlesex, by Licence

November 20 Robert Scott of St Saviours Southwark co. Surry & Dorothy Ford of the same parish. Licence

26 Benjamin Harling of St Mary Aldermary London & Rebecca Taylor of St Mary Le Bow London. Licence

26 John Bellas of St Michael Crooked Lane London & Jane Wigg of St Martin Orgars London. Licence

March 14 Gregory Stevenson of Henley upon Thames co. Oxon & Sarah Worley of the same parish. Licence

February 21 Thomas Bishop of St Salvator Southwark & Constantia Marsh of Lambeth co. Surrey. Licence

1710 April 11 John Wrench of the par. of Trinity in the Minories & Sarah Oldis of St Peters Cornhill London

24 Thomas Askin of St Pauls Shadwell co. Midd^x & Judith Noulton of the same. Licence

27 John Smith of St Salvator Southwark co. Surry & Barbara Adams of St Sepulcher, London

May 2 William Baylis of St Giles Cripplegate co. Midd^x & Mary Clarke of St Bottolph Aldersgate. Licence

4 Robert Austin* of Shallford co. Surry & Mary Ludlow of St Bridgett al's Brides London. Licence

June 20 Thomas Hudson of St Saviour Southwark co. Surry & Susanna Perkins of Lambeth in s^d co^y. Licence

July 25 Richard Taylor of Allsaints the Great, London, & Dorcas Prince of Mile End co. Midd^x

August 6 Henry Hodgson of St Bridgetts al's Brides London & Marrabella Pine of the same parish

September 5 Richard Holme of St Buttolph Aldgate London & Sarah Fogg of St Andrew Wardrobe London

17 William Holyday of St Martins Ludgate London & Anne Armatage of St Bridgett al's Brides London

October 22 George Otway of St Anne & Agnes London & Anne Kendall of the same parish

12 John Hungerford of Standhurst co. Kent & St John Top of Camberwell co. Surry

31 Charles Brett of Cowley co. Glouc^r & Elizabeth Gauden of St James in the fields co. Midd^x

December 2 William Costen of St Buttolph Aldersgate London & Mary Sympson of the same. Licence

21 Thomas Wattson of St Olives Southwark co. Surry & Elionor Fepound of this parish. Licence

22 William Blackey of Deptford co. Kent & Sarah Hartley of the same. Licence

January 28 Samuel Boswell of Stepney co. Midd^x & Elizabeth Mason of Allsaints Barkin London. Licence

* He second son of George Austen of Shalford by Elizabeth, daughter of Sir Robert Anstruther of co. York, died 1718, *sans* issue. She second daughter and coheir of Henry Ludlow of Bramley, co. Surrey, by Margaret, one of the three daughters and coheirs of John Caryl of Tangley, co. Surrey, buried at Bramley July 25, 1721.

Years.	Month.	Day.	Names.
1710	January	31	Thomas Rogers of St Sepulchers London & Ann Gardiner of St Bridgett al's Brides London. Licence

Years. Month. Day. Names.

1710 January 31 Thomas Rogers of St Sepulchers London & Ann Gardiner of St Bridgett *al's* Brides London. Licence

February 7 Jeremia Rububs of St Giles in the Fields co. Midd. & Elizabeth Honnor of St Dunstan's Stepney in same co^y Licence

March 1 Henry Tomkins of Whitechappell co. Midd. & Jane Beebe of St Bridget *al's* Brides London. Licence

1711   25 Abraham Bishop of St John Zachary London & Anne Ballinger of the same. Licence

25 William Vaughan of Stepney & Martha Cheyney of the same

April 2 Ludovicus de La Haye of St Martins in the Fields & Anne Hemming of the same. Licence

8 Nathaniel Marven of St Anne Blackffryers London & Mary Bradly of the same. Licence

23 John Bowen of this parish & Sarah Nutcher of the same, by Banns

July 14 John Corrance of Kensington co. Midd. & Penelope Thursby of the same. Licence

September 11 John Barnes of Stepney co. Midd. & Judith Turner of the s^d parish. Licence

12 Thomas Northey of the parish of St Nicholas Olives London & Mary Strange of the parish of St Bridgetts *alias* Brides London, by Licence

18 Joseph Potts of St Giles in the Fields co. Midd. & Mary Hickinbottom of St Mary Whitechappel in s^d Co^y. Licence

November 13 Richard Grundy of St Pauls Shadwell co. Midd. & Mary Allen of the same parish. Licence

22 William Scholey of St Martins in the Fields co. Midd. & Elizabeth Harper of St Faiths London. Licence

24 Francis Hyde of St Bridgetts *alias* Brides London & Millicent Foster of White Chappell co. Midd^x. Licence

December 11 Thomas Lake of Stepney co. Midd. & Mabell Turner of the same parish. Licence

February 4 Jacob Griffes of St Olives Southwark co. Surry & Rose Sefton of St Mary Abchurch London. Licence

9 John Gough of St Botolph Bishopsgate London & Margaret Tyler of St Giles in ye Fields. Licence

March 4 Roger Elliot of St Martins in the Fields London & Charlott Elliot of the same parish. Licence

1712   27 Charles May of St Bridgetts London & Rebecca Symon of ye same. Licence

July 5 George Wanley of St Dunstans in the West London & Mary Watson of St Bridgetts *alias* Brides London. Licence

13 Thomas Gouldsmith of St Margaretts Westminster co. Midd. & Mary Adams of St Sepulchres London. Licence

13 Joseph T . . . y of Shipton Mallett co. Somersett & Mary Tolson of Bromley co. Kent. Licence

August 2 Robert Randall of St Bridgetts *alias* Brides & Rebecca Cooke of the same parish. Licence

24 Robert Marsh of St Andrews Holborne London & Mary Branch of St Peters Cornhill London. Licence

October 23 Anthony Dapilly of St Giles in the Fields co. Midd. & Judith Ware of the same. Licence

January 2 Christopher Ford of St Leonard East Cheap London & Susanna Russell of St Peters Cornhill London. Licence

Years.	Month.	Day.	Names.
1712	January	1	John Stubblay of St James Clerkenwell co. Midd. & Sarah Hancock of St Giles in the Fields in the same co^y. Licence
	February	10	Thomas Lovelidge of Colchester Essex & Elizabeth Mills of St Botolph Bishopsgate co. Midd. Licence
		11	Hugo Dovellson & Sarah Baldock both of St Pauls Shadwell, co. Midd.
1713	April	7	Thomas Freke of St Bartholomew the Great & Sarah Cooper of St Mary Aldermanbury London. Licence
		21	John Johnson of Stepny co. Midd. & Sarah Love of ye same parish. Licence
	May	7	James Beldon of St Andrews Holborne co. Midd. & Mary Bayly of St Gregory London. Licence
		17	Randulph Pratt of St Mary Somersett London & Mary Stacey of St Salvator London. Licence
	June	17	John Thompson of Stockden Durham & Jane Pearce of St Botolph Aldgate. Licence
	August	13	Thomas Smith & Anne Chorley, both of St Bridgetts al's Brides London. Licence
	September	25	William Smith & Hannah Cowley, both of this parish, by Licence
	November	12	William Miller an Hann,* both of Ratcliff co. Middlesex, by Licence
	March	18	James Spiltimber of Little Hallinbury co. Essex & Mary Mills of Harlow in same co^y. Licence
1714	April	29	William Children of St Mildred in the Poultry & Elizabeth Johnson of this parish. Banns
	May	9	Thomas Knight & Mary Noar, both of this parish. Lic.
		13	John Ilenn of St Sepulcher London & Elizabeth Ingram of St Gregory Southwark
		14	Francis Bayley of St Dunstans in the West & Margaret Slemaker of Stepney co. Midd.
		24	Benjamin Holloway of St Martins in the Fields & Elizabeth Kent of St Leonards Shoreditch co. Midd. Licence
	July	14	Thomas Skeggs of Chelfield co. Kent & Sarah Nuwitt of the parish of St Saviour Southwark co. Surry
	August	26	Edward Maber of St Mary White Chappell co. Midd. & Mary Chapman of this parish. Licence
	September	7	Anthony Adams of Greenwich co. Kent & Susanna Cole of the same. Licence
		9	John Holiday of Milton co. Kent & Mary Gyles of the same
	October	2	Edward Lance of St Botolph Aldgate & Mary Bale of St Brigetts London
		30	Daniel Day of St Dunstans in the East London & Anne Beaumont of St Leonard Shoreditch co. Midd^x Licence
	November	25	Samuel Bloss of St Paul Shadwell co. Midd. & Elizabeth Mary Jeff of St John Wapping in s^d co^y. Licence
	October	19	Thomas Beckett of St Mary White Chappell co. Midd. & Elizabeth Williams of the same. Licence
	January	15	Samuel Peter of St Giles Cripplegate co. Midd. & Hannah Hatton of the same. Licence
	February	19	Leonard Pead of St Mary Cole Church London & Anne Halstead of the same. Licence
		20	George Male of Bridwell precinct & Sara Longworth of St Brides London

* Sic.

Years.	Month.	Day.	Names.
1715	April	18	Daniel Tevoyce of St Mich. Bassishaw London & Mary Tarrant of Stepney co. Midd. Licence
	May	5	Francis Barefoot of St Margaretts Moses London and Catherine Rogers of the same. Licence
	June	2	Thomas Leveridge of St Andrews Holborn co. Midd. & Mary Winhover of St Mary Magdalen Bermondsey co. Surry. Licence
		4	Benedict Horsely of St Mary Abchurch London & Mary Grove of the same. Licence
		14	Beresford Baker of St Augustines London & Anna Maria Cressy of Houghton Regis co. Bedford. Licence
		23	Oughton [John] of St Giles in the Fields co. Midd. & Elizabeth Mason of St Brigetts (*alias* Brides) London. Licence
		25	James Miles of St James Westminster & Elizabeth Smith of St Martins in the Fields. Licence
	July	5	Jasper Lidgate of the parish of St John Hackney in the county of Middlesex and Mary Leatherland of the same, by Licence
		18	William Russel of Stepney co. Midd. & Mary Booth of the same. Licence
		31	Henry Busby of St Salvator Southwark co. Surry & Jane Shell of Shadwell co. Midd. Licence
	September	4	Benjamin Wilson of All Saints at the Wall London & Hanna Taylor of St Peters Cornhill London. Licence
		22	Josiah Maber of St Mary White Chappell co. Midd. & Susanna Mussell of the same. Licence
		27	John Barlow of the Town of Derby & Mary Jackson of Theobalds co. Hertford. Licence
	October	1	John Herring of St John Wapping co. Midd. & Elizabeth Nurden of Coventry. Licence
		10	Joseph Palmer of Hawley co. Surry & Elizabeth Arter of the same. Licence
		26	William Thompson of St Giles in the Fields co. Midd. & Delicia Butler of St Clements East Cheap London, by Licence
	November	1	Thomas Pilling of All Saints at the Wall London & Anne Style of Iver co. Bucks. Licence
	December	18	John Lenham of Malling co. Kent & Lydia Johnson of St Dunstans in the East London. Licence
	January	19	James Wright of St Dunstans in the East London & Mary Adams of the same. Licence
		24	Patrick Balnevis of St Martins Outwich London & Ann Halsted of Edmunton co. Midd. Licence
	February	14	Richard Luellyn of Wickham co. Bucks & Elizabeth Bromwich of St Martins in the Fields. Licence
		14	Stephen Mercer of St Olives Hart Street London & Sarah Smith of St Johns Wapping Middx. Licence
	March	2	Thomas Dillingham of St Botolph Bishopsgate London & Elizabeth Warren of White Chappel co. Midd. Licence
1716	April	29	Thomas Kirke of St Gregory London & Elizabeth Land of St Mary Magdalene Old Fish Street London. Licence
	May	27	Thomas Pritty & Elizabeth Husey both of Eaton co. Bucks. Licence
	June	17	Thomas Watson & Elizabeth English, both of St Pauls Shadwell co. Midd. Licence

Years.	Month.	Day.	Names.
1716	April	17	John Caroll of St Olives Southwark co. Surry & Anne Ewell of the same. Licence
	October	22	Joseph Jarrin of St George Southwark co. Surry & Anne Toon of St Mary Somersett London. Licence
	December	28	Giles Cook of St Giles Cripplegate co. Midd. & Mary Davis of this parish, by Banns
	January	27	William Robinson of Stepney co. Midd. & Isabella Hillard of the same. Licence
	February	21	Thomas Stanton of St Leonards Shoreditch co. Midd. & Anne Beamont of ye same. Licence
1717	June	2	Tobias Harbrough of St Mary Whitechappell co. Midd. & Rebecca Wood of the same. Licence
	August	8	Thomas Riste of St James Clerkenwell co. Midd. & Anne Bouden of St Mary Whitechappell in same Co^y. Lic.
		29	William Caslon of St Botolph Aldgate co. Midd. & Sarah Pearman of St Michael Rude Lane London. Licence
	September	1	Richard Jee of St Brigetts *alias* Brides London & Rebecca Armitage of the same. Licence
		5	William Gregory of St Peters Cornhill London & Elizabeth Mason of the same
	October	17	William Roberts of St Olives Southwark & Sarah Toovey of St Botolph Bishopsgate co. Midd. Licence
	November	80	Josias Snowden of St Bennetts near Pauls Wharf London & Anne Hook of St Mary Athill London. Licence
	February	16	Peter Allston of St Catherine Cree London & Elizabeth Thomas of St Giles Cripplegate London. Licence
		18	Robert Glyn of St Andrews Holborne co. Midd. & Frances Gardiner of the same. Licence
		23	Edward Henderson of St Olive Southwark co. Surry & Sarah Chaire of St Peters Cornhill Lond., by Banns
		25	Thomas Sharp of St Margarett Westm^r & Amy Monk of St Anne Westminster. Licence
1718	April	27	George Norton of St Olives Southwark co. Surry & Mary Williams of ye same. Licence
	May	25	John Hiott of St Gregory London & Isabella Barnes of St Edmond Lombard Street London. Licence
	July	22	Thomas Edwards of St Catherines Coleman London & Mary Rose of the same. Licence
		27	James Randall of St Dunstans Stepney co. Midd. & Easter Mell of ye same. Licence
	August	10	William Robinson of St Mary Magdalene Barmondsey co. Surry & Mary Finchett of the same. Licence
		19	Robert Geary of St Mary Hill London & Sarah Chapman of Low Layton Essex. Licence
	September	23	John Swain of St Andrews Holborn co. Midd. & Eliz. Marchant of ye same. Licence
	October	7	William Smith of Westham co. Essex & Rebecca Fox of ye same. Licence
		23	Amos Mills of St Dunstans Stepney co. Midd. & Elizabeth Miles of ye same. Licence
		28	Nicholas Gurr of St Gabriel Fanchurch Street London & Mary Gilbert of ye same. Licence
		30	John Harrison of St James Duke Street London & Martha Gratrix of St Mary Aldermanbury Lond. Licence
	December	7	James Colner of St Olives Southwark co. Surry & Eliz. Blowen of ye same. Licence

Yeare.	Month.	Day.	Names.

1718 December 11   John Hughes of St James Westminster co. Midd. & Margaret Swaddell of ye same. Licence

                  22   Edward Oddy of Walthamstow co. Essex & Elizabeth Wattson of St Matthew Friday Street London. Licence

    January   1   Abraham Phillips of Bridewell London & Mary Stephens of St Botolph Aldersgate London. Licence

    February   1   Joseph Humphrys of St Bridgetts al's Brides London & Jane Woodcock of ye same. Licence

                  2   John Tatnal of St Catherines near ye Tower London & Eliz. Mills of Westham Essex. Licence

                  3   Christopher Bradbury of Hampton co. Midd^x & Mary Perkins of Richmond co. Surry. Licence

                  3   James Gall & Hannah Bradburne, both of St Leonards Shoreditch

    November 18   William Nicholl of St Mary Whitechappell co. Midd. & Anne Bradnee of St Bridgetts alias Brides London. Licence

                  20   Francis Fairchild of Putney co. Surrey & Jane Street of Streatham co. Surry. Licence

         These two by a mistake were entered out of course.

1719 March   26   Thomas Tyndall of Bartholomew the Less London & Eliz. Dawson of Aldermanbury London. Licence

    May   1   Alexander Taylor of St Mary Newington co. Surry & Eliz. Alchorne of ye same. Licence

                  28   Wm Stubbs of St Mary Magdalene Barmondsey co. Surry & Hannah Story of ye same. Licence

    June   7   Jabez Gurnell of ye Minories London & Catherine Bagg of Dukes Place co. Midd. Licence

                  21   Thomas Walker of St Dunstans Stepney co. Midd. & Mary Gale of ye same. Licence

    July   4   Joseph Tarbox of St Peters poor London & Susanna Duke of the same. Licence

                  14   Henry Ewstice of St Dionis Backchurch London & Catherine Hill of St Peter Cornhill. Licence

                  23   Wm Mayo of St Mary Somersett London & Sarah Mitchell of St Bennett Pauls Warf. Licence

    September 8   James Pointing of St Christopher Le Stooks London & Rebecca Townly of the same. Licence

    October   15   William Leeson of St Martins in the Fields co. Midd. & Mary Dalby of St Anne's Westm^r. Licence

    December 19   John Evans of Stepney co. Midd. & Mary Porter of St Helens London. Licence

    January   21   James Clift of Stepney co. Midd. & Elizabeth Finney of ye same. Licence

    February   27   George Towers of St Martins in the Fields co. Midd. & Sarah Lynam of St John Hackney in ye same co^y. Licence

1720 April   28   William Buckmaster of St Dunstans in the East London & Sarah Jarvis of Newington Butts co. Surry. Lic.

    February   11   Isaac Proute of Aldgate co. Midd. & Ellis Phipps of this parish, by Banns

    May   3   Daniel Cock of Colchester co. Essex & Letitia Lane of ye same. Licence

                  12   James Morson of St Annes Aldersgate London & Anne Goodrick of St Mary Whitechappel co. Midd. Licence

Years.	Month.	Day.	Names.

1720 July 12 John Wright Esqr of the Inner Temple London & Mary Heywood of Holywell Oxon. Licence

26 Thomas Hills of Stansted mount Flitchett co. Essex & Jane Paxton of Stepney co. Midd. Licence

August 2 John Hare of Westham co. Essex & Ruth Moor of ye same. Licence

4 Seymor Stocker of St Dunstans Stepney co. Midd. & Susanna Clark of St Paul Shadwell. Licence

September 29 Andrew Phillips of St Andrew Hubbard London & Elizabeth Holdroide St John Le Evangelist of ye same. Licence

November 17 Edward Hamm of St Dunstans Stepney Midd^x & Anne Norman of Bow co. Essex. Licence

22 Samuel Hanson of St Saviours Southwark co. Surry & Susanna Gotman of St Mary Abchurch London. Lic.

24 Richard Allen of All Saints on ye Wall London & Anne Bradshaw of St Botolphs Bishopsgate London. Lic.

25 Francis Wilson of Edmonton co. Midd. & Anne Lindsey of St Laurence old Jury London. Licence

December 1 William Clark of Deptford co. Kent & Dorothy Blundell of ye same. Licence

14 Abraham Campbell of Aldgate London & Mary Adams of ye same

20 William Bevan of St Faith London & Elizabeth Birdwhisle of St Botolphs Bishopsgate Lond^n. Licence

22 Benjamin Wilmot of St Martins in ye Fields Midd^x & Elizabeth Ross of St Andrews Holborn Lond^n. Licence

January 1 William Tompkinson of St Peters Cornhill London & Elizabeth Burridge of ye same. Licence

2 Reeve Gale of St Peters Cornhill London & Elizabeth Bateman of ye same

5 Jos. Harrison & Anne Ross. Licence

5 Thomas Hutt of St Saviours Southwark co. Surrey & Mary Brinkley of St M. Whitechappel Midd^x. Licence

31 William Newton of St Gyles Cripplegate London & Catherine Smith of ye same. Licence

February 14 William Allen of St Martins Le Grand London & Mary Wigginton of ye same. Licence

1721 April 20 William Dye of Waltham Abbey Essex & Mary How of De Wheel in ye same co^y. Licence

25 John Crossier of Ikenham Midd^x & Sarah Gregory of St Albans co. Hertford. Licence

May 16 Gyles Tuckey of St Botolphs Aldgate London & Grace Ashmore of ye same. Licence

June 1 Thomas Gill of De Eaton co. Bucks & Catherine Shirley of ye same. Licence

August 19 Matthew Thompson of St Peters Cornhill London and Elizabeth Hunt of ye same. Licence

September 24 James Cotton of St Margaretts West^r & Sarah Nicholls of ye same. Licence

December 4 Samuel Greene of All Saints Lombard Street London & Sarah Godman of St Saviours Southwark co. Surrey. Licence

1721 October 19* John Franks of Stepney co. Midd. & Susanna Wescott of St Peters Cornh. Lond. Licence

February 4 Stephen Jackson of Stepney co. Midd. & Elizabeth Green of St Botolph Bishopsgate. Licence

* Sic.

Yeare.	Month.	Day.	Names.

1721 February 4 John Green of St Pauls Covent Garden Midd^x & .... Loton of Nasing co. Essex. Licence

1722 July 21 Morris Goulston of Kingston on Thames co. Surrey & Mary Ashton of St Clemens Danes Midd^x. Licence

August 5 Simon Hawkins of Whitechappel Midd^x & Jane Phillips of St Dunstans Stepney. Licence

11 William Diggs of Cliffords Inn London & Sarah Ottley of St Georges Southwark co. Surry Licence

16 Jonathan Barnes of St Margaretts Westm^r & Elizabeth Cuthbert of St Annes Westm^r. Licence

21 Peter Blake of St Leonard Shoreditch Midd^x & Mary Blake of ye same. Licence

October 7 Samuel Herring of St Pauls Shadwell Midd^x & Eliz. Richards of ye same. Licence

18 William Cox of St John Wapping Midd^x & Rebecca Stile of ye same. Licence

November 3 William Ashmore of St Annes Aldersgate Londⁿ & Eliz. Gray of St Dunstans Stepney co. Midd^x. Licence

8 Martin Smith of St Bartholomews ye Great London & Elianor Morrice of St Martins in ye Fields Midd^x. Lic.

17 Ducy Hungerford of Henly upon Thames co. Oxon, & Mary Hanson of ye same. Licence

24 John Butler of Gravesend co. Kent & Mary Hall of Milton in same co^y. Licence

25 George Purkos of St Christophers Le Stocks London & Hannah Poplewell of St Peters Cornhill London. Lic.

January 24* Benedict Rose of St Laurence Jewry London & Mary Upp of Hertford co. Hertford. Licence

29 George Stringer of All Saints Lombard Street London & Mary Hill of St Peters Cornhill of ye same. Licence

February 5 William Whitelock de Waltham Abby co. Essex & Judith Crake of ye same. Licence

10 Thomas Lancaster of St Dionis Backchurch London & Hannah Cowley of St Peters Cornhill London. Lic.

21 Thomas Hall of St Mary Ax London & Eliz. Cordwell of ye same. Licence

1723 April 2 Edwd Pickard of White Friars London & Sarah Pagett of ye same. Licence

10 Isaac Gibbs of St Botolphs Aldgate London & Mary Harris of St Mary Ax London. Licence

June 12 Richd Parkes of St Saviours Southwark & Sarah Morgan of St Georges Southwark in Surry. Licence

July 25 Paul Calton of St Barthol. behind ye Change & Catherine Bembow of Deptford co. Kent. Licence

October 1 John Harris of Shadwell co. Midd. & Eliz. Brooks of St Peters Cornhill Londⁿ. Licence

7 Daniel Dyche of Bethnall Green Midd^x & Mary Ramsden of St Peters Cornhill Lond., by Banns

19 Joseph Stent of St Bridgetts (*alias* Brides) London & Eliz. Prichard of St Andrews Holborn. Licence

29 Richard Rogers of St Martins in ye Fields Midd^x, & Eliz. Shapshire of Malbrough Wilts. Licence

31 Thom. Hollis of Kingston Surry & Mary Brookes of the same. Licence

---

* The Register from January 24, 1722, to January 23, 1727, is subscribed " Jo. Carliol, Parson Commendat' ;" and from April 27, 1728, to August 5, 1731, " Jo. Carliol, Parson."

Years.	Month.	Day.	Names.
1723	November	5	John Elliot of St Olives Southwark Surry & Mary How of St Gyles Cripplegate Midd^x. Licence
		23	Workman Hoskins of Greenwich Kent & Catharine Bray of ye same. Licence
	January	12	Wm Axe of Bromley in Kent & Mary Dry of All Saints Lumberstreet London. Licence
		16	Jonas Holliday of Stepney Midd^x & Sarah Willison of ye same. Licence
		23	Richd Starkey of St Andrews Holborn Midd^x & Mary Stephenson of ye same. Licence
	February	2	Tho. Emes of St Andr. Holborn Midd^x & Marg^t Gardiner of St Peters Cornhill, by Banns
		6	Tho. Oxley & Catharine* both of St Peters Cornhill, by Banns
		9	Thomas Jenkes of St Catherine Cree London & Eleonor Freeman of St Andr. Holborn. Licence
		22	Robert Keylway of St Gyles in ye Fields Midd. & Susanna Nicholson of St Bridgetts (*alias* Brides). Licence
	March	8	Richd Smith of Henley upon Thames Oxon & Eliz. Pigeon of the same. Licence
		15	Peter Feather of St Peters Cornhill London & Mary Hodgson of St Martins in ye Fields Midd^x. Licence
1724	April	28	John Eglon jun^r of St Rumwald in Colchester Essex & Eliz. Richardson of St Peters Colchester. Lic.
	May	9	John Bedwell of Dagenham Essex & Mary Miller of ye same. Licence
		19	Robert Blewett of White Chappel Midd. & Mary James of ye same. Licence
	June	2	Martin Cowart of Sr Dunstans Stepney Midd. & Jane Carey of ye same. Licence
		16	Samuel Hanson of St Edmonds King & Eliz. How of St Mary Magdal. Barmondsey Surry. Licence
		25	John Scrimshire of St Antholins London & Sarah Spencer of Stepney Midd. Licence
		28	Isaac Gentill of St Dunstans Stepney Midd. & Mary Battaill of St Philip in Bristol. Licence
	July	9	John Rayner of All Saints ye Great London & Jane Murray of St Mary Abchurch Lond. Licence
	August	2	John Walter of St Gyles in ye Fields Midd. & Olive Clifton of St Peters Cornhill Lond. Licence
		20	William Macklellen of St Martins in the Fields Midd. & Martha Barber of ye same. Licence
	September	8	Jo. Glanvill of St Stephens Coleman Street London & Eliz. Andrews of ye same. Licence
	October	18	William Elliot of St Peters Cornhill Londⁿ & Jane Hine of ye same. Licence
	January	10	James Povall of St Mary le Bow London & Mary Turvell of St Peters Cornhill of ye same
		14	Thomas Balley & Rachell Crisp of St Peters Cornhill London, by Banns
1725	March	31	Henry Waller of Horsham Sussex & Martha Longlinest of ye same. Licence
		31	Abraham Cooper of Horsham Sussex & Henrietta Yexley of Worth, of ye same

* Sic.

Years.	Month.	Day.	Names.
1725	April	18	Michael Robinson of St Saviours Southwark Surry & Mary Norton of St Olives Southwark. Lic.
	May	9	Abraham Beamont of St Buttolph's Aldgate London & Mary Rivers of ye same
		16	James Bovey of St Bottolph Aldgate London & Grace Shotling of ye same. Licence
	June	17	Matthew Deane of St Gyles Cripplegate Midd. & Mary Julian of ye same. Licence
		24	Joseph Pummerroy of St Gyles Cripplegate Midd. & Mary Spencer of Stepney in same coy. Licence
		29	Tho. Arewater of Waltham Abby Essex & Mary Nightingale of the same. Licence
	October	17	Samuel Craxell of St Clements Dane London & Releife Craddock of St Martins in the Fields Midd. Licence
	November	16	Jenkin Davies of St James Westminster Middx & Eliz. Long of St Giles in ye Fields, same coy. Licence
	February	21	Wm Sheepey of St Dionis Backchurch London & Eliz. Redford of Barking in Essex. Licence
		6	Samuel Bowyer of St Peters Cornhill London & Eliz. Stocker of ye same parish. Licence
	March	14	Wm Winrowe of St Mildred in the Poultry London & Susanna Hall of St Mary Whitechappel Midd., by Licence
1726	April	20	Thos Legge of Deptford Kent & Eliz. Waller ditto. Lic.
		27	Charles Brown of St Olave Hartstreet London & Elizth Hunt of St Botolph Aldgate London. Licence
	May	12	Joseph Amey of St Giles Cripplegate London & Joan Keightley of St Mary Rotherhith in Surry. Lic.
	July	12	Wm Chilwell of Lambeth in Surry & Mary Dalling* of Westerbam in Kent. Licence
	August	6	George Hill of Doctors Commons London & Sarah Richardson of St Botolph Bishopsgate Lond. Licence
		21	Samuel Atkins of St Dunstan in the West Lond. & Alicia Stafford of St Brides Lond. Licence
	September	6	Wm Curlews of St Swithin London stone & Mary Stephens of St Olave Southwark Surry. Licence
	October	6	Josiah Mitchell of St Leonard Shoreditch Middx & Margaret Lucas of Stepney ditto. Licence
		9	Joseph Woodhouse of St Clements Danes Middx & Eleanor Morgan ditto. Licence
	November	1	Richd Tryce & Dove Grosvenour, both of this parish, Lodgers. Licence
		1	Peeter Greening of St Martin in ye Fields & Jane Hibdon of St Andrew Holborn London. Licence
		19	Joseph Jackson of St Mary Whitechappel & Elizth Sprigmore of Stepney Middx
	December	13	Richard Parkins of St Dunstans in the East London & Judith Mainwaring of St Saviours Southwark Surry. Licence
		27	Jno Thorne of Wellington co. Somerset & Anne Streater of Waltham Abbey co. Essex
	February	2	Edward Littleton of Eaton co. Bucks & Frances Goode of ye same. Licence

* She daughter of John Dalling of Westerham, Mercer (probably the same person who was baptised there July 25, 1678, as "John son of John Dauling," and buried there Oct. 19, 1750), baptised there Aug. 20, 1706.

Years.	Month.	Day.	Names.
1726	February	4	Jeremiah Smith of St Andrew Hubbard London & Mary Pealin of Mark Lane London. Licence
1727	April	4	Thos Banister of Great St Bartholomews London & Margaret of St Pancrace Soper lane London Lic..
	May	11	Richard Weedon & Constantia Parker, both of St John Wapping in Middx.
		16	Wm Smith of St Katharine Coleman London & Mary Morson of St Mary Whitechapple Midd. Licence
	June	1	Wm Brown & Winefred Mayo both of ye parish Servants, by Banns
		29	Robert Gill & Deborah Cruse, both of St George the Martyr co. Surry. Licence
	July	6	John Batcheler & Margaret Coleman both of ye old Artillery Ground in ye Liberty of the Tower of London. Licence
	October	30	Thos Hodsden of Croydon co. Surry & Alice Heyward of Wooldingham in same coy. Licence
	December	31	Richard Wright of Wanstead in Essex & Anne Johnson of St Peters Cornhill London. Licence
	January	23	Jno Marshall of Wapping Middx & Colleberry Abell of Ham near Kingston Middx. Licence
1728	April	27	Alexander Bolton of St Clements Danes Middx & Elizth Stayner of Westham Essex. Licence
	May	5	Jno Williams of Greenwich in Kent & Mary Green of the same. Licence
	June	26	Carew Weekes of St George ye Martyr Southwark & Anne Wright of the same. Licence
	August	23	Jno Corbett of St Brides Lond. & Sarah Templar of St Andrew Undershaft Lond. Licence
		27	Thos Wight & Cassandra Leigh, both of Barking in Essex. Licence
		29	Wm Clifford of St Andrews Holborn & Anne Arters of Stratford in Essex. Licence
	September	19	Wm Coombs of St Giles Cripplegate Midx & Mary Seabrook of St Peters Cornhill Lond. Licence
		19	Thos Davis of Allhallows Bread Street & Ruth Hart of St Peters Cornhill London. Licence
		19	Harry Pope Blount of Twickenham Midx & Anne Cornwallis of St James Westminster. Licence
	January	12	Jno Howell of St Giles Cripplegate Midx & Mary Frost of St Mary at Hill London. Licence
		21	Edward Miles of St Andrew Holborn London & Sarah Gift of St Botolph Aldgate Midx. Licence
		23	Wm Searle Bright & Sabina Campbell, both of St Katherine Creechurch London. Licence
		26	Jacob Mosley & Elizth Pain, both of St Dunstans Stepney Midx. Licence
	February	1	Roger Clarke of St Sepulchre's Midx & Mary Thomas of St Mary Magdalen Bermondsey Surry. Licence
	March	6	Joseph Hooper & Elizabeth Hurt, both of St Mary White Chapple Midx. Licence
1729	May	8	James Ougham of All Saints Maldon Essex & Mary Argent of Kelldon in same coy. Licence
	August	26	Wm Edden & Sarah Ward, both of St Sepulchres London, p' Mr Fiddes. Licence
	October	12	Wm Beaty of St Andrew Holborn London & Sarah Davis of St Saviours Southwark co. Surry. Licence

Years.	Month.	Day.	Names.
1729	October	14	Jnº Davis of Allhallows Staining & Rebecca Bunce of Crutchet Fryars London. Licence
		16	Thoˢ Wright of Coventry & Lydia Halpenny of Sᵗ Clements Danes co. Midˣ. Licence
		24	John Creighton of Sᵗ Olaves Southwark Surry & Elizᵗʰ Hamnet of Sᵗ Georges Southwark. Licence
	December	7	James Atkinson of Sᵗ Mary Whitechappell Middˣ & Elizᵗʰ Fletcher of this parish. Licence
	January	1	Edward Frith of Sᵗ Mary White Chappel Midˣ & Mary Dick of Stepney Midˣ. Licence
	February	6	James Porter of Sᵗ Andrew Holborn Midˣ & Mary Barton of Sᵗ Brides London. Licence
		8	Abraham Gibbs of Deptford in Kent & Eliza. Martin of Allhallows Barking Lond. Licence
1780	April	19	Joseph Feepound of Sᵗ Mary White Chappel Middˣ & Mary Harris of Sᵗ Sepulchres London. Licence
		28	Nathanael Delander & Hannah Henshman, both of Sᵗ Michael's Cornhill Lond. Licence
	May	12	Wᵐ Rayment of Barking co. Essex & Frances Allyn of the same. Licence
		17	Cornelius Hinton & Mary Rowe, both of Sᵗ Margarets Westminster. Licence
	June	18	Jnº Copping Vicar of Heybridge in Essex & Mary Gregg of Putney in Surry. Licence
	August	27	William Reeve of Sᵗ Botolph Aldgate London & Jane Carr of Sᵗ Gregory London. Licence
	November	1	Thoˢ Butler & Jane Cotton, both of Chigwell in Essex. Lic.
		9	Amos Swaisland & Mary Bargrove, both of Southfleet in Kent. Licence
	January	9	Nicholas Smith of Sᵗ Gregory's London & Penelope Slater of Sᵗ Dunstans in yᵉ West London. Licence
	February	6	Thoˢ Atwood of Sᵗ Clement Danes Midˣ & Maria Eleanora Glasier of Allhallows Bread Street London. Lic.
1731	April	21	Daniel Elkin & Elizᵗʰ Garret, both of Dagenham in Essex. Licence
	May	13	John Cooper of Sᵗ Mary Magdalen Bermondsey in Surry & Lætitia Holloway of Sᵗ Peter Cornhill Lond. Lic.
	July	4	George Sibley & Mary Brett, both of Sᵗ Katherine Coleman London. Licence
		19	James Morgan & Mary Saunders, both of Waltham Abbey Essex. Licence
	August	5	Francis Brooke of West Malling Kent & Mary Cox of Stanstead in Kent. Licence
	September	5*	Danˡˡ Everit of Sᵗ James Clerkenwell Middˣ & Jane Smith of Sᵗ Peters Cornhill London, by Banns
	October	12	Joseph Lamb & Sarah Smith, both of this parish, by Banns
		27	Peter Bowyer & Elizᵗʰ Dade, both of Sᵗ Dunstan Stepney Middˣ, by Mʳ Lawrence. Licence
		80	Wᵐ Conway of Sᵗ Mary Aldermanbury & Mary Davis of Sᵗ Bartholomew yᵉ less. Licence
	November	20	Anthony Haynes of Sᵗ Ann Blackfryars & Mary Morris of Sᵗ Gregory London. Licence
	December	12	Samuel Kynaston of Bethnall Green in par. of Sᵗ Dunstan Stepney & Mary West of Sᵗ Peters Cornhill, by Banns

* The Register from September 5, 1731, to September 30, 1786, is subscribed "Jnº Higgate, M.A., Curate."

Years.	Month.	Day.	Names.
1731	February	11	Michael Lally of St Andrew Holborn Mid^x & Elizth Bigg of Reading Berks. Licence
1732	April	16	Jno Robinson of St Olave Southwark & Anne Watson of this parish. Licence
	May	13	Jno Jackson, Clerk, of Simpson co. Bucks & Margaret Roberts of Haversham in same co^y. Licence
		18	Jno Rew of St Georges Mid^x & Anne Edwards of St Botolph Aldgate London. Licence
		25	Jno Fairbrother of St Michael in Cornhill Lond. & Rebecca Walter of this Parish. Licence
		28	Thos Hunt & Ruth Cricks, both of this parish, by Banns
	December	16	Sam^{ll} Barker of St Giles Cripplegate London & Freelove Burton of St Mary Cray Kent. Licence
		17	Edwd Seabrooke of St Peter at St Albans Herts & Ann Langley of St Vedast Foster lane Lond. Licence
		19	Wm Rice of Richmond Surry & Jane Fitzwater of ye same place. Licence
1733	April	19	Joseph Meadows & Elizth Crick, both of this parish. Lic.
	June	9	Jno Glasscock of Standford Rivers Essex & Susan Perry of Edmonton Midd^x. Licence
	August	25	Paul Pepper of Allhallows Barking & Catharine Smith of St Michael Wood street. Licence
	September	11	Joseph Marchant of Barking Essex & Ann Whiting of the same place, p' Mr Fiddes. Licence
	October	17	Thos Pearce of Xst Church Lond. & Mary Sprigmore of St Mary White chapple Mid^x. Licence
	December	14	Job Wiseman of Newington Butts Surry & Sarah Dash of the same. Licence
	February	22	Jasper Orchard of Kensington Midd^x & Elizth Cooke of ye same. Licence
		26	Ambrose Skinner & Ann Pittman, both of Barkin in Essex. Licence, p' Mr Fiddes
	March	24	James Bosley of this parish & Mary Jacobs of St Olave Southwark Surry. Licence
1734	April	4	Willm Woolley of St Michael in Cornhill & Dorothy Smith of St Antholin London. Licence
		16	Thos Spencer of Isleworth Mid^x & Margaret Tutin of this parish, by Banns
	May	21	Nathaniel Maning* of Croydon Surry & Ann Nash of Warlingham in same co^y. Licence
	June	8	Wm Leach of Bromley St Leonard Mid^x & Lucy Baker of Nutwell near Exon Devon. Licence
	August	8	Jno Pate of St Saviour's Southwark Surry & Ann Creighton of the same. Licence
	October	1	Jno Lardner of St Ann Limehouse Mid^x & Alice Buckston of St Mary Rotherhithe Surry. Licence, p' Mr Awdley
		10	Jno Gregory of St James Westminster Mid^x & Sarah Wilson of St Ann Blackfryars London. Licence
	December	16	Robt Emmet of St John Wapping Midd^x & Bethia Parson of the same. Licence

* He purchased lands in Titsey, co. Surrey, April 15, 1726; Will dated Nov. 30, 1741, proved by Ann his widow Jan. 22, 1742.   She daughter of Thomas Nash, of Warlingham, and Olive his wife, born March 20, 1713-14, baptized at Warlingham March 31st following.   [A note in the margin of the register of her baptism records her marriage, but gives the date May 27.]   She died Jan. 1764, having remarried in 1742, Sir John Humphrey of Beckenham, co. Kent, who was buried July 15, 1764.

Years.	Month.	Day.	Names.
1734	January	1	Roger Evans of St Paul Shadwell Mid^x & Anna-Maria Shaler of St Mary le Bone Mid^x. Licence
		4	George Hitchcock of St Clements Danes Midd^x & Mildred Shakleton of St George in same co^y. Licence
	February	27	Francis Hooker of St Luke Midd^x & Jane Taylor of Deptford in Kent. Licence
1735	April	5	Merry Pronting of St George Botolph lane London & Martha Hodgson of St Andrew Holbourn. Licence
	May	10	Adam Rutherford of St Jno Wapping Midd^x & Jane Hilder of St Mary Whitechappel. Licence
	June	27	Thos Woodruffe of St Martin in ye fields Midd^x & Frances Woodruffe of St Peter in Colchester Essex. Licence
	July	1	Calvert Benn of St Botolp Bishopsgate London & Ann Titchborne of Croydon Surry. Licence
		10	Charles West of Putney Surry & Sarah Tyler of the same place. Licence
	August	26	Mark Carpenter of St Olave Southwark Surry & Ann Tarry of Xst Church Surry. Licence
		31	Wm Thomas of St Jno Wapping Midd^x & Elizth Bell of St Peter Cornhill London. Licence
	September	16	Jno Trinder of St Michael crooked Lane Lond. & Mary Browne of ye same. Licence
		28	Bartholomew Wood of St Sepulchre's Midd^x & Mary Chambers of St Bartholomew behind ye Royal Exchange Lond. Licence
	October	25	Jacob Loot of St Botolph Algate Mid^x & Mary Southham of St Leonard Shoreditch Mid^x. Licence
	November	13	Jno Stanley of St Andrew Holborn Mid^x & Elizth Thompson of St George Mid^x. Licence
	December	14	Henry Farrington of St Mary Magdalen Bermondsey Surry & Mary Peachie of the same. Licence
		21	Major Robinson of St Olave Southwark Surry & Elizth Potter of ye same
	January	6	Thomas Cooke of St Trinity in ye Minories Mid^x & Sarah Freeman of this parish. Licence
		31	Jno Marriot of this parish & Mary Dawson of Greenwich Kent. Licence
	February	19	Thos Sexton of St Botolph Bishopsgate Lond. & Priscilla Mackris of Endfield Mid^x. Licence
1736	May	2	Charles Ayres & Mary Grantham, both of this parish. Licence
	July	17	Thos Baxter of St Olave Hartstreet Lond. & Elizth Wynn of Ludlow co. Salop. Licence
		22	Jno Markham of St Brides Lond. & Ann Thompson of St George Mid^x. Licence
	September	16	Joseph Child of St Faith's Lond. & Ann Brears of St Ann Limehouse. Licence
		30	Robert Writon of Westham Essex & Jane Graham of St Katharine Creechurch London. Licence
	October	17*	Moses Waite & Sarah Hughson, both of St George the Martyr Southwark Surry. Licence
		19	Thos Mason of ye old Artillery Ground in ye Liberty of ye Tower London & Rebecca Hunt of Broughton Wilts. Licence

* The Register from October 17, 1736, to January 15, 1743, is subscribed "Richd Thomas, M.A., Curate."

Years.	Month.	Day.	Names.
1736	October	17	Richd Freelove & Alice Freelove, both of this parish, by Banns
	November	11	Jno Berkley of St Giles in ye fields & Alice Belshaw of St Mary Whitechappel. Licence
	February	3	George Russell & Rebecca Love, both of St Mary Rother-hithe Surry. Licence
		22	Abraham Whitchurch of St Botolph Aldergate Lond. & Sarah Chidley of St James Garlick-hith. Lic.
	March	15	Robert Wastfield & Elizth Powell, both of Mile-End in the par. of St Dunstan Stepney Mid^x. Licence
1787	April	25	Thomas Tyler, Widower, & Elizabeth Bush, sp^r, both of Essex. Licence
	May	20	Robert Kimpton, Bach^r, & Martha Smith, Sp^r, both of St Botolph Bishopsgate London. Licence
		29	James Best of Lincolns Inn co. Midd., B^r, & Elizabeth Lomax of St Clement Danes, Sp^r, in same county. Licence
	August	21	Hayter Scrivener, Bach^r, & Anne Piercy, Sp^r, both of St Mary Magdalen Bermondsey Surrey. Licence
	September	13	Edward Hurdle of Westham Essex, Wid^r, & Ann Marshall of ye same, Sp^r. Licence
		18	Henry Sanders of St Dunstan Stepney co. Midd^x, Bach^r, & Elizabeth Chandler of the Old Artillery Ground, sp^r
	October	6	Richd Warrum of Greenwich in Kent & Mary Beresford of this parish, by Banns
		16	Richd Maskell of St Clements East Cheap London, Bach^r, & Sarah Glenn of St James Westm^r, sp^r. Licence
		28	John Pristo, bach^r, & Susannah Stone, Sp^r, both of this parish, by Banns
	November	5	Thomas Goodwyn of St Sepulchres, bach^r, & Mary Wiggins of this parish, sp^r, by Banns
		6	William Lewis of St Paul Covent Garden co. Midd^x, bach^r, & Mary Jones of ye same parish, sp^r. Licence
		25	John Sawbridge of Richmond co. Surry, wid^r, & Margaret Perry of St Dunstan in the East London, widow. Lic.
	December	21	Richd Thomas of St Michael Crooked Lane London, bach^r, & Jane Groves of St George ye Martyr Surry, Widow, by Licence
	January	12	Thomas Manning of St Matthew Friday Street London, bach^r, & Elizabeth Bagnall of St Olave Southwark Surry, Widow
	February	2	Joseph Ennever of Beauchamp Roothing Essex, bach^r, & Mary Gridley of Blackmoor in ye same co^y, Widow. Licence
		2	James Clark of St Botolph Aldgate, bach^r, & Susannah Mason of this p'ish, sp^r, by Banns
		14	Thomas Randle of St Jno Wapping Midd^x, Wid^r, & Jane Barrett of St Helens London, sp^r. Licence
1738	June	18	Samuel Cowley of Christ Church Midd^x, bach^r, & Mary King of St Botolph Bishopsgate, sp^r. Licence
	August	5	Richard Allen of St Mary White Chappel co. Midd^x, Wid^r, & Mary Wright of St Botolph Aldersgate, sp^r. Licence
		29	Thomas Summerhayes of this p'ish, Wid^r, & Patience Ware of St John Wapping Midd^x, sp^r. Licence
	October	30	Thomas Young of St Thomas Southwark Surry, Wid^r, & Lydia Smith of St Olave d^o, Sp^r. Licence
	November	28	Francis Holmes of Queen Hith London, bach^r, & Anne

Years.	Month.	Day.	Names.

Roberts of St Catherine precinct near ye Tower, Widow. Licence

1738 December 2 — Anthony Leyrisse of St Martins in ye fields Mid^x, Wid^r, & Dorothy Jackson of St Andrew Holborn Midd^x, Sp^r. Licence

11 — Jury Wacklin, Bach^r, & Martha Pix, Sp^r, both of this parish, by Banns

23 — Edward Norris of St Mary le Bow London, B^r, & Mary Norman of St Saviour's Southwark in Surry, Sp^r, by Licence

January 27 — Froward Cowell of Allhallows Barkin London, Bach^r, & Sarah Wilkins of ye same, Sp^r. Licence

February 21 — Joshua Hubbart of St Gabriel Fenchurch street London, Wid^r, & Frances Fawson of St Dunstans in ye East London, sp^r. Licence

March 5 — Christopher Shackleton of Barking Essex, Bach^r, & Martha Carter of ye same parish, sp^r. Licence

6 — Richd Collins of Hendon Midd^x, Bach^r, & Abigail Weaver of St Andrew Holbourn London, Sp^r. Licence

1739 April 22 — Henry Bacon, Bach^r, & Rachel Kirton, Sp^r, both of this parish, by Banns

26 — William Whitaker Esqr of ye Middle Temple London, Bach^r, & Isabella Rebekah North of St Bennet Fink London, Sp^r. Licence

July 5 — Robert Mills of St Dunstan Stepney Midd^x, Bach^r, & Mary Stumphousen of ye same parish, Sp^r. Licence

October 9 — George Payne of St Peter Cornhill, Bach^r, & Elizabeth Mason of St James Westminster, Sp^r

16 — William Cheeseman of Peckham Kent, Bach^r, & Anne Golding of ye same, Sp^r

December 27 — Richd Lockett, Bach^r, & Anne Purse, sp^r, both of this parish

1740 May 3 — John Jaques of Christ Church London, Bach^r, & Mary Hiorne of St Bartholomew ye Less London, Sp^r.

15 — Richd Aguttar of Huntingdon, Bach^r, & Priscilla Forster of ye same, sp^r

17 — Richd Gibbons of St Brides London, Bach^r, & Elizabeth Some of St Andrew London, Sp^r

July 24 — Thomas Mercer of St Peter in Cornhill, Bach^r, & Anne Hunt of St Andrew, sp^r

August 26 — Richd Thomas of St George Southwark, Wid^r, & Abie James of Camberwell, Widow

November 9 — James Poor, Bach^r, & Mary Crawford, Sp^r, both of this parish

January 26 — Arthur Perkins of St Bot. Aldersgate London, Bach^r, & Priscilla Abbott of this P'ish, Widow

1741 June 2 — John Blood of Bromley Midd^x, Bach^r, & Elizabeth Mann of Stratford in Essex, Sp^r

20 — Edmund Drayton of Rotherhith, Wid^r, & Elizabeth Knowles of ye same, Widow

September 29 — Peter Ford of St John's Southwark, Wid^r, & Mary Fitchett of ye same, Sp^r

29 — Peter Burrough of St Botolph Aldgate, Bach^r, & Mary Sturgis of ye same, Widow

October 6 — Charles Griffiths of St Botolph Bishopsgate, Bach^r, & Hannah Denton of St George Hannover Square, Mid^x, Sp^r.

Years.	Month.	Day.	Names.
1741	November	3	Lewin Grave of Stansted Herts, Bach^r, & Elizabeth Sibthorp of Widford in d^o, Sp^r
	December	24	Robert Stevens, Bach^r, & Mary Adams, sp^r, both of this parish
1742	April	18	Harman Camberwell of Christ Church Spittlefields, Bach^r, & Sarah Cope of this parish, Sp^r
	May	11	Samuel Jemprett of St Edmund ye King London, Bach^r, & Alice Lee of St Mary Le Bow, Sp^r
	June	11	Jno Austin of Oundell Northamptonshire, Wid^r, & Mary Digby of St James Westminster, sp^r
		22	Henry Wall of St Mary White Chappel, Wid^r, & Elizth Hull of ye same, Widow
	July	20	Francis Oliver of St Mary Sommersett London, Wid^r, & Edith Jones of St Andrew Holbourn, Sp^r
	August	30	Richd Shakeshaft, Bach^r, & Anne Shaw, Sp^r, both of this parish
	October	14	David Hardie of St Clements Danes, Bach^r, & Mary Boosey of St Bot. Bishopsgate, Widow
	November	29	Henry Granger of St Andrew Holbourn, Bach^r, & Betty Lyford of St Martins in ye fields, sp^r
	December	14	Benjamin Mott of Allhallows ye Great, London, Bach^r, & Mary Longland of St Michael Royal, sp^r
1743	April	29	Henry Sympson of St John's Wapping, Bach^r, & Anne Fletcher of ye same, sp^r
	October	18	John Fawler of Deptford Kent, Bach^r, & Mary Poole of Sheerness, Sp^r
	November	8	Anthony Rushton of St Geo. ye Martyr, Widower, & Susannah Sherrot of St Stephen Coleman, Sp^r
		20	George Webster of St Dunstan in ye East London, Bach^r, & Mary Carpenter of Allhallows Barkin, Sp^r
	December	17	Thomas Bigg of Allhallows Barkin, Bach^r, & Anne Evans of ye same, Widow
		21	John Neale of Preshut co. Wilts, Wid^r, & Anne Edwards of Stanfield Hall co. York, Widow
		26	Zebedee Pitney of St Peter's Cornhill London, Bach^r, & Mary Tanner of Allhallows Lombard street, Sp^r
	January	15	Richd Cross of St Mary White Chappel, Bach^r, & Sarah Robinson of ye same, Widow
		28*	Thomas Hubbard of St Austin London, Bach^r, & Mary Greenwell of ye same, Sp^r
	February	6	William Bedford of Hampstead, Wid^r, & Dorcas Butler of ye same, Sp^r
		7	Richd Jarvill of St Peters Cornhill, Bach^r, & Sarah Wakeling of Orpington Kent, Sp^r
1744	June	11	Robert Williams of St James Clerkenwell, Bach^r, & Sarah Killeslye of this parish, Sp^r
	July	29	Sam^{ll} Balmano of St Bot. Aldgate London, Wid^r, & Sarah Walker of D^o, Sp^r
	August	28	Henry Blazer of St Paul Covent Garden, Bach^r, & Elizabeth Chitch, sp^r
	September	29	William Taylor of St Dunstan in the West, Bach^r, & Anne Smith of St Andrew Holborn, Sp^r
	January	5	Christopher Burrows of St Gabriel Fenchurch street, Bach^r, & Susannah Stevens, sp^r
		6	Ambrose Sparrow of this Parish, Bach^r, & Mary Sholl of St Mary le Bow, Sp^r

* The Register from January 28, 1743, to August 8, 1745, is subscribed " R^d Wynne, Curate."

Yeare.	Month.	Day.	Names.
1744	January	31	Benjamin Clark of this parish, Bach^r, & Susan Phillips of the same, Sp^r
	February	5	Samuel Pitchford, Bach^r, & Anne Taylor, both of this Parish
		13	Daniel Woodriffe of All Hallows Barking, Bach^r, & Elizabeth Whiting of the same, Sp^r
1745	May	20	Thomas King, Bach^r, & Susanna Bosden, Widow, both of Edmonton, Midd^x
	June	30	John Tapperell, Bach^r, & Martha Shallys, Sp^r, both of this parish
	July	8	Francis Scott, Bach^r, & Martha Tustin, Widow, both of St James Westminster
	August	8	John Barber of St Catherine Cree Church, Bach^r, & Hannah Wilson of St Faith, Spinster, by Licence
	December	9*	John Bates, Bach^r, & Henerietta Kenton, Sp^r, both of this parish, by Banns
		16	Richd Keir, Bach^r, & Mary Biggs, sp^r, both of this pp'sh, by Banns
		21	Samuel Rusbatch of All Hallows Barking & Eliz. Mascall of St Mary Ax, by Licence
	January	21	Simon Bockcumb of St Andrew Holborn & Anne Clark of All Hallows the Great, by Licence
1746	April	11	David Kennard & Elizabeth Bodman, both of St Johns Southwark, by L.
	August	3	John White of this parish, Bach^r, & Sarah Shurman of X^t Church Spittlefields, Sp^r, by Banns
	March	10	Joseph Atkinson of this parish, Bach^r, & Frances Sandwell, Sp^r, of St Mary Cole church, by Licence
	May	7	Abraham Youell of Cree Church, Bach^r, & Jane Atkinson of this parish, Sp^r
	July	16	John Johson, Bach^r, & Rebecca Martin, Wid.
	September	14	Thos Constable of St Andrews Holborn & Sylvaster Marsh of St Botolph Bishopsgate, by Licence
		15	Richd Collins of Epping, Bach^r, & Anne Champain of the same parish, Sp^r, by Licence
	February	23	Thos Porter & Mary Taylor, Both of this Parish, by Bands
	March	6	William Richards of St Botolphs Bishopsgate London, Wid^r, & Catherine Carey of the same parish
1748	April	12	Nicholas Peterson of St Catherine near the Tower London, Wid^r, & Susanah Hardman of St Clements East Cheap
	May	24	John Dove of St Botolph Aldgate co. Midd., Bach^r, & Alice Jemmet of Allhallows Barking London, widow, by Lycence
	August	16	Jonas Briggs of St Edmunds the King, Bach^r, & Mary Scrims of Rye co. Sussex, Sp^r, by Lycence
		16	Edmund Dawson of St Olive Southwark co. Surry, Bach^r, & Anne Ellis of St Johns Southwark in the co^y afs^d, Sp^r, by Lycence
		24	Georg Shakeshaft of St Mathews Fryday Street London, Bach^r, & Ane Bricknell of the same parish, by Lycence
	September	3	Thomas Whitaker of Kingston co. Surry, Bach^r, & Mary Tell of St Georges Southwark, Widow, by Lycence
	October	20	George Smith of Feversham co. Kent, Bach^r, & Martha Hegwin the younger of St Nicholas Deptford, Sp^r, by Lycence

* The Register from December 9, 1745, to March 24, 1754, is subscribed " Willm Shackleford, M.A., Curate."

Years.	Month.	Day.	Names.
1748	March	5	John Presland & Thomasin Beckley, both of this Parish, by Banns
1749	July	8	Andrew Barlow of St Saviours Southwark & Margaret Ellis of St Olave Southwark, by Licence
		13	Richard Ilwins of St Giles Cripplegate & Rebecca Cook of St Mary Rotherhith, by Licence
	August	27	Edmund Keckner & Sarah Rushforth, both of this parish, by Banns
1750	April	29	Richard Pearson & Elizabeth Hayton, both of Xt. Church in Midd^x, by Licence
	May	1	John Munday & Edith Wilce, both of St John Southwark, by Licence
1749*	September	21	James Higgs & Jane Taylor, both of y^s parish, by Banns
	December	19	Walter Rie & Sarah Brown of St Martin Le Grand, by Lic.
	February	25	James Fisher & Mary Locton, both of this parish, by Banns
1750	May	6	Charles Thos Duncomb & Deborah Conduit, by Licence
		7	Joseph Clark & Ann Cock, by Licence
		15	Harvey Combe & Christian Jarman, by Licence
	August	6	John Brown & Hannah Brown, by Banns
		16	John Seguin & Mary Taylor, by Licence
	October	4	John Alcock & Elizth Sharp, by Licence
	December	20	Henry Sutton & Mary Read, by Banns
	March	3	Saml Lindsey & Mary Osmond, by Licence
1751	April	25	Gilbert Ford & Mary Stevenson, by Licence
		27	Xtopher Hind & Mary Archer, by Licence
	May	30	Benjⁿ Boone & Ruth Holloway, by Licence
	December	14	John Scott & Mary Frances Henderson were married by a Special Licence by Robt Lamb Dean of Peterborough
1752	April	26	Willm Smith & Margaret Jones, by Banns
	June	15	Joseph Allin & Sarah Layer, by Banns
	October	29	Thomas Watkinson & Ann Silverwood, by Licence
	November	16	Thomas Griffiths & Mary Langthorn, by Licence
1753	February	4	John Roof & Elizth Jenning, by Banns
	April	10	Henry Wall & Sarah Taylor, by Licence
	May	26	John Stump & Elizth Bell, by Licence
	July	11	Joseph Blackwell & Mary Reeves, by Licence
	August	2	John Lemon & Susannah Nelson, by Licence
		27	James Blizzard & Ann Cannon, by Banns
	September	20	Willm Biley & Sarah Selby, both of St Olave Southwark, by Licence
		30	Hill Burton of Low Layton co. Essex & Elizabeth Kinnimond of St Mary Whitechappell, by Licence
	November	18	Robert Swaysland of St Bartholomew ye less & Mary Hughes of St Peter le Poor, by Licence
1754	January	31	Newton Lucas of St George in Midd^x & Rebecca Adey of this parish, by Licence
		31	Thomas Martin of East Moulsey & Mary Sawkins of Wimbledon co. Surrey, by Licence
	February	12	Richard Bexley & Ann Barret, both of this Parish, by Banns
		25	Charles Reynolds & Mary Waller, both of this parish, by Banns
		25	Henry Beaumont & Phillis Parker, both of this Parish, by Banns
		26	John Ward & Sarah Lewis, both of this Parish, by Banns
	March	24	Edward Saunders of St Andrew Holborn, Bach^r, & Mary Meyer of the same parish, a Minor, by Licence

* Sic.

Burials.

Year.	Month.	Day.	Names.
1667	May	9*	Elizabeth Buck wife of James Buck, in the North Ile near her child
	June	10	Ann Rugby the younger, in the West Churchyard
		15	Ann Rugby the elder, in the West Churchyard
		26	Elizabeth Banes, widow, a penc'oner, in the same Churchy^d
	August	8	Susanna dau. of John Beard, Sugar baker, in the North Ile
		11	Elizabeth dau. of Thomas Woodward, Cook, in the West Churchyard
		30	Mrs Blackmore the elder, in the Cloyster
	October	22	Elizabeth dau. of William Ingall, Cooper, & Elizabeth his wife, in the West Churchy^d
		27	Widow Whitney, in the East Churchyard
	November	15	Matthew Searle servant to Mr Henry Chitty, Merchant, in the West Churchy^d
	December	4	Henry son of Henry Jordan (by Trade Tallow Chandler), & Alice his wife, in the West Churchy^d
		18	William son of Samuell Pooke, Weaver, & Elizabeth his wife, in the West Churchy^d
		24	Anne Rancez servant to Alice Only, widow, in the same Churchy^d
	February	16	Nathaniel Langley son of John Langley Esq. (of the Company of . . . .) and . . . . his wife, in the Chancell
			. . . . Thrift . . . . of the Parish of St Olave Hart street, in the South Ile
	March	8	Henry Jordan, Barber Chirurgeon (by trade Tallow Chandler), in the South Isle
		24	Beniamin Benson a poor man (who died at Mr Motteirs in Leadenhall), in the East yard
1668	April	7†	Elizabeth Dormer servant & kinswoman to . . . . Gerrard, in the East yard
		16	Elizabeth Cage, widow, mother to Mr Cornelius Cage, Vintner, in the South Isle
	May	15	Jervas Smith, merch^t taylor, in the Middle Isle
		22	Joane wife of William Payne, Butcher, in the midd. Isle
	July	17	A male Child taken up in Mr Chitty his yard, buryed in the East Churchy^d. M'd this child was left in the p'ish on Monday the 13 of this instant July
			William son of William Broman, Victualler, & Margaret his wife, in the Cloyster
	August	1	An abortive male Infant fro' Mr Braggs house (in the Green yard), interred in the East yard

---

* The Register from May 9, 1667, to March 24, 1667-8, is subscribed "Mr Richard Blackburne, Churchwarden."

† The Register from April 7, 1668, to September 16, 1669, is subscribed "Mr Timothy Rosse, Churchwarden."

Years.	Month.	Day.	Names.
1668	October	1	.... wife of Thomas Woodward, Cook, in the East yard
		4	Richard Stone
		6	Elizabeth wife of William Sherrington, Esq., in the middle Isle
		19	John son of William Bookey, Merch[t] taylor, & of .... his wife, in the middle Isle
	November	19	Thomas Lane, Vintner, in the South Chapel
	January	1	Rich. Catham (servant to Tho. Allison), in the East Churchy[d]
		5	William Stumbells (dying passing as a Vagrant in his chaire at M[r] Gerrard the Constables dore), in the East yard
		23	Thomas Hanson, Grocer, in the South Isle
		20	Tobias Knowles, Pewterer, in the middle Isle
	February	3	Theodore Pepys and William Pritchet, in the East Church yard
1669	April	24	M[r] Deputy John Chevall (Draper), in the middle Isle
	May	2	Christopher son of Christopher Tillard, Vintner, in the South Chapel
		13	Eliz. Hinton, widow, in the South Chapel
		17	M[rs] .... Gardner, in the Chancell
		10	James Wych, in the Chancell
		27	John son of Thomas Rolfe, mariner, in the South Isle
	June	17	Sara Dorman, widow, in the Cloyster
		22	Thomas Wilson son of William Wilson, in y[e] middle Isle
	July	9	Alexander Horton (serv[t] to M[r] Horton, fishmonger), in y[e] East yard
		13	Richard son of Richard Palleday, Haberdasher, in the South Isle
		23	John Smith serv[t] to M[r] Robert Rowland, in the East yard
		30	Ellis Nolder, Carpenter (a lodger in the green yard), in the New Churchyard in Bedlam
	August	13	Clement Bacon, Clarke, of this p'ish, in the East yard
	September	12	John son of John Adams, Cook, in the South Isle
		16	Edward son of Rich. Phrip, Gent., in the middle Isle
	October	1*	James son of James Buck, in the North Isle
		2	Dorothy wife of Jn[o] Ladd, Bricklayer, in y[e] West yard
		2	Eliz. .... serv[t] to M[r] Sam[l] Wickens, in y[e] East yard
		3	Jn[o] Hawkins serv[t] to M[r] Lewis Wilson, Vintner, in the East yard
		20	Gerrard Whorwood, Drap', in the South Chapel
		24	Robert Ferne, Tanner, in the New Churchy[d]
	November	9	Isaiah Broman son of W[m] Broman, in y[e] Cloyster
		19	Andrew James son of Jn[o] James, Armourer, in the South Isle
	December	19	Rowland son of Rob[t] Wairing, Sadler, in y[e] middle Isle
		20	Jn[o] French serv[t] to M[r] Jn[o] Price, in y[e] Cloyster
		26	Jn[o] son of Tho. Wickersham, in the Cloyster
		30	Mary dau. of James Blat the elder, in y[e] South Isle
	January	23	One abortive male child of W[m] Tighe, Haberdasher, in the East yard
	February	10	Susanna dau. of Beniamin Maynard, fishmonger, in the East yard
		15	Eliz. dau. of Henry Jordan, in y[e] South Isle
		18	Mary wife of Jn[o] Alder, Drap', in the South Isle
		20	Ann wife of Rob[t] Russell, Innholder, in the East yard

* The Register from October 1, 1669, to August 16, 1681, is subscribed " Will. Beveridge, parson;" and from August 16, 1681, to March 20, 1703, " Will. Beveridge, D.D., parson."

Yeare.	Month.	Day.	Names.
1669	February	26	William son of Richard Bartlet, in the South Isle
	March	1	Susanna daughter of George Grigman, in the East yard
		13	Adry dau. of Richard Phrip, Gent., in the middle Isle
1670	April	12	Randall serv^t to Mr Jno James, in the East Churchy^d
		23	Jno serv^t to Mr Cornelius Cage, East Church yard
	May	4	Gilbert serv^t to Mr Waring, East Church yard
		19	Beniamin son of Beniamine Shute, South Isle
		21	Katherine dau. of Walter Young, Church yard
		22	Mary dau. of Robert Rowland, South Isle
		24	A ffoundlin Buried
		28	Mary another ffoundlin Buried
	July	6	Robert Samber serv^t to Mr Tho. Child, Cloyster
		12	ffrances dau. of Will'm Smith, South Isle
		23	Susannah dau. of Edward Rich, South Isle
	August	15	Thomas Smith, in the North Isle
	September	6	Timothy Rosse, in the South Chappell
		6	Elizabeth Blagrave, in the South Chappell
		7	Sarah Purchas, in the Middle Isle
		18	Judith dau. of Henry Gulliford, South Chappell
		28	Thomas Birkhead, in the Middle Isle
	October	27	Roady Purchas, in the Middle Isle
		28	Phillip son of Aldm' Langley, Chauncell
	November	9	Samuell son of William Willson, Middle Isle
		10	Cornelius Cage, in the South Isle
		14	Robert Mason son of Jo. Mason, Ch. yard
	December	1	Alice Onely, in the Cloister
		21	Ann dau. of John Silke, Middle Isle
	February	19	Mary dau. of Richard Shelley, South Chappell
	March	3	Isaac Brooman, in the Cloister
1671		29	ffrancis Meaddopp, in the South Chappell
	June	21	Martha Germin, Church yard
		29	Richard Snow, South Isle
	July	14	Elizabeth Medly, North Isle
	August	12	Susanna ffoster, South Isle
		30	Elizabeth Buck, at the West end
	September	16	George Cockeram, South Isle
		17	Elizabeth Paine, Middle Isle
	October	20	William Rugby, Church yard
		21	John Smith, South Isle
	November	2	Ann Seale, Cloister
		7	Abraham serv^t to Mr Thomas, Church yard
		22	Mary serv^t to Mr Mason, Church yard
	December	13	North Darleston, Church yard
		24	Jno serv^t to Mr Hill, Ch. yard
		27	Ann Palladay, South Isle
	January	2	Elizabeth Rowland, South Isle
		18	Robert Rowland, South Isle
			Walter son of Henry Gullifer
			Edmund son of Richard Porter

[A blank space occurs here.]

1672	May	22	Debora dau. of Robert Rowland, South Iyle
		28	Nicholas Conyers son of Nicholas Conyers of S^t Mi'les Cornhill
	June	2	James son of John Couper, in the East Churchy^d
		15	John Molinen, East Church yard
		15	Judith dau. of Henry Gulliford, South Chappell

Years.	Month.	Day.	Names.
1672	June	26	Juda dau. of Thomas Deane, East Church yard
		29	Ann dau. of John Potts, South Iyle
	July	1	William Hudson, South Iyle
		5	Richard son of George Gregman, in the East Church y^d
		8	Ann Pale, in the Church yard
		9	Midleton Hudson son of William Hudson, South Ile
		9	Benjⁿ son of Benj. Majnard, East Church yard
		30	John Barnes. serv^t to Mr Alder, East Churchyard
	August	15	Henry son of Henry Gulliford, South Chapel
		27	Richard Smyth serv^t to Mr Will' Parker, East Churchy^d
		30	Reb' dau. of Will' Langham, in middle Iyle
	September	20	Richard Palleday, South Iyle
	October	10	Presilla Parker, East Church yard
		11	Sarah the wife of Sam. Bicker, Chancell
		15	Judith wife of Mr Richard Goulding, South Chappell
	November	21	.... Langlye wife of .... Langley, in the Chancell
		19	John Heylyn, Esq., Chancell
	December	5	Tobias Baxster, Church yard
		6	John Smyth, East Church yard
		20	Elizebeth dau. of Mr Will' Willson, Middle Ile
	January	4	Benjⁿ Shute son of Benj. Shute, middle Ile
		9	Will. Gulleford son of Mr Henry Gulleford, South Iyle
			Rebecka dau. of Mr Henry Palmer, South Iyle
	February	21	Elizabeth wife of Mr William Hinton, Middle Iyle
		22	Nathanell Clagget, North Iyle
	March	4	Richard Shelly, South Iyle
		19	John son of Benjⁿ Majnard, East Church yard
1673	April	4	Hestor dau. of Jno Potts
		10	Elizabeth Domvill, West yard
		26	Kathern Domvill dau. of Charles Domvill, West Church yard
	May	3	Ann dau. of Thomas Abine, South Iyle
	July	2	John Haukins, South Iyle
		2	Will. son of Rob. Waring, Middle Iyle
		3	Zacharia Bertrand, North Iyle
		16	Rebecca wife of Will. Carter, South Iyle
		25	Thomas Barker, South Iyle
	August	5	Barbary Bard, tabernacle in ye Church yard
	July*	10	John Garbrand, son of Tobias Garbrand, South Chappell
	August	11	Kath. Browman dau. of Will. Browman, in the Cloisters
		25	Penelope dau. of Jno ffoster, South Iyle
		31	Thomas Wells, tabernacle Church yard
	September	8	Edmand Welch son of Edmond Welch, East Church y^d
		12	Ann dau. of Jno Mason, tabernacle
		21	Rebecca Scott, South Iyle
		26	James Blatt, South Isle
	October	8	Edwd Godfrey, in the Church yard
		18	Elizabth Moise, in the Church yard
		29	Richard Greene, in the North Isle
	November	16	Richard Abrathat, in the Middle Isle
		18	John Meteire, in the Middle Isle
		26	James Symons, in the Tabernacle
		27	Mary Stackhouse, in the p'ish Church of St Mary Mounthaw
		29	Mary Blackmore late ye wif of Sr Jno Blackmore, in the Cloysters

* Sic.

Years.	Month.	Day.	Names.
1673	December	11	John Paine, in the Tabernacle
		26	Morris Roch, in the Churchyard
		29	Thomas son of Tho. Dorman, in the Churchyard
	January	30	Robert son of Robt Rowland, in ye South Isle
	February	21	Rich^d son of Robt Rowland, in ye South Isle
		22	Sarah North, in the South Isle
	March	6	James Adams, in the South Isle
1674	April	8	Martha Newarke, in ye Church yard
		9	Marg^t late wife of Fran^s Walker, in South Chappell
		11	Robert Pagett, in the Church yard
		13	Faith Taylor, in the Church yard
		16	Nathan. Gayes, in ye South Isle
		19	Tho. Bockie, in ye Tabernacle
		23	Edwd son of Edwd Bull, in ye Church yard
	May	14	John Newark, in the Church yard
		18	Thomas Trigg, in the Church yard
		22	Eliz^a Robson, in the South Chappell
		26	Martha Cockram, in the South Isle
		27	Thos Burkett, in the Middle Isle
	June	25	Sarah dau. of Edwd Bull, in the Church yard
		28	W^m son of Sam^ll Purchase, in the Middle Isle
		29	Peter son of Osmund and Mary*
	July	20	Francis Cox, in the Churchyard
	August	26	Charles son of Samuell & Mary Purchase, in the Middle Isle
	July	27	Elizabeth dau. of John Newark, in the Churchyard
	October	1	Katherine dau. of Jno Thomas, in the Tabernacle
		7	Deborah dau. of Robt Rowland, in the South Isle
		25	Mary dau. of Sam^ll Purchase, in the Middle Isle
	November	27	Ann Abrathat, in the Middle Isle
	December	4	Mary Clark, in the Church yard
		12	Margate Twiney, in the Tabernacle
	January	9	Wm Gibbins, in the South Isle
		18	Anne Graves, in the Churchyard
		23	Mary Boogis, in the South Chapell
	February	9	Tho. son of Jno Meriton, in ye South Chapell
		10	Richd Goulding, in the North Chapell
1675	March	28	Sam^ll son of Anth^e Hall, in the Middle Isle
		29	Edwd Rugby, in the South Isle
		30	Alice Taylor, in the Middle Isle
		30	Elizab^th Kinton, in the middle Isle
	April	11	Moses Bartlett, in the Church yard
		13	Tho. Dighton, in the Church yard
		18	Robt Russell, in the Tabernacle
	May	9	Ann Adams, in the Church yard
		21	Ann Hill, penc'oner, in the church yard
	June	14	Tho. Allison, in the North Isle
		29	James son of Tho. Abny, in the Middle Isle
	July	6	Hester Mateire in the Middle Isle
	August	8	Tho. Anger, in the New Church yard by the Artillery ground
		12	Tho. Cowes, iu the Church yard
		12	Mary Cole, in the Church yard
		20	Martha Cockram, in the South Isle
	September	6	John Browman, in the Cloysters

* Sic. See note to Weddings, p. 55.

Years.	Month.	Day.	Names.
1675	September	16	Hanah Caster, in the Churchyard
		23	John Seal, in the Tabernacle
	October	14	Elizab' Wood, in the Churchyard
		24	Elizab' Wickersham, in yᵉ Church yard
		31	Elizab' Bromridge, in yᵉ Church yard
	November	23	Geo. Brewer, in the South Isle
		28	John son of Richᵈ Pagett, in the Churchyard
	December	12	Thomas Coves, in the Church yard
		17	Elizabeth Lardner, in the South Isle
		24	Elizabeth Peters, in the Church yard
	January	19	Tho. Abny, in the South Isle
		27	John Mason, in the Tabernacle
	March	2	Henry Chitty son of Henry Chitty, in the Middle Isle
		8	Edward Colt, in the North side
		12	John Lucas, in the Church yard
1676		26	Sarah dau. of Robᵗ Rowland, in the South Isle
	April	13	Mathew James, in the North Isle
	June	2	Wᵐ son of Edwᵈ Bull, in yᵉ Church yard
		7	John son of Robᵗ Wareing, in yᵉ South Isle
		14	Mary Lovegrove, in the Churchyᵈ of Sᵗ Ethelborough
	July	12	Joseph Buck son of James Buck, in the middle Isle
		12	Sarah dau. of Georg & Sarah Atwood, in the Churchyard
		13	Tho. Beach, in the Church yard
	August	9	Katherine dau. of John & Elizabᵗʰ Price, in the South Isle
		11	Samuell son of Nichᵒ Bendy, in the middle Isle
		23	John Rawleson, in the North Isle
		31	John son of Thomas & Juda Weeks, in the North Chapell
	September	19	Richard Cardall, in the Church yard
	October	1	Joseph son of Samˡˡ Purchase, in the middle Isle
		5	Roger Greene, in the Church yard
		6	Mary wife of Alexʳ Snapes, was buried in the Church of Alhallows Lumbard Street
		20	Robert Welch, in the Church yard
	November	8	Will'm son of Mʳ Tho. Lardner, in the Middle Isle
		11	Elizabeth wife of Mʳ Tho. Lardner, in the Middle Isle
		26	Wᵐ Falkner, in the Church yard
	December	2	Geo. Birkhead, in the middle Isle
		5	Ruthe Parker, in the Church yard
	January	26	Andrew Rowland, in the middle Isle
	February	3	Susanna Gibbons, in the South Isle
		9	Sarah Gray, in the Church yard
		10	Elizabeth dau. of Benjamin & Mary Thorowgood, in the Chancell
		18	Hannah Jones, in the North Isle
		23	Abigall Cowes, in the Church yard
	March	2	Roger Rolph, in the North Isle
		18	Mary ffloyd, in the North Isle
1677		31	Margaret Helmes, in the South Isle
	April	3	Lucie Langham, in the South Isle
		29	Sarah Adams, in yᵉ Church yard
	May	6	Mary Purchase, in yᵉ middle Isle
		8	Elizabeth Booker, in yᵉ Church yard
		10	Elizabeth Wilson, in yᵉ North Isle
		13	Rebecca Atwood, in the Church yard
	June	9	John servᵗ to Mʳ Chittie, in the Church yard
		10	Thomas Wilson, in yᵉ Church yard
		19	Johanna Spinage, in the North Chapel

Years.	Month.	Day.	Names.
1677	June	28	Hester Potts, in the South Isle
		30	William Roseby, in yᵉ Church yard
	July	21	George Atwood junʳ, in yᵉ Church yard
		22	Honor Baker, in yᵉ Church yard
		23	Samuel Purchase junʳ, in yᵉ Church yard
		29	Hester ffenn, in the Church yard
	August	1	Elizabeth Beauchamp, in yᵉ South Isle
		6	John Purchase, in the Churchyard
		30	Anne Darlston, in the Church yard
	September	4	Anne Russell, in the Church yard
		4	Joseph Wibourne, in the Church yard
		9	William Tigh, in the Middle Isle
		22	Susanna Wareing, in the Church yard
	October	8	James Dalton, in the Church yard
		19	ffrancis Hall, in the North Isle
	November	4	Hannah Caster, in yᵉ Church yard
		5	Elizabeth Lardner, in the Church yard
		22	Thomas Thornton, in the North Isle
		28	John Knowles, in the Church yard
	December	2	Thomas White, in the Church yard
		12	John Adams, in the South Isle
		16	Elizabeth Bartlett, in the South Isle
	January	6	Joseph ffreeman, in yᵉ Church yard
		18	William Pirkin, in the Church yard
	February	12	Humphry Merriton, in yᵉ Middle Isle
		19	Sʳ Richard Langley,* Knight, in yᵉ Chancell
	March	19	Ann Page, in the Church yard
1678	April	8	Charnel Green, in the Churchyard
		13	Eleanor dau. of Thomas & Bridgett Phipps, in yᵉ Churchyᵈ
		19	ffrances Watts, widow, in the Churchyard
		23	Mary dau. of John & Dorcas Adams, in the Churchyard
	May	5	Susan wife of ffrancis Simms, in the Churchyard
		7	Jane wife of George Manayrd, in the Churchyard
		19	Ann dau. of Robert & Ann Clarke, in the Churchyard
		23	Elizabeth dau. of Thomas Bristow, in the Churchyard
	June	2	Elizebeth dau. of Alexander Caster, in the Churchyard
		10	Richard Thorrowgood, in yᵉ Chancell
	July	16	John Crouch, in yᵉ Churchyard
		21	Henry & Ann Latham, in yᵉ Churchyᵈ
		28	Richard Kettle, in the Churchyard
		30	Kathrine Orton, in yᵉ Churchyard
	August	15	Elizabeth Willson, in yᵉ Church
	September	20	ffrancis Lamb, in the Churchyard
		30	William Paine, in yᵉ Middle Isle
	October	17	Susanna Donvill, in yᵉ Churchyard
		17	John Brandon, in yᵉ Churchyard
	November	3	Daniell Hunt, in the Churchyard
		5	Samuell Smith, in the Churchyard
		14	Elizabeth Cooke, in the Churchyard
		21	John ffaron, in the Churchyard
		29	Lem son of James Vtbure, in the Churchyard
	December	6	Thomas Purchase, in the Churchyard
		15	Benja. Clarage, in the Churchyard
		23	. . . . Bacon, in yᵉ Churchyard
		27	ffrancis Walker, in yᵉ South Chapel

* Son of Alderman Langley; knighted at Whitehall March 15, 1672.

Years.	Month.	Day.	Names.
1678	January	2	Joseph Pell, in yᵉ Churchyard
		8	Thomas son of Thomas & Elizabeth Lardner, in the Church
		17	Wᵐ Carter, in yᵉ Churchyard
		18	Edward son of Robert & Elizabeth Rowland, in yᵉ middle Isle
		23	Richard son of John ffaron, in yᵉ Churchyard
	February	9	Ann dau. of John and . . . . Morris, in yᵉ middle Isle
		10	Alice Bayes, in the Churchyard
1679	March	28	Wᵐ Browman, in yᵉ Churchyard
	May	21	Elizabeth Bendy, in yᵉ middle Isle
	June	12	John James, in yᵉ middle Isle
		19	Mary Nicholds, in yᵉ middle Isle
		27	Ann ffilewood, in yᵉ Churchyard
	July	6	Elizabeth dau. of John & Mary Loyd, in yᵉ middle Isle
		12	Hellena dau. of Thomas & Bridgett Phips, in the middle Isle
		20	Sarah dau. of Charles & Katherine Domvill, in yᵉ Churchyᵈ
	August	5	Elizabeth dau. of Marthew & Elizabeth Ricraft, in the Churchyard
		8	John son of William & Margery Browman, in the Church yard
			Joseph son of John and . . . . Meriton, in the Church
		12	Thomas Seale, in the Churchyard
		19	John son of John & Mary Weston
		28	ffrances dau. of Andrew & Elizabeth Heriott, in the middle Isle
		28	Samuell son of Henry & Bridget Palmer, in the middle Isle
	September	30	Edward Goulding, in the Churchyard
	October	1	Wᵐ son of Anthony & Joyce Hall, in the middle Isle
		5	Susanna dau. of Tho. Phipps, in middle Isle
		26	Wᵐ son of Wᵐ & Hanna Tye, in the South Isle
	November	3	Mary Jones, in the Churchyard
		6	John son of John & Ann Starkey, in the Churchyard
		16	Mary Studare, in the Churchyard
		19	Katherine dau. of Thomas & Martha Witherden, in the Church
		19	Elizabeth Simson, in yᵉ Churchyard
	December	5	Henry son of Henry & Bridget Palmer, in the South Isle
		11	Margarett Bonham, in yᵉ Church
		13	John Aylett, in the South Isle
		15	Thomas son of Thomas & Judeth Weekes, in the North Chapell
		19	Susan dau. of Andrew & Susan Boult, in the middle Isle
		20	Daniell Meddows, in the Churchyard
		21	Margarett the dau. of John & Mary Lloyd, in the middle Isle
	January	1	William Hammon, in the North Chapel
		30	William son of Richard Blackburne, in the North Isle
	February	27	Peter son of Thomas & Bridget Phipps, in the Churchyᵈ
	March	7	Thomas son of Thomas & Elizabeth Lardner, in the middle Isle
		9	Robert Welch, in the Churchyard
		20	Mary Wing, in the Churchyard
1680	April	8	Richard Tharp, in the Churchyard
	May	10	ffrances the late wife of Doctor William Beveridge, in the Chancell
		14	John Knowles, in the North Isle
		16	Peter son of John Wiburne, in the Churchyard

Yeare.	Month.	Day.	Names.
1680	June	14	Honour North, in the Churchyard
		23	Edmund Chillington, in the Churchyard
		28	Ann dau. of Josua & Mary Williams, in the Churchyard
		29	Charles son of John & Mary Weston, in the Churchyard
	August	13	Isaac Aylet, in the North Isle
		20	Mary Tillery, in the Churchyard
		21	Andrew son of Andrew & Elizabeth Harjot, in the Churchy^d
		31	William Blagrave, in the South chapel
	September	9	William son of William & Mary Cox, in the middle Isle
		25	Percivall Thomas, in the Churchyard
		26	William Stable, in the Churchyard
	October	4	Corney ffrowde, in the South Isle
		21	Elizabeth Paine, in the Churchyard
	November	4	Stephen Thornely, Esq., in the Chancell
		14	Elizabeth late wife of Philip Stowers, in the middle Isle
		30	Ann late wife of Charles Weekes, in the middle Isle
	December	1	Mary dau. of Edward Wing, in the Church yard
		2	Anthony Hall, in the middle Isle
		5	Samuell Heath, in the Churchyard
		7	John Clarage, in the Churchyard
		14	Mary the late wife of Thomas Alder, in the South Isle
		14	Benjamin Low, in the Churchyard
		22	Miriam Smyth, in the North Isle
	January	9	Andrew son of John Baxter, in the South Isle
		11	John son of John Radams, in the Church
		12	Elizabeth Tharp, in the Churchyard
		23	ffrancis Lenord, in the Churchyard
		25	Presilla Orton, in the Churchyard
	February	3	Elizabeth Peters, a foundling, in the Churchyard
		5	Ann Parish, in the Churchyard
		23	William Bendy, in the middle Isle
		26	Robert Armitage, in the Churchyard
	March	6	Elizabeth Porter, in the Church
		24	Mary Gray, in the Church
1681		27	Mary Lane, in the Church
	April	1	Richard Wing, in the Church
		17	Samuell Ellet, in the Churchyard
	May	1	Thomas Gouge, in the Churchyard
		18	Thomas Alder, in the Church
		19	Elizabeth Colier, in the Churchyard
		23	Thomas Salter, in the Church
		31	Mary Beuchamp, in the Church
	July	2	William Packer, in the Churchyard
		6	Benjamin Shut, in the Church
		22	Ann Davis, in the Church yard
	August	1	Robert Smyth, in the Churchyard
		2	John Searle, in the Churchyard
		16	Mary Parrot, in the Church
		16	ffrancis Sims, in the Churchyard
		18	Thomas Taylor, in the Churchyard
	September	13	Joseph Couper, in the Churchyard
		18	Thomas Seale, in the Churchyard
		20	Ann Hollyday, in the Churchyard
	October	6	James Gray, in the Churchyard
		18	Alexander Caster, in the Churchyard
		20	Ann Yates, in the Churchyard
		25	Ambros Jones, in the Church yard

Years.	Month.	Day.	Names.
1681	October	27	Benjamin Thorowgood, in the Chancell
	November	9	William Wonham, in the middle Isle
		20	John Lun, in the Churchyard
	December	3	Mary Weston, in the middle Isle
		4	Alice Barker, in the Churchyard
		8	John Morris, in the Church
		9	Ann Seale, in the Churchyard
		19	Ambros and William Rowland, in the South Isle
	January	8	Thomas Spence, in the Churchyard
		17	Richard Acton, in the middle Isle
		22	Elizabeth Dyton, in the Church yard
		24	Thomas Person, in the Church yard
		26	John Murry, in the Churchyard
	February	2	Robert Acton, in the middle Isle
		14	Sarah Cockeram, in the middle Isle
		21	Jn° Young, in the Churchyard
	March	16	Mary Pitts, in the North Isle
		19	ffrancis son of ffrancis Sims, in ye Churchyard
1682		28	Elizabeth Cooke, in the Churchyard
		30	Richard son of Philip Stubs, in the South Isle
	April	10	Wm Longford, between the North & South doors
		21	Mary dau. of William & Mary Pagget
		23	Katherine Dobbs, in the Church yard
	May	25	Sarah Wiburne, in the Church yard
	June	4	Elizabeth dau. of Thomas & Elizabeth Larner, in the South Isle
		24	John son of John & Sarah Blunt, in the Churchyard
		26	Thomas son of Thomas & Judith Weekes, in the North Isle
	July	14	Mary dau. of Wm & Mary Cox, in the middle Isle
		14	ffrances dau. of William & Philip Chase, in the Church yard
		21	Thomas Tharpe son of Arbella Tharpe, in the Churchyard
		25	Ann dau. of Nicholas & Ann Swingler, in the Churchyard
		26	Elizabeth Young, in the Churchyard
	August	21	Elizabeth Colwell, in the South Isle
		22	Richard son of Richard Shaw, Vintner, between the North & South doors
		25	Margaret Langmore dau. of William Langmore, in ye middle Isle
	September	8	Elizabeth dau. of Samll & Ann Guinn, in the Churchyd
		16	A female Chrisome of Henry Murrey, Victualler, in the Churchyard
		19	John Blackburne Curate at St Micha Cornhill, in the middle Isle
		19	A stillborn son of Thomas Andrews, in the North Isle
	October	10	Joseph son of Ralph & Elizabeth Smyth, between the North & South doors
		17	Bartholomew son of Bartholomew Pigot, in the Churchyd
		29	Stephen son of Thomas Armitage, in the Churchyard
	November	2	Robert Carpenter, in the South Isle
		5	Nathaniel Draper, in the South Isle
		19	Ann Davis, in the Churchyard
		22	Edward son of Richard & Ann Acton, in ye Middle Isle
		26	Sarah Peters, a foundling, in the Churchyard
		30	Henry ffookes, in the Churchyard
	December	1	A stillborn son of Richard Wareing, between the North & South doors

Years.	Month.	Day.	Names.
1682	December	8	Gabriel son of William Wenham, between the North & South doors
		24	Ann dau. of John Graves, in the Churchyard
	January	9	Ann Brjan, in the Churchyard
		12	Two abortive Children of ffrancis Kirby
		19	William son of William & Katherine Spinage, in the North Isle
		23	Hester dau. of Richard Bartlet, in the South Isle
		28	Elizabeth wife of Robert Rowland, in the South Isle
		31	Anna Lawelling, in the middle Isle
	February	8	Rebecca Person dau. of Paul Person, in the Churchyard
	March	1	Joseph son of Joseph & Elizabeth Gray, in the South Isle
		2	Cariell son of Samuell & Ann Shute, in the South Isle
		3	Jacob son of Samuell & Elizabeth Clarke, in the Churchyard
		3	William Garaway, in the Churchyard
		9	Susan dau. of Samuell & . . . . Smyth, in the Churchyard
		21	Thomas Atwood, in the Churchyard
1683		30	James son of Thomas & . . . . Abny, in the South Isle
	April	5	John Thomas, between the North & South doors
		13	Henry Tilley, in the Churchyard
	May	7	John Sturt, in the middle Isle
		10	John son of Andrew & Bridget Yates
		23	ffrancis son of Samuell & Ann Shute, in the South Isle
	June	3	Susanna dau. of Andrew & Susanna Bolt, in the South Isle
	July	17	Stephen son of Samuell & Katherine Smyth, in the Churchyard
	August	15	Hannah dau. of William & . . . . Tigh, in the middle Isle
		22	Abraham son of Abraham & Jane Hemingway, in the South Isle
	September	1	Jacob son of Philip and Ma . . . Stubbs, in the middle Isle
		23	Elizabeth dau. of Thomas & Elizabeth Chamberlin, in the middle Isle
	October	2	Henry Latham, in the Churchyard
		2	Martha dau. of James & . . . . . ffremantle, in the Churchyard
		10	Charles son of James & Debora Vtburt, in the midd. Isle
	November	11	Dorithy Wingfeild, between the North & South doors
		25	Mary Dover, in the Church yard
	December	10	Elizabeth dau. of Benjamin and Mary Thorowgood, in the Chancell
		18	John Waukelin, betw. the North & South doors
		18	William son of William & Jane Knight
		19	Elizabeth Whittle, in the Churchyard
		19	Benjamin son of John & Sarah Cockeram, in the midd. Isle
		27	Martha dau. of John & . . . . Radhams
	January	8	Alder dau. of William & Elizabeth Court, in the Churchyard
		8	Roger Pitts, in the middle Isle
		11	Elizabeth Dalton, in the Churchyard
		13	John Snosden, in the Churchyard
		26	Mary dau. of Benjamin Thorowgood, Esqr, & Mary his wife, in the Chancell
		23	Mary Streete, between the North & South doors
	February	9	John son of Andrew Boult, in the South Isle
		19	Thomas Edgerly, in the east Churchyard
		24	Ann Broadbent, between the North & South doors
		27	James son of James & Debora Vtburt, in the middle Isle

Year.	Month.	Day.	Names.
1683	February	29	Levine dau. of John & Levine Gentry, in the Churchyard
	March	4	Samuell Smyth, in the Churchyard
		5	Thomas Gujon, in the Chancell
		14	Ann Latham, in the Churchyard
		14	Samuell son of Samuell & Elizabeth Clarke, in the Churchy^d
		21	John Sturt, in the middle Isle
1684		30	William Rowland, in the middle Isle
	April	8	John Dodd, in the North Isle
	May	1	Robert son of John & Elizabeth Hayward, in the Churchy^d
		4	Mary dau. of Walter & Elizabeth Parsons
		13	Ann dau. of William & Alice Langmore
	June	12	Thomas Derleston, in the Churchyard
		22	Thomas Blott, in the Churchyard
		23	John son of Barnet & Ann Trance, in the Churchyard
		28	Mary dau. of John & Elizabeth Ingle
	July	14	Minn. dau. of ffrancis & Elizabeth Kerby, in the Church
		30	William Babham, in the South Isle
	August	6	Humphry son of Richard & Martha Wareing, in ye North Isle
		13	Philippia dau. of William & Philippia Chase
		19	Bridget dau. of Richard Bartlet
	September	21	Martha dau. of Richard & Ann Marjot
	October	6	Sarah late wife of John Cockeram
		10	Thomas Careless, in the Churchyard
		10	William Mason, in the Churchyard
		25	Thomas Thorneton, in the North Isle
		26	John Buck, between the North & South doors
		26	Richard Stable, in the middle Isle
		30	Elizabeth dau. of William & Mary Packer, in the Churchyard
	November	2	Elizabeth Hariot, in the middle Isle
		6	Philip Price, in the Churchyard
		16	Elizabeth Spence, in the Church yard
		21	Jane Paulett, in the North Isle
		21	Samuell Rowland, in the Church yard
		30	Thomas Spence, in the Churchyard
		30	John King, in the Churchyard
	January	20	Cave Linch, in the South Isle
	February	13	Richard Blackburne, in the North Isle
		13	John son of Henry & Bridget Palmer, in the middle Isle
		14	Joseph son of John & Elizabeth Morris
	March	2	Susan'a Bucke, between the North & South doors
		19	Walter Kurby, between the North & South doors in the Church
685	April	1	Charles Stubbs, in ye South Isle
		8	Elizabeth Brickland, in the Churchyard
		8	Agnis wife of William Hall, in the South chapel
		9	Thomas Wardner, in the chancell
		14	Thomas Shenton, in ye Church yard
		29	Elizabeth ffilewood, in the Churchyard
		29	Mary King, in ye Churchyard
	May	5	Ralph Trunket, in ye North Isle
		6	Thomas Clement, in ye Churchyard
		16	John Ingle, betw. the North & South doors
	June	4	Emma dau. of Robert & Emma Sanderson, in the South Isle
		5	William Hanson, in ye Churchyard

Years.	Month.	Day.	Names.
1685	July	7	Susan'a dau. of Oliver & Susanna Andrews, in the North Chapel
		17	Agnes dau. of William Hall, in the South Chapel
		21	Thomas Lackham, in the North Chapel
		23	Sarah dau. of Ralph & Elizabeth Smyth, in the Church
		30	Andrew son of James ffremantle, in the Churchyard
	August	1	Elizabeth dau. of John & Elizabeth Howard, church yard
		4	Henry son of Andrew & Bridget Yates, in the Church yard
		12	Elizabeth dau. of Edward Pitts, in the Churchyard
		23	John son of John & Mary Loyd, between the North & South doors
		23	Richard son of John & .... Smyth, in the midd. Isle
		26	Elizabeth late wife of Mathew Ricroft, in the North Isle
	September	1	Elizabeth dau. of Mathew Chitty, in the North Isle
		8	Thomas son of William & Leah Holyday, in the Church yard
		14	William son of William & Elizabeth Hardy, in the Church-yard
		14	William son of Andrew & Bridget Yates, in the Church yard
		17	Elizabeth dau. of Thomas & Hannah Leach, in the Church-yard
	October	8	Mary Thorneton, in the South Isle
	November	4	John Lewis, in the Churchyard
		8	Thomas son of Paul Person, in the Churchyard
		12	Samvel Shute, Esqr, in the North Isle
		25	John Smyth, in the Churchyard
	December	20	Nicholas son of Nicholas Bendy, in the middle Isle
		22	Leah wife of William Hollyday, in the Church yard
		23	Samvell Clarke, in the Churchyard
	January	7	James Buck, between the North & South doors
		9	Dorithy dau. of Richard & Martha Wareing, in the Church-yard
		16	John son of Randolph & Susan Vodry, in the Churchyard
		17	Sarah dau. of Thomas & Elizabeth ffreeman, in the Church yard
	February	22	Sarah dau. of Thomas & Sarah Abney, in the North Isle
		28	Rebecca dau. of Oliver & Susan'a Andrews, in the N. Isle
		28	James Latham, in the Church yard
	March	7	Katherine wife of Richard Ilive, between the North & South doors
		7	John Cockeram, in the middle Isle
		14	James son of George & Han'ah Smyth, in the Church yard
		21	William Woodcocke, betweene the North & South doors
1686		26	Mathew son of James and Mary fformantle, in the Church yard
	April	6	Charles Blackburne, in the North Isle
		23	James son of Joseph & ffrances Goodale, between the North & South doors
	May	30	John son of John & Ann Dauson, in the Church yard
	June	3	Thomas son of Andrew & Agnes Hamilton, in the Church yard
		3	John son of John & Elizabeth Shaw, between the North & South doors
		20	Katherine Coote, between the North & South doors
		29	Joseph Shute, in the North Isle
	July	9	Mary dau. of Richard & An' Marjot, in the Churchyd
		10	John Starkey, in the South Isle

Years.	Month.	Day.	Names.
1686	July	24	George Rose, in the Chancell
		24	ffrances Rose, in the Chancell
		25	Gilburt son of Gilburt & Han'ah Lascy, in the midd. Isle
	August	1	Dorithy Graytray, in the North Isle
		28	Robert Sanderson, in the North Isle
		31	Robert Tompson, in the Church yard
	September	16	John and Philip sons of Philip & Mary ffincher, between the North & South doors
		16	Ann dau. of Peter & Susan Vansitt, in the Churchyard
		19	Stower son of John & Elizabeth Weston, in the Church
	October	5	Charles Cooke, in the South Isle
		12	William son of Thomas & Elizabeth ffreeman, in the Church yard
		19	Martha dau. of Edward & Jone Howard, in the Church
		27	Edward ffounds, in the Chancel
	November	5	Mildred Smyth, in the Churchyard
		7	Stephen son of Henry & Mary Harford, in ye Churchyd
		19	Stephen Bye, in the Church yard
	December	8	Margaret Willson, in the middle Isle
		9	Paul Person, in the Church yard
		15	Ann dau. of William & Ann Layton
		19	Charles Chappell, in the Church yard
	January	16	John son of Simond Linch, in the Churchyard
		23	Barbara Stable, in the middle Isle
		24	Joseph Gray, in the South Isle
	February	23	Eliner dau. of Thomas & Elizabeth ffreeman, in the Church-yard
		24	Mary dau. of Thomas & . . . . Lardner, in the North Isle
	March	22	Joseph Nichols, in the middle Isle
		25	William son of Charles & Katherine Domvil, in the Church yard
1687		26	Elizabeth dau. of Calveley and Dorithy Bewicke, between the North & South doors
		30	James Smyth, between the North & South doors
	April	12	Thomas Greene, in the Churchyard
		21	ffulke Rose son of ffulke Rose, in the Chancell
		28	Thomas Andrews, in the South Isle
	May	13	Alice Weaver, in the Churchyard
	June	20	Ann wife of John Dauson, in ye churchyard
	July	1	Ann Young, in the Churchyard
		6	Judith Weekes, in the North Isle
	August	31	Robert Shaw, between the North & South doors
	September	19	John Simpson, in the churchyard
		27	Mary dau. of Nich. & Mary Exton, in the Churchyard
	October	9	James son of James & Mary ffromantle, in the church yard
		10	Mary Parker, between the N. & S. doors
		11	Coling Bendy, in the Chancell
		22	Mary Williams, in the Churchyard
	November	11	Andrew Lamburt, in the churchyard
		22	Susanna dau. of Gilburt & Hannah Lacey, in the churchyard
		24	Mary Stringer, in the middle Isle
		26	Abigal Archer, in the churchyard
	December	3	John son of John Cooper, in the Church
		8	Mary dau. of Charles & Mary Lane, in ye Church
		25	Mary Wiburne, in the churchyard
	January	10	Massa Auston, in the Churchyard
		22	Richard Shaw, in the North Isle

Years.	Month.	Day.	Names.
1687	February	9	Bridget Moore, in the Churchyard
		12	Ann Hilliard, in the South Isle
		19	Elizabeth dau. of Charles & Mary Lane, in the Church
1688	March	28	Margaret Baily, in the churchyard
		31	Elizabeth Dodwin, in the Church
	April	19	Sarah dau. of John Webster, in the Church
	May	4	John son of Oliver Andrews, in the Church
	June	20	Elphree Crooke, in the Church
		25	Daniell Whetston, in the Churchyard
		26	Jane Thornly, in the Chancell
	July	18	Edmund son of John & ffrances Gardner, in the Church yard
		24	James Ashton, in the Churchyard
		28	Samuell Onecell, in the North Isle
	August	13	Robert Hermitage, in the Churchyard
		19	Randolph Drew, in the North Isle
	September	8	Jane dau. of John Parrat, in the North Isle
		12	Thomas son of Abraham & Elizabeth Lee, in the Church yard
		14	Thomas son of Thomas & Elizabeth Lowes, in the Church yard
	October	5	James Vtbure, in the middle Isle
	November	1	William Stable, in the middle Isle
		23	Alice James, in the Church
	January	2	ffrances Loman, in the North Isle
		29	Jane Bencher, in the Church yard
	February	3	Elizabeth dau. of Joseph & ffrances Goodale, between the North & South doors in the Church
		14	John Graves, in the Church
	March	7	George Powell, in the Churchyard
1689	May	5	Thomas son of Thomas Willcox, in the Churchyard
		5	Mary dau. of Henry Harford, in the Church
		20	Ann Chetwood, in the Church
		29	Joannah late wife of John Butler, in the Churchyard
	June	2	Catherine dau. of John Blizard, in the Church
	July	4	William Browne, in the Church
		23	John Willmore, in the church
	August	1	Mary dau. of John Parrot, in the North Isle
	September	8	Hannah late wife of Thomas Leech, in the Churchyard
		20	William Hinton, in the middle Isle
		22	Elizabeth dau. of John ffilewood
		30	Richard son of Richard & Katharine Wing
	October	2	Nathaniell son of Robert & Hannah Porter, in the Church-yard
		17	William son of Henry Gilburt, in the Church
		31	Mary Timber, in the Churchyard
	November	12	Elizabeth Horsman (dau. of Mr William Hudson an Antient parishioner of this parish, an Vpholder by trade), was burd in the South Isle
		18	Henry Gilburt, in the Churchyard
		24	William Brotreman, in the Churchyard
		26	John Brinkely, in the South Isle
		29	Samuell Paine, in the Churchyard
	December	2	ffrancis Toplady, in the Churchyard
		30	Henry Walker, in the Churchyard
		31	Mary Porter, in the Church
	January	9	Elizabeth dau. of John Gardiner, in the West church yard

Years.	Month.	Day.	Names.
1689	January	10	Mary wife of John Baber, from St Mary Aldermanbury, in the middle Isle

Years.	Month.	Day.	Names.
1689	January	10	Mary wife of John Baber, from St Mary Aldermanbury, in the middle Isle
		23	William Tigh, in the middle Isle
		26	Martha dau. of John Gardiner, in the West Church yard
		31	Christopher Elliott, in the West Church yard
	February	2	William Pitts, in the middle Isle
		10	John Holcomb, a Traveller from the Spread Eagle Inn, in the W. yard
1690	March	25	Richard Young, in the West Yard
	April	2	William Davy, in the West yard
		3	Thomas son of William Turtle, in the west yard
		6	Stephen Tanner, in the west yard
		8	Heritage Harford, in the North Chapel
		15	Ellen dau. of John & Mary ffern, in the paved passage near the Church door
		21	Benjamin son of Mathew Roycroft, in the Churchy^d
		25	Christopher Colt, parish Clark, in the North Isle
			Nicholas Dawes, in the Middle Isle
			Anne dau. of Richard & Elizabeth Parrot, in the North Isle
		29	Stephen Orchard, a Stranger, in the east yard
	May	7	Hannah dau. of Thomas & Elizabeth Willcox, in the Church between the 2 doors
		9	Mary Wan of this parish, in the west yard
		17	John Carter son of John Carter, in ye west churchyard
		20	Mary wife of Uriah Arnell, in the South Isle
	June	3	Samuell Leeke, a Stranger, in the East Church yard
		24	Cathren dau. of Abraham Brand & Dulcebella his wife, in the East yard
	July	11	Isaac Butler son of John & Marcy his wife
	August	1	Griffith Edwards, Linen draper, in the South Isle
		14	Daniel son of John & Elizabeth Ingle, between the 2 doors in the Church
		15	Abraham Truncket, Upholsterer, in the South Isle
		18	James Oakes, a Stranger, in the North Isle
		20	Elizabeth Marth, a Servant Maid, in the East Yard
		29	Alexander son of Alexander & Mary Parratt, in the North Isle
		29	Ralph Copdaine servant to John fferne, in the West Church Yard
	September	6	Robert Rowland, a Stranger, in the West Church yard
		17	Henry son of James Latham & Mary his wife, in the West church yard
		23	Elizabeth dau. of John & Mary ffern, Upholder, in the Cloister
	October	14	William Smith, in the Middle Isle
	November	11	Jane Graves servant to Jacob ffranklin, in the West church yard
		25	George Smith, Taylor, in the South Isle
	December	11	Mary wife of William Mathews, in the east Church y^d
		12	Katherine wife of Thomas Good, in the Church between the two doors
		14	John Turton, in the W. Church yard
	February	11	Thomazin dau. of Richard Wing, in the Church Yard
		19	Humphry Hoskins, in the East Ch. yard
		20	Abigail wife of William Weater, in the West Church y^d
		22	Thomas Whitman, a stranger, in the West Church yard
		24	William Cobb, a Stranger, in the west Church yard

Years.	Month.	Day.	Names.
1690	March	10	Philidelphia dau. of Crane & Katherin Complin, in the Church yard
		15	Anne dau. of John Sparkes, in the Church yard
		18	Edward Townesend, in the Church betw. the two doors
1691	April	12	Mary dau. of John & ffrancis Gardiner, in the west Church yard
		27	Anne dau. of William & Priscilla Grove, in the west Church yard
	May	3	Rowland Kirby, in the west Ch. yard
		5	Elizabeth dau. of James & Elizabeth Smith, in the South Isle
		13	Elizabeth Smith, Widow, in the Church between the north & south doors
		15	Thomas Cooke, a Stranger, in the west Church yard
		28	Rebecca Tillman, a stranger, in the Chancell
	June	2	William Langham, in the middle Isle
		23	Sarah dau. of Thomas Weekes, in the north Chapel
		24	Joan Morecocke, in the West Chu. Yard
	July	13	Anne Steffe, a stranger, in the Church
	August	12	James son of Thomas Alford, in the east Church yard
		25	Elizabeth Graves, Widow, in the east Church yard
		29	Henry Palmer, in the middle Isle
	September	2	James & Elizabeth, twins, Children of Hen. Rosser, Barber, in the east Church yard
		6	Thomas son of Thomas Pain, Uphold^r, in the east Church yard
		11	John son of John & Sarah Atkins, in the east Church yard
	October	12	Daniel son of Henry & Anne Sanders, in the west Church yard
		19	Jane Leach, a stranger, in the West Church yard
		25	Sarah Saint, a Stranger, in the west Church yard
		27	Mary wife of William Dash, in the east Church yard
	November	2	Elisabeth wife of James Smith, in the Church in the South Isle
		6	Robert son of Robert ffowler, Junr, in the Church between the 2 doors
		20	Jane wife of Richard Smith, a stranger, in the east Church yard
	December	11	John son of Thomas & Bridgett Phipps, in ye middle Isle
		15	John Smallman, in ye east Church yard
		16	Elisabeth daughter of Abraham & Jane Hemingway, in the South Isle
		20	Robert Watt, a Stranger, in the Church yard
		27	Elisabeth, a ffoundling, in the Church yard
		28	William son of Richard & Alice Partridge, in the middle Ile
		31	Jane dau. of William & Jane Hemingway, in the South Isle
	January	6	Elisabeth Townesend, a Stranger, in the Church between ye 2 doors
		11	Elisabeth dau. of John Bookey, in the north Isle
		14	Elisabeth Moye mother of Richard Moye, in the Church by the Steeple door
	February	1	Rebecca Baynard, Widow, in the East Church yard
		19	Elisabeth dau. of Edward Bridge, Apothecary, & Elisabeth his wife, in ye north Isle
	March	1	John son of Henry & Anne Sanders, in the east Churchy^d
		9	Robert ffowler, Senior, Hosier, in the Church by the sidesmans pew

Years.	Month.	Day.	Names.
1691	March	13	William Pomfret, a Stranger, in the east Church yard
		15	James Levitt son of Robert Levitt, a Butcher, in the West Church yard
		17	ffowke son of Henry & Anne Rosser, Barber, in the paved passage
		19	John son of Humphry & Mary Overton, Upholdster, in the Middle Isle
		19	Sarah the relict of Coleing Bendy, Linen Draper, in the Chancell
		20	Richard son of Richard & Elisabeth Parrott, Haberdasher of hats, in the north Isle
1692	April	3	Susanna wife of ffrancis Thomson, Joyner, in the West Church yard
		14	Mary dau. of Thomas & Bridget Phipps, Linen Draper, in the mid. Isle
	May	1	Isaac son of James & Mary ffromantel, ffactor, in the east Church yard
		7	Samuell Blower servant to Thomas Manning, Vintner, in the West Church yard
		11	Sarah White, in the east Church yard
	June	2	Nicholas Grey, Victualler, in the Church by the Belfry door
		8	John son of John Crofts, Upholder, & Mary his wife, by the ffont
		8	Martha dau. of John Bertles, Linen draper, & Susanna his wife
	July	4	Thomas son of Alexander Parrott, Haberdasher of Hats, & Elizabeth his wife, in the north Isle
		22	Anne wife of Walter Lane, Joyner, in the East Church yᵈ
	August	14	Joningham Biggs, a travailer at the Bull Inn, Leadenhall street, in the west Church yard
		18	Richard Elliott, a Stranger from Rob. Porters house, an Apothecary, in the west Church yard
	October	31	Nash son of Philip ffincher, Ironmonger, & Mary his wife, in the Church
	November	7	Elizabeth wife of Edward Timson, a Butcher, in the east Church yard
		26	Elizabeth Philips, in the east Church yard, Servant to Calverley Bewick
	December	1	Rebecca Hinton, Widow, in the middle Isle
		11	Thomas Woodward, Cook, in the east Church yard
		12	Anne Waters, a stranger, in the Church yard
		12	A stillborn Child of Thomas Hunsdon, Cheesemonger, in the east Church yard
		19	Anne Hains, a stranger, in the east Church yard
	January	26	Anne wife of Robert Levit, a Butcher, in the east Church-yard
	February	16	Edward Howard, a shoemaker, in the east Churchyard
		22	John son of Joseph Barker, Innholder, & Mary his wife, in the west Church yard
	March	9	An abortive Child of John ffilewood, Poulterer
		16	Mary Sexton sister of Samuel Sexton, Haberdasher of Hats, in the east Churchyard
		22	John Ellet the younger, a porter, in the west Church yard
		24	John Parker, wax chandler, in the Church by the font
		31	Elizabeth dau. of James Branch (& Martha his wife), a poulterer, in the Church near the steeple door

Years.	Month.	Day.	Names.

1693 April 4   William son of John Tilley, Cabinet Maker, in the Church near the ffont

8   John son of John Purchass (and Penelope his wife), a Poulterer, in the east Church yard

16   Katherine Manning, Widow, a Lodger, in the east Church yard

20   John Reyner servant to Richard Moy, Leatherseller, in the Church by the steeple door

May 5   Richard son of George Burnham, a Porter, & Elizabeth his wife, in the west Church yard

18   Anne dau. of Oliver Andrews, Linen draper, & Susanna his wife, in the South Chapel

31   Sarah dau. of Thomas Pain, Upholdster, & Judith his wife, in the east Church yard

June 18   Mary dau. of William Chase, Haberdasher of Small Wares, & Philip his wife, in the east Churchyard

July 2   Mary dau. of Henry Rodes, a Lodger in the Market, in the west Church yard

9   Alice wife of William Sapsford, a Bacon seller, in the east Church yard

12   A Chrisome son of John Clements, ffishmonger, in the east Church yard

20   Elizabeth dau. of John Cole, Victualler, & Mary his wife, in the east Church yard

23   Mary dau. of Thomas Alford, Vintner, & Anne his wife, in the east Church yard

August 20   Judeth dau. of William Rowlandson, a Tapster, & Judeth his wife, in the west Church yard

26   Mary dau. of Enoch Porter, factor, & Mary his wife, in the west Church yard

September 8   Robert Wareing, in the Chancell

24   Richard son of Richard Patridge (& Alice his wife), Brasier

November 4   Isabella Place, a stranger, in the east Church yard

17   Lidia wife of Moses Cowley, Comb maker, in the east Church yard

28   Mary dau. of John Mirfin, Butcher, in the east Churchy^d

28   Elizabeth wife of John Morris, Brasier, in the middle Isle

January 6   Tabitha Bucke dau. of James Bucke, Esqr, in the Church by the North door

14   Catherine dau. of John Crofts & Mary his wife, in the Church at the lower end

14   Lidia dau. of Robert Porter (& Hana his wife), Apothecary, in the east Church yard

26   William Langmore, Upholder, in the Middle Isle

February 8   Mary dau. of Humphry Overton (& Mary his wife), Upholdster, in the mid. Isle

10   Thomas Johnson, Marchant, a stranger, in the middle Isle

March 4   Mary Bedford servant to Thomas Cowes, Millen', in the east Church yard

6   Robert Lawrence, a Barber, in the Church by the South door

14   John son of John Bookey, Linen drap', & Anne his wife, in the North Isle

14   Amabella dau. of John Bertles, Linen draper, & Susanna his wife, on the south side of ffont

1694 29   ffoulke Rose, Marchant, in the Chancell, North side

Years.	Month.	Day.	Names.
1694	April	1	Sir Benjamin Thorowgood,* knight and Alderman, in the Chancell on the North side
		5	Richard Porter, Poulterer, in the South Isle
		8	Thomas son of Calverly Bewick, Grocer, & Dorothy his wife, in the Church by the Churchwardens pew
		15	Susanna dau. of Matthew Roycroft, Stationer, & Elizabeth his wife, near the Churchwardens pew
		19	John Turpin, a Butcher, in the west Church yard
	June	3	Joshua Bolt son of Andrew Bolt decd formerly of this parish, Linen draper, in the South Isle
		7	Sarah wife of Thomas Smith, a Butcher, in the east Church yard
		9	Mary wife of Daniel Hewlin, Baker, in the west Church yd
		23	Jane Thorne servant to Dan. Hewlin, Baker, in the west Church yd
	July	10	John Ploughman, in the west yard
		16	John Dews, oilman, in the Church behind the Churchwardens pew
		22	Edward fford servant to Richard Marriot, in the West Church yard
		24	Mary Peters Servant to Andrew Yates, Sexton, in the east Church yd
		26	Walter Parsons, a Butcher, in the east Church yard
	August	6	Elizabeth Gudgeon a Girl from William Packers, Victualler, in the east Church yd
		16	Anne Darlston, Widow, in the east Church yard
		16	Anne dau. of William Grove, Porter, in the west Church yard
		23	William Grove, Porter, in the west Church yard
		26	Urian Arnold, in the South Isle, a Poulterer
	September	1	Mary Bridges sister of Thomas Bridges, Surgeon, in the north Chap. by the Vestry door
		6	Nicholas Guillim, in the East Church yard
		7	Katherine wife of Charles Carter, Cooper, in the east Church yard
	October	21	Thomas Good, a furrier, behind the sidesman's pew
		21	John son of William Chase, near the same place
		26	Mary dau. of Daniel Oakes, a Glover, in the west yard
		30	Mary dau. of Charles Weston, a Potter, in the Church by the Steeple door
		30	John Threadcroft Servant to Tobias Garbrand, Linen draper, in the South Chapel
	November	18	Elizabeth wife of William Hardy, a Barber, in the east Church yard
		25	George Burnham, a Porter, in the W. Church yard
	December	2	Roger Chapman, a Packer, in the Chancel
		4	Edward son of Edward Bull, a stranger, in the east Church yard
		7	Elizabeth dau. of Philip ffincher, Ironmonger, in the Church betw. the two doors
		10	Abigail wife of ffrancis Tolson, a Taylor, in the Church by the south door

* Of Woodford in Essex, Sheriff of London, 1685. Knighted at Windsor Castle, Aug. 13, 1685. Built three shops in 1682, at the west end of St. Peter's Church, and settled them upon the Parish for the maintenance of an organ and organist to play in time of Divine service on Sundays and Holidays. His mother buried May 22, 1695.

Years.	Month.	Day.	Names.
1694	December	21	Susanna Thomson, Widow, in the east yard
	January	6	Samuel Clutterbuck servant to Henry Hartford, Pewterer, in the east Church yard
		9	Hannah dau. of Henry Barton, Wyer drawer, in the east Church yard
		10	Thomas son of Richard Cooke, Sword Cutler, in the east Church yard
		11	Rebecca Claridge, Widow, in the east yard
		16	Robert son of Robert Hart, Tobacconist, in the east Church yard
	February	6	John Garland, Gent., a stranger, in the Church behind the Churchwardens pew, he shot himselfe with a pistoll being distracted
		7	Henry ffairbrother, Victualler, in the Church near the font
		17	Sarah Dod, a stranger, in the west yard
	March	3	Mary Smith, a stranger, in the east Church yard
		12	Thomas Simson, Victualler, in the Church behind the Churchwardens pew
		24	ffrances Burton, an infant, in the West Church yard
1695	April	2	Abraham Hemingway, a Scrivener, in the South Isle
		4	Henry Allibone, Victualler, in the East Church yard
		9	Benjamin son of John Clements, ffishmonger, in the east Church yard
		15	ffrederick ffrowd, Gent., a stranger, in the south Isle under the pews on the north side
	May	9	Roger Chapman son of Roger Chapman, Packer, dec^d, in the Chancell
		19	Charles son of Charles Duell & Eliz. his wife, in the east Church yard
		21	An abortive Child of James ffromantel
		22	Elizabeth Thorowgood, Widow, Sir Benja' Mother, in the Chancell
	June	7	William son of John Cooper, Linen draper, & Elizabeth his wife, in the North Chapel by the vestry door.
	July	29	Anne dau. of William Paget, Baker, and Mary his wife
	August	30	Thomas Couse, Millener, in the east Church yard
	September	6	Hannah dau. of Nicholas Gillam & Hannah his wife, Lodgers, in the east Church yard
	October	28	Beatridge Carstairs servant to Edmund Chrislow, Victualler, in the east Church yard
	November	7	Thomas ffowler son of Robert ffowler, Hosier, in the Church near the sidesmen's pew
		19	Mary Hamon, a stranger, in the east Church yard
		26	Henry Sanders, a porter, in the west Church yard
		28	Thomas son of William Layton, ffishmonger, in the East Church yard
	December	20	Jane dau. of Robert Porter, Apothecary, in the east Church yard
		28	Elizabeth Parker, Widow, a stranger, in the east Church yard
		29	Bartholomew Pigot, a Patten Maker, in the South Isle
	January	4	Anne dau. of Lingham Arkesden, a Barber, in the Church by the Steeple door
		14	William son of Richard Parteridge, Brasier, in the Middle Isle
		26	John Sculthrop the elder, Barber, in the east Churchy^d
	February	14	Richard son of Oliver Andrews, in the South Chapel, Linen draper

Years.	Month.	Day.	Names.

1695 February 11 Mary dau. of Robert & Mary Garbrand, Linen draper, in the S. Chap.

15 Josias son of Josias Bainton & Anne his wife, factor, in the South Isle

20 John ffilewood, Poulterer, in the East yard

March 1 William Packer, Victualler, in the Church near the South door

5 John son of Benjamin Elford, Grocer, in the Middle Isle

15 Elenor dau. of John Sparkes, w. yard

20 Mary Minard, a child, a stranger, east yard

1696 April 9 Sarah dau. of William Chase and Philippa his wife, Haberdasher of small wares, in the East yard

18 A Chrisom female Child of John Owen, Woollendraper, in the east Church yard

22 Elizabeth Chapman, Widow, in the Chancell

28 Elizabeth dau. of Robert Seal, Upholdster, in the East Churchy^d

May 1 A female Child of Rowland Bois

8 John son of Edward Short and Jane his wife, Leatherseller, at the West end of the Church near the north door

14 William Bingham, a Butcher, in the east Church yard

June 4 Henry Nicholls servant to Richard Williams, a Packer, in the West Church yard

10 James Smith, Servant to Richard Stockwell, Victualler in the west Church yard

19 Richard Thorowgood, Gent., in the Chancell

19 Henry son of Henry Kelsey, Linendraper, in the north Chap.

July 3 Elizabeth dau. of William Cock, Vintner, in the north Isle

14 Zachary ffreeman servant to William Simmons, a Butcher, in the West Church yard

26 Arthur Wright, a Butcher, in the west Church yard

27 Enoch son of Enoch Porter, a Porter, in the west Churchyard

August 26 Thomas Joyce servant to Edward Bull, ffishmonger, in the West Church yard

September 9 Abraham Halford servant to John Abbott, Couler man, in the west Church yard

10 Elizabeth Morris servant to Matthew Roycroft, Stationer, in the West Church yard

October 17 Beverly, son of Elisha Dod, a Lodger, in the East Churchy^d

18 Rebecca Birtles daughter of John Birtles, in the Church near the ffont

29 Ann wife of John Smith, a Packer, in the Middle Isle

November 2 An abortive dau. of Stephen Cole, a Lodger

11 Mary wife of Charles Willia'son, Grocer, in the West Church yard

11 Elizabeth dau. of Elizabeth Cowes, Widow, in the east Church yard

December 5 Elizabeth Walker servant to John Cooper, Linen draper, in the east Church [yard]

6 Thomas Naseby, Porter, in the east Church yard

8 John Lilly, a Pewterer who dyed in the Hospitall, in the east Ch. yard

29 John Garnet (a Lodger at Christopher Backhouse, a Coffee man), in the east Church yard

Years.	Month.	Day.	Names.
1696	January	24	Henry son of John fford, Poulterer, in the east Church yard
	February	10	Jasper son of Jasper Waters, in the Church behind the sidesmen's pew
		14	Richard Marriott, a Gauger, in the South Isle
		18	Dorothy wife of Calverly Bewicke, Grocer, in the Church near the ffont
		24	Penelope dau. of Robert Porter, Apothecary, in the east Chu. yard
	March	14	Martha dau. of Philip ffincher (& Mary his wife) Ironmonger
		17	Edward Bright a Stranger from the Bull head in Leadenhall street, in the west Church yard
		21	Vincent Hebb, Vintner, in the West Church yard
1697		28	Randolph Vodrey, Victualler, in the middle Isle, near the Pulpit
		30	Mary wife of Henry Yeomans of Enfeild, Gent., in the South Chappell near her ffather Benjamin Shute
	April	20	Elizabeth Rolfe, Widow, aged 92, in the west Church yard
		21	Elizabeth Clark, in the west Church yard, a stranger from Mr Willmotts
	May	2	Mary dau. of John Cowper, Linen draper, in the North Chapel
		4	Susanna wife of Oliver Andrews, Linendraper, in the South Chapel
		18	Samuell King, Tallow Chandler, in the East Church yard
		19	Mary Showers, a Child in the west Churchyard
		23	William Ramsden, a tapster from the Spread Eagle Inn, in the east Churchyard
	June	27	Samuell Richardson, a stranger from the Bull head in Leadenhall str.
	July	27	Lewis son of Lewis Willson, Vintner, in the Middle Isle
		29	Elizabeth wife of John Ingle, Linendraper, in the Church by the South door.
		29	Josiah Rock, an Infant, in the east Churchyard
		31	William Martin, a stranger, in the west Churchyard
	August	9	Robert Kerrington, a Linendraper, in the North Isle
		26	William Dash, ffishmonger, in the Church near the north door
	September	21	Mary dau. of John Ainesworth, Linendraper, in the east Church yard
		21	Mary dau. of Richard Jennings, Drugster, in the South Isle
		30	Philippa wife of William Chase, Haberdasher, in the Middle Isle
	October	12	Joseph Simson, a poor boy taken up in Leadenhall, in west Ch. yard
		12	William the supposed son of Will. Stevenson, a stranger, in the W. yard
		17	Elizabeth dau. of Thomas Warham, Cook, in the West C. yard
		19	Mary dau. of Charles Domvile, Undertaker, in the east Church yard
	November	4	John Ellott, a Porter, in the West yard
	December	13	John son of John West, a Tapster, in the east Church yard
		29	Matthew Roycroft, Stationer, in the Middle Isle

Years.	Month.	Day.	Names.

1697   January   14   Richard son of Moses Cowley, Combmaker, in the east Church yard

17   Anne wife of Richard Acton, Linendraper, in the Middle Isle

18   Alice Smith, Widow, in the east Church yard

20   Henry son of Henry Twyford, in the west Churchyard

27   John Dee servant to Charles Yate, Linendraper, in the east Church yard

February   23   Sarah Pippen servant to Mary Izard, Widow, in the Church behind the Sidesmens pew

March   1   Anne dau. of Anne Dash, Widow, behind the Sidesmens pew

17   Thomas Smith, a Packer, in the Middle Isle

18   Dame Sarah Abney the wife of Sir Thomas Abney, knight and Alderman, in the S. Chapel

1698   30   Isaac son of Isaac Cole, Confectioner, in the Church yard

April   19   Anne wife of John Mustern, in the Church yard

June   13   Elizabeth dau. of Humphry Patty, Butcher, in the west yard

15   Thomas Threadcroft, Brother in Law to Robert Garbrand, Linendraper, in the South Chapel

29   Sarah Pigot, Widow, in the South Isle

July   8   John son of Robert Hart, Tobacconist, in the east Church yard

26   Sarah dau. of Edward Johnson, Linendraper, in the Middle Isle

28   Mary Crispe Widow, in the west yard

30   William son of William Kempster, in the west yard

30   Richard son of Richard Jenings, Drugster, in the South Isle

August   11   Mary dau. of Mary Smith, widow, in the Church near the north door

21   Matthew Roycroft, Confectioner, from the parish of St Ethelburgh, in the Middle Isle

September   2   Randolph Vaudry son of Randolph Vaudry, decd, in the Middle Isle

August   25   Thomas Byat servant to Jasper Waters, Linendraper, in the Church near the ffont

September   2   Mary Wyatt dau. of William Wyat, Ironmonger, in the Church near the ffont

18   Thomas Hollis servant to ffrancis Tolson, Taylor, in the west Church yard

October   12   Robert Rawlins servant to Thomas Jones, Exchangeman, in the Church at lower end

21   Rebecca dau. of William Elliot, porter, in the Church yard

November   15   John son of Daniel Cooper, Upholdster, in the east Church yard

December   2   Anne dau. of John Birtles, Linendraper, in the Church nr the font

19   Mary dau. of Henry Pike, Mariner, in the east Churchyard

19   Mary dau. of William Cock, Vintner, in the North Isle

January   6   Joyce Hall, dau. of Joyce Dalton, by her first husband Anthony Hall, in the north Chapel

9   Robert Seal buried in Bunhill ffeilds, Upholdster

12   Mary wife of Roger Martin, Sadler, in the east Churchyd

15   John son of John Cooley, Poulterer, in the east Churchyd

Years.	Month.	Day.	Names.
1698	January	31	Martha wife of Roger Burrough, Linendraper, in the Chancell, from St Leonards Eastcheap
	February	12	Anne Cheston, Widow, in the Church by the Belfry
		16	Elizabeth Lansdale, Widow, in the East Church yard
		17	Elizabeth wife of Richard Parrot the Beadle of Lime street Ward, in the Church
		20	Hannah dau. of Robert Porter, Apothecary, in Bunhill ground
	March	14	Anne dau. of Jasper Waters, Linendraper, in the Church near the north door
		21	Edward son of George Allen, a Packer, in the Church near near the ffont
1699	May	5	Elizabeth dau. of Richard Jennings, in the south Isle
		18	William son of Richard Stockhal, in the West yard
		27	Anne ffalconer, Widow, one of the pentioners, in the West yard
	June	5	William Langhton, ffishmonger, in the West yard
		5	Jane dau. of Edward Short, Leatherseller, in the Church
		16	Owen Willson, Vintner, in the Middle Isle, at the upper end
	July	11	Isaac son of Isaac Cole, Victualler, in the west yard
		17	Mary dau. of Robert Hart, Tobacconist, in the east yard
		22	Elizabeth dau. of Alexander Parrott, Haberdasher of Hats
		22	Jane dau. of Matthew Taylor, a Porter, in the east Church yard
	August	10	Catherine dau. of Peter and Priscilla Motteux (Lodgers), in the Churchyard
	September	13	Esther dau. of Charles Starmer and Martha his wife, Poulterer, in the Churchyard
		15	Lydia a foundling, in the Churchyard
	October	17	Gregory Barber, Vintner, in the east Churchyard
		22	Phœbe dau. of Robert Garbrand, Linendraper, and Mary his wife, in the South Chapel
	November	9	Robert Griffith, Gent., in the North Isle
		28	Sarah dau. of William and Anne Matthews, a Taylor, in the Churchyard
	December	17	Richard Williams, a Packer, in the middle Isle
		17	Jane ffettiplace, Widow, in the North Isle, the Mother of John Cowper, Lin. drap.
		25	Rebekah dau. of Henry Pike, in the east Church yard
		27	Thomas Vodry, in the Middle Isle, upon his father Randolph Vodry, Victualler
		28	Richard Parrot, the Beadle of Lime street Ward, in the North Isle
	January	10	Susannah Hoskins dau. of Hanna Hoskins, Widow, in the east Church yard
		14	Jane Toplady, in the Church by the steeple door
		29	Sarah wife of Edward Johnson, Linendraper, in the Chancell
		31	Richard Cream, a traveller, from the Bull Inn, in the east Church yard
	February	4	Isaac Cole, Victualler, in the east church yard
1700	May	8	Jane wife of Charles Danvers, woollendraper, the dau. of Lewis Willson, Vintner, in the middle Isle
		20	Mary dau. of Richard Moy, Leatherseller, in the Church by the Steeple door
		22	John Packer, in the east Churchyard

Years.	Month.	Day.	Names.
1700	June	21	John son of John Cooper (& Ann his wife), Victualler, in the east Church yard
		27	Thomas Cotton, Plaisterer, in the east Church yard
		29	Hannah Porter wife of Robert Porter, Apothecary
	July	13	Elizabeth dau. of Robert Brooke, Tapster, in the east Churchy^d
	August	3	Jane dau. of John Cowper, Linendraper, in the North Chapel
	September	9	Mary wife of ffrancis Ray, Victualler, in the east yard
		15	Margaret dau. of Sarah ffilewood, Widow, in the east yard
	October	1	ffrancis son of William Wyat, Ironmonger, in the Church by ye font
		5	Peter Southey (Lodger), in the Church betw. the two doors
		26	Mary the wife & Rebecca the Child of James ffromanteel, in the south Isle
		31	Dorcas Heyton, dau. of James Buck, Esqr, in the Church n^r the North door
	November	24	Richard Williamson son of James Williamson, Bodies mak', in the east Church yard
	December	6	Elizabeth Neal, a gentlewoman from Leeds in Yorksh., in the Chan'.
		14	Sarah dau. of Robert Woodney, Haberdasher of hats, in the Church at the lower end
		14	William son of Philip ffincher, Ironmonger, near the font
	January	6	Jane dau. of John Roberts, Vintner, in the Middle Isle
		30	Sarah dau. of William Kettle, Pattern drawer, in the east Ch. yd.
	February	2	Abigail Peck a Lodger, under the Pews in the South Isle
	March	21	John Peters a parish child, in the Church yard
1701	May	1	Johanna Day, a stranger, buried in Bunhill ffields
		2	Benjamin Conley, Victualler, in the east Church yard
		7	John Bookey, Linen draper, in the North Isle
		13	John Ingle, Linendraper, in the Church by the south door
		18	John Glanfeild a stranger, servant to the Lady Luckin, in the west yard
	June	3	James Smith son of Hannah Smith, Widow, in the south Isle
		14	Edward Padbury servant to Jacob ffranklin, in the Church yard
		16	John son of Jasper Waters, Linen draper, in the Church near the font
		20	Elisabeth ffenn Widow, a stranger, in the east Church yard
	July	21	Sarah dau. of John Pierce & Elisabeth his wife, in the east Churchyard
		22	Richard Beard, a strangers Child, in the west Church yard
		27	Richard son of Thomas Pain, Upholdster, in the East Church yard
		29	Sarah dau. of John Sculthrop, Barber, in the West Church yard &
		29	Anne a foundling, in the same grave
		31	Elizabeth dau. of Thomas Smith, in the east Churchyard
		31	Gentry, taken up in Corbits Court, in the east yard
	September	8	Anne dau. of Jacob (& Deborah) Spooner, Gro', in the S. Chap.
		15	Christian Peterson servant to Rob' Atkins, Linendraper, in the North Isle

Years.	Month.	Day.	Names.
1701	September	22	Richard son of James Boseley, Linendraper, in the east Churchyard
		27	Jane dau. of Peter Motteux a Lodger, in the east Churchyard
		28	Jonas Hillis a Lodger, in the east yard
	October	7	Martha dau. of John Cowper, Linendraper, in the N. Chap'
	December	2	John son of John Cantrell, Poulterer, in the east Churchyard
		14	John son of Richard Benington, Victualler, in the east Church yard
	January	1	Matthew a ffoundling, in the West yard
	February	22	Elizabeth dau. of Richard Allum, a Lodger, in the west Ch. yd.
	March	1	Elizabeth Stockhall sister of Rich. Stockhall, Cook, in the east Ch. yard
		4	Adam Calhoon, Gent., in the south Isle
		8	John son of Roger Chillingworth, Taylor, in the west Church yard
1702	April	20	Richard Bartlet, Drugster, in the N. Isle
		26	Alice dau. of Richard Stockhall, Cooke, in the east Church yd.
	May	12	Elizabeth Scampton Mother of ffrancis Scampton, Cutler, east Ch. yard
		31	Priscilla wife of Robert Gainesford, Cutler, in the east Church yard
	June	19	George Probert servant to Robert Paget, Victualler, in the West yard
		19	Anne dau. of Philip Presbury, Barber, in the east Church yard
		20	Edward Chandler kinsman to Joseph Chandler in Bethlehem
	July	6	Isabella Blagrave, Widow, in the south Chapel by her husband
		13	Hannah dau. of John Bainham, Barber, in the west Church yard
		20	Elizabeth Blackburn, Widow, in the north Isle by her husband
	August	3	William son of Moses Cowley, in the east Church yard
		9	John son of John North, ffishmonger, in the west Church yard
		19	Bithiah dau. of Josias Bainton (in the south Isle), ffactor
		21	ffrancis son of ffrancis Clifton, Baker, in the Church yard
	September	2	Sarah dau. of George Hague, Victualler, in the east Church yard
		15	Nathanael son of Nathanael Norris, ffishmonger, in the east yard
		16	Robert son of Robert Gravenor, Stationer, in the east yard
		20	Elisabeth dau. of John Pierce, Barber, in the east yard
	October	1	Anne dau. of William Holyday, Tallow Chandler, in the east Church yard
		6	Thomas Jones Exchange man, in the middle Isle
		13	Susanna dau. of John Pierce, Barber, in the east Church yard
		16	Samuell Spendlove, Linen draper, in the south Isle
		25	John Abbot, Colourman, in the Middle Isle
		27	Samuel son of the above written Samuel Spendlove, by his ffather

Years.	Month.	Day.	Names.
1702	November	13	Anna Maria dau. of Thomas Edwin, Tallow Chandler, in the east Church yard
		23	Robert Lloyd, Gent., in the Church at the lower end
	December	4	James Cooke servant to William Weston, Vintner, in the west yard
		22	Elizabeth dau. of John Lloyd, perfumer, by the font
		23	Richard son of Henry Burridge, Butcher, in the east yard
	January	3	Mary dau. of Benjamin Cowley, Victualler, in the east yard
		15	Richard son of Richard Partridge, Brasier, in the middle Isle
		23	John Birtles, Linen draper, behind the sidesmens pew
	February	1	Elisabeth Clarke a Lodger at Nathanael ffrench's, Merchant, in the north Isle
		11	John son of Susanna Pepis, Wid', in the east Church yard
	March	9	Anne-Margaret dau. of Nicholas Jarvis, Poulterer, Ch. yard
		10	Tobias Garbrand, Linen draper, in the south Chapel
		10	Elizabeth Jackson servant to Wᵐ Kettle, pattern drawer, west yard
		16	Elizabeth dau. of John Bainham, Barber, west Church yᵈ
		19	Robert son of Robert Hart, Tobacconist, in the West Churchyᵈ
		23	Thomas Whinfield, Ironmonger, in the Church by the Belfry
1703	April	9	Mary dau. of Charles Weston, in the Church by the south door
		11	Sarah Levison servant to Henry Hartford, pewterer, in the west yard
		11	Sarah dau. of Charles Norris, Box maker, in the west Church yard
		24	Joseph son of John Purchass, Poulterer, in the east Church yard
		28	John son of Henry Kelsey, Linendraper, in the south Chapel
	May	7	George Andrews, Esqʳ, in the Chancell on the north side, from Hammersmith
		20	John son of ffrancis Tuckwell, Mealman, in the Church yard
	June	21	Mary dau. of William Hardy, Barber, in the east yard
		28	Jane dau. of Richard Moy, Leatherseller, in the Church by the Belfry door
	July	25	William Cock, Vintner, in the north Isle
	August	3	Henry son of Henry Pike, Mariner, in the east Church yard
		11	Bridget dau. of Edward Serle, Merchant, in the Middle Isle
		25	Susanna-Tabitha dau. of William Hayton, Merchant, in the Church near the North door
		26	Anne Glover servant to Richard Plomer, Coffee man, in the east yard
	September	5	John Heath, perfumer of Gloves, in the east Church yard
		5	Mary wife of Charles Weston, Potter, in the Church by the south door
		21	Martha dau. of William Sherrington, Junior, Esqʳ, in the Middle Isle
		24	George son of George Coning, Merchant, in the east Church yard
		24	Elizabeth dau. of John Martin, Victualler
	November	16	Thomas son of Alexander Crudge, Vintner, in the Church near the ffont
		17	Robert Brooke, Victualler, in the east Church yard
	December	12	Mary dau. of Joan Howard, Widow, in the east Church yard
		25	Mary Sculthorp, Widow, in the west Church yard

Years.	Month.	Day.	Names.
1708	January	15	William Carpenter, a Lodger, in the east Church yard
		16	John Orton, Victualler, in the east yard
		20	ffrances dau. of James Bosely, Linen Draper, in the North Isle
		28	James Levingston, a Lodger, in the east Church yard
		25	Richard Arnold, ffruiterer, in the West Church yard
	February	18	Elizabeth wife of ffrancis Scampton, Cutler, in the east Church yard
		24	John son of Thomas Grant, Victualler, in the West Church yard
		26	Lydia wife of Nathanael ffrench, Merchant, in the North Isle
	March	6	Martha wife of Richard Trenance, Victualler
		15	Henry Buxton, behind the Churchwardens pew, Gent., a stranger
		21	Richard Acton, Linen draper, in the Middle Isle
		20	Mary dau. of Roger Chillingworth, a Taylor, in the west Church yard
		22*	ffrances Hunter servant to Steph. Heely, Surgeon, in the west yard
1704		29	Samuell Clayton a Lodger, in the west Church yard
	April	6	Mary dau. of Henry Burridge, a Butcher, in the east yard
		16	Thomas Alvey, M.D., in the north Isle behind the pulpit
	May	25	Alice Sweat, Widow, a Lodger, in the west Church yard
	July	27	Thomas son of Thomas Skinner, Linen draper, in the middle Isle
		6	William Child, Senior, Trunkmaker, in the south Isle
	August	8	Amey Betts servant to Richard Acton, formerly of this parish, in the Church near font
		17	Mary Segar servant to Mrs Norman in little Queen, in the west Church yard
		17	Dinah dau. of Samuel Dufresnay (& Dinah his wife), Mercer, in the West Churchyard
	September	20	Roger Chillingworth, a Taylor, in the West Church yard
	October	11	Martha dau. of Richard Trenance, in the East Church yard
		15	Elionor wife of John Nasby, in the East yard near the Gate
		19	Joyce dau. of William Kettle, in the East Church yard
		25	Edward Abney son of Sir Thomas Abney, in the South Chapel near the Step
		26	Benjamin Palmer, Esqr, in the middle Isle
	November	15	Joseph Prigg, a Calender, in the South Isle
		24	Walter Adamson, an Attorney at Law, in the middle Isle
	December	5	A female Child of Mr Daniel Cowper, in the East yard
		14	Samuel Kettley servant to Mr Clifton, Baker, in ye east yard
		22	William Matthews, a Taylr, in the East yard
	January	27	Elizabeth Gravener dau. of Robert & Ruth Gravener, in the east yard
		11	Elizabeth Bourn a Child, in ye Church yard
		11	Edward Browne a Child, in the Church yard
	February	7	Francis Grunwin a Child, in the West yard
		9	Thomas son of William & Anne Kittley, in the east yard
		11	Richard Buridge a Child, in the East yard
		18	James Martin son of Christopher & Mary Martin, in ye West yard

* The Register from March 22, 1703, to January 6, 1722-3, is subscribed "John Waugh, D.D., Parson."

Years.	Month.	Day.	Names.

1704 February 25 Elizabeth dau. of Christopher & Mary Martin, in the West yard

March 20 Letitia dau. of William & Anne Kettle, in the East Ch. yard

23 Elizabeth dau. of John & Elizabeth Bainham, in the West yard

1705 28 William son of William & Susanna Simons, in the East yard

30 Elizabeth dau. of John & Elizabeth West, Lodger, in the East yard

April 22 George son of William & Anne Matthews, in the East yard

24 Mr John Smith, in the middle Isle

29 James Timpson, Bacheler, in the East yard

May 25 Alice dau. of Elizabeth & William Langmore, Upholster, in the middle Isle

June 6 Samuel Cooke son of Thomas & Christian Cook, in the West yard

7 Mary Pricktow, Chandler, in the West yard

23 George Langmore, Linen draper, in the middle Isle

July 10 Anne dau. of John & Mary Day, in the East yard

20 Anne Elliott, Widow, in the West yard

20 Thomas son of John & Elizabeth Sculthorp, in the West yard

29 Mary Short, in the East yard

August 8 Emma Sanderson, Widow, in the North Isle near ye middle

10 Martha Hunsden, in the middle Isle near the Black Stone

30 John Pott, an Oyle man, in the Bellfry

September 4 Katherine dau. of Richard & Sarah Stockall, in the East yard

12 Robert son of Alice & Robt Woodney, near ye Bellfry

12 John son of John & Hannah Rising, near the Font

20 Richard son of John & Elizabeth Frampton, in the North Isle

October 9 Anne dau. of Thomas & Katherine Griffin, in the South Chapel

2 Samuel son of Francis & Agnes Clifton, in ye East yard

November 20 Charles son of George Haigh, in the East yard

21 Thomas Archer, poulterer, in the Church near the Font

25 John son of Charles & Anne Dunvell, in the East yard

December 4 Hannah dau. of Alexander & Hannah Crudge, near Mr Fowlers stone

6 Margarett Garbrand, under the Books in the South Chapel

January 6 James son of Benjamin & Mary Phillips, Barber, West y^d

22 Sarah dau. of Thomas & Mary Smith, Butcher, East yard

23 Peter Douse a Stranger, at the bottom of the Church near the South door

28 Joseph son of Daniel & Rebecca Cowper, Upholster, in the East yard

1706 April 4 Mrs Joyce Dalton, in the North Chapel n^r the vestry door

May 2 Roger Filewood, in the East yard

June 4 Deborah dau. of Daniel & Harris Minshull, in the West yard

7 John son of John & Anne Looker, in the West yard

9 Robert son of John & Elizabeth Sculthrope

11 Anne Mount, in the West yard

13 Anne Cox a Stranger, in ye East yard

July 17 Mary dau. of Thomas & Magdalin Grant, in the East yard

21 George son of John & Mary Day, near the Font

Years.	Month.	Day.	Names.
1706	July	21	John son of William Allett, in the West yard
	August	7	Hannah dau. of Christopher & Mary Martin, in yᵉ West yard
		30	Anthony son of George & Elizabeth Conning, in the East yard
	September	7	Elizabeth Orton, Widow, in the East yard
	October	5	Jane dau. of Joseph & Rebecca Caryl, in the South Chapel near the Books
		9	William Spinage, in the Church near the South door
		18	William son of William and Anne Kettell, in the East yᵈ
		18	Robert Waring, Gentleman, Attorney at Law, in the Chancell near the Ministers pew
	November	15	William Shirrington, Esqʳ, in the middle Isle
	December	16	John son of Robert and Eliz. Grosvenor, in the East yard
	March	2	Dorcas Rycroft, Widow, in the Middle Isle
		3	Elizabeth dau. of William & Anne Kettle, in the East yard
		16	Mʳ Richard Acton, in the middle Isle above the black stone
		18	Elizabeth dau. of John & Anne Gore, on the south side of the font
1707		26	Mʳˢ Hester Walters, in the middle Isle
	April	2	Francis Brerewood,* Esqʳ, Treasurer of Christs Hospital, in the Chancell
		25	John son of John Nasby, in the East yard
	May	4	Roger Middleton, Hosier, in the East yard
		11	Jane dau. of William & Mary Molden, in the West yard
		23	John Atwood, in the West yard
	June	24	Robert Rowland, Brasier, in the South Isle
	July	17	John son of John & Susanna Adee, in the East yard
		21	Lydia dau. of Lydia & Benjamin Cooke, in the West yᵈ
		25	Frances dau. of John & ffrances Nasby, in the West yard
		27	John son of Alexander & Hannah Crudge, in the Church near the Font
	August	18	Philip son of Henry & Hannah Sharp, in the East yard
		31	Bridgett Yates, in the East yard, close to the Church
	September	5	Sarah Kelsey, in the North Chapel near the Dʳˢ pew door
		7	John Perry, Render in the little Vestry
		8	Elizabeth dau. of Thomas & Katherine Griffin in the South Chapel
		18	Martha dau. of John & Mary Day, near the Steeple door
	October	9	Leonard Short, a Cook, in the East Ch. yard
	November	12	Thomas Abney, Esqʳ, son of Sʳ Thomas Abney, in the South Ally under the Books
	December	2	Elizabeth dau. of John and Sarah Forde, in the West yard near the Gate
		8	Mʳ Wᵐ Briggs, in the South Chapel towards the Chancel
		12	Edward son of Edward & Bridgett Searle, in the North Isle towards the Reading pew
	January	16	Mary wife of John Gooding, Lodger, in the East yard
		23	Thomas Daws, in the west yard, Butcher
	February	5	Elizabeth dau. of Thomas & Susannah Skinner, In yᵉ Isle between the two middle pillars
		20	George son of William & Elizabeth Langmore, in the middle Isle
	March	22	Anne dau. of Charles & Anne Domvile in the East yard

* Treasurer from 1700 to 1707.

Years.	Month.	Day.	Names.
1708	May	12	Sarah dau. of Thomas & Sarah Oland, in the East yard
		19	Mary wife of Robert Garbrand, in the South Chapel
		23	Charles Williams, Grocer, in the West yard
		24	Joseph son of Joseph & Sarah Hicks, in the West yard
	June	2	Mary dau. of John & Sarah Smart, in the East yard
		3	Cicelia dau. of John & Hannah Rising, against the great Vestry door
	July	9	Frances dau. of James & Jane Bosely, in the East yard
	August	8	Barbara wife of John Sparks, in the East yard
		9	Sarah Ingle, in the Church by the South door
		24	Sarah dau. of Michael & Jane Gregory, in the West yard
	September	8	John son of Josiah & Sarah Lutman, in the West yard
		10	Hannah Tigh, Widow, in the middle Isle against the reading desk
		16	Anne dau. of John & Anne Looker, in the West yard
		24	Martha Pitts, in the North Isle behind the reading desk
	October	10	Elizabeth dau. of John & Elizabeth Cantrill, in the East yard
	November	3	Hanah dau. of Daniel & Rebekah Cowper, in the East y^d
		4	John son of John & Mary Day, in the middle Isle, Linen draper
		30	John son of Richard & Elizabeth Chase, near the great Vestry
	December	5	Ralph Palmer, near the Belfry
		8	Anne Gullyford, in the West yard
		29	Jane Miller, in the West yard
	January	2	John son of Charles & Mary Chapman, near the Font
		4	Mary dau. of Robert Garbrand, in the South Chapel
		10	Isabell Hutchinson, in the middle of the South Isle
		18	Robert Tredcroft Garbrand son of Robert & Mary Garbrand, in the South Chapel
		23	Anne dau. of Henry & Anne Ford, in the South Isle
	March	2	Waterman Osborne, in the East yard
		3	Elizabeth dau. of Samuel & Susannah Christie, in the West yard
		14	Josiah Lutman, in the West yard
		21	Mary dau. of Edward & Bridgett Searle, in the midd. Isle
1709	April	24	Elizabeth dau. of Charles & Anne Donvile
		27	Ann wife of Matthew Taylor
	May	17	James son of John & Elizabeth Buchanan, near the Font
		19	Jane dau. of William & Mary Pumroy
	June	3	Jane dau. of William & Susanna Simons, in the East y^d
		14	Bennett Colt, in the North Isle
		17	Margarett dau. of Anthony & Anne Ferris, near the Font
	July	2	Elizabeth dau. of Matthew & Elizabeth Barnard, near the great Vestry
		13	David Mead, Apothecary, in the East yard
		15	John son of Charles & Sarah Hoyle, near the Churchwardens pew
	September	9	Alice Langmore, widow, in the middle Isle
		16	Grace dau. of James & Lydia Osborn, in the East yard
		17	John son of Christopher & Mary Imber, in the West yard
	November	13	John son of Christopher & Mary Martin, in the West yard
		28	Mary Warren, Lodger, in the East yard
	December	23	George Conning son of George & Elizabeth Conning, whose father George Conning, Linen draper, was buried July 11th of this year

Yeare.	Month.	Day.	Names.
1709	January	2	Jane Swallow, in the West yard, Lodger
		7	Thomas Rawlinson, in the West yard
		25	Elizabeth dau. of Edward & Mary Mitchel, in the West yard
	February	4	Elizabeth da. of John & Anne Gore, Apothecary, near ye Steeple door
1710	March	26	John Edee, in the East yard
	April	4	John Snart, in the East yard, Fishmonger
	May	14	Mary dau. of Roger & Rebecka Walter, in the West yard
		23	Joseph son of Joseph & Rebecka Caryle, in the South Chapel
		26	Thomas son of John & Margarett Parsons, in the West yard
		31	Thomas Bendish of St Andrews Holborn, in the South Chapel
	June	1	Elizabeth dau. of John & Anne Gore, near the Tower door
		27	Mary wife of Francis Tolson, near the South door
		29	Margarett dau. of Joseph & Sarah Mallard, in the East yard
	July	4	William son of John & Elizabeth Bainham, in the West yard
		10	Mary Purchas, near the great Vestry door
		18	Mary Evans, in the West yard
		25	George Dinzdell, in the East yard
		30	Elizabeth Clark, in the East yard
	August	10	Mary dau. of Anthony & Mary Wybird, the East yard
		14	Elizabeth Rowland, in the West yard
		21	Catherine Wallett, in the East yard
		23	John son of Matthew & Elizabeth Barnard, by the Font
		26	Walter son of Walter & Rhoda Tredway, in the middle Isle
		29	Sarah Day, dau. of John & Mary Day, in the middle Isle
	September	8	Christian dau. of Robert & Sarah Hanson, in the East yard
		10	Thomas Hunsden, Cheesemonger, in ye middle Isle
		24	John Hine son of John & Anne Hine, parish Clerk
		25	Bridgett Daughter of John and Elizabeth Waugh, parson of this parish, on the north side of the Communion Table within the Rails
	October	5	Peter son of Samuel & Dina Dufresnay, Mercer, in the East yard
		9	Robert son of Henry & Elizabeth Forde, in the South Isle
	November	1	Thomas Pinnock, under the Gallery near ye North door
		2	Bridgett Nesby, Widow, in ye East yard
		9	Alice late wife of Robert Woodney near the Belfry door
		20	. . . . dau. of Robert Woodney, near the vestry door
		22	Thomas son of Thomas & Susanna Skinner, Linen draper, in the West Isle
		23	James Bosely, at the West end of the South Isle
	December	3	Elizabeth dau. of John & Anne Looker, in the West yard
		10	Bray D'Oyly, in the West yard
		10	Jane Cock, wife of William Cock
		20	Sarah dau. of Michael & Jane Gregory, in the West yard
		28	William son of William & Mary Pomroy, by the South door
	January	11	Anne Brethaver, in the Chancell under the pew by the little Vestry

Years.	Month.	Day.	Names.
1710	February	11	Anne Child, in the Middle Isle
		16	Elizabeth Rolfe, in the North Isle
		20	Elizabeth Meachell, in the West yard
		21	Dorothy Fulford, in the Chancell under the pew on the North side of the Altar
	March	10	John Everard, Silversmith, under the Organ Loft
		21	Thomas Coles, in the West yard
		22	John Cantrell, in the East yard
		24	Thomas Norris, under the Organ Loft
1711		29	Mary Pate, in the East yard
	April	7	Ralph Hickes, Dr of Physick, in the East yard
		18	Anne Pickard, in the South Chapel
		28	Rebecka Barnes, in the middle of the South Isle
	May	9	William Holiday, in the East yard
		24	Raymond Beck son of Justus & Rachel Beck, in the Chancell at the South side of the Altar
	June	5	George son of John & Frances Nesby in the East yard
		10	George son of Richard & Sarah Stockall, in the East yard
		30	Sarah late wife of Mr Reading
	July	20	William Sherington, Esqr, in the Middle Isle
		21	James son of Roger & Rebecca Walter, West yard
		24	Christopher Backhouse, in the South Isle
	August	23	Richard Pell, a porter, in the West yard
		23	Elizabeth wife of William Langmore, middle Isle
	September	20	Ann dau. of John & Mary Parish, W. yard
		30	Richard son of Richard & Bridgett Knight
	October	25	William son of Thomas & Susanna Skinner
		28	John Buckeridge, in the East yard
		28	William Tayler, Vintner, in ye South Isle
	December	6	Jane dau. of Robert & Mary Brookman
		11	Mary dau. of Robert & Mary Nicholl
		19	Lancelott son of Thomas & Martha Unwin, in the North Chapel
		28	Joseph Waters, in the middle Isle
	January	15	Jane Smith, in the East yard
		18	Mary Parish, in the West yard
	February	5	Elizabeth Mitchell, in the West yard
		18	Thomas Son of William & Mary Pumroye, by the South door
		19	Anne wife of Henry Haford, East yard
		24	Elizabeth wife of John Cowper, Linendrapr
	March	24	Thomas son of William & Susanna Simons
1712	April	27	Francis son of Francis & Eliz. Underwood
		30	Samuel Purchase, West yard
	May	15	Daniel Ulye, Baker, West yard
	July	17	Edward son of Edward & Bridgett Searle, Merchant, in ye middle Isle
		17	Samuel son of Walter & Rodah Tredway, in the middle Isle
		20	Sarah Stringer, in the West yard
	August	6	John Cowley, in the East yard
		21	Joseph Osborn, in the East yard
	September	5	Mrs Bridgett Daws, in the middle Isle over against the reading desk
		8	Charles Freeman, in the West yard
	October	4	Thomas Skinner, in the Middle Isle
		5	Anne Buchanan, by the Font

Years.	Month.	Day.	Names.
1712	October	14	James Backhouse, in yᵉ East yard
			Elizabeth West, in the North Isle
	November	29	Samuel Waters, in the middle Isle
	December	18	Mʳˢ Jane Thornbury, Widow, in yᵉ middle Isle
		22	Thomas Oland, in the East yard
		25	Rebecca Williams, in the West yard
	January	8	John Skinner, Middle Isle
		11	Thomas Goodier, in the East yard
		17	Anne Bird, in the North Isle
		25	John Rickards, in the West yard
		30	John Jones, Sexton, in the West yard
	February	6	William Hooper, in the North Isle
		9	Elizabeth Mitchell, in the West yard
	March	15	Judah Paine, in the North Isle
		17	Richard Skikelthorp, Lecturer, by the Little Vestry door
		21	Samuel Porter, in the paved passage
		24	John Phillips, in the West yard
1713	April	3	William Pagett, Baker, in the East yard
		20	Jane Wilson, in the Middle Isle
		22	Mary Carryle in the South Chapel
	May	4	Robert Reeve, in the West yard
		26	Henry Wayte, in the West yard
		30	Richard Sadler, in the South Isle
	June	6	Mary Bloyton, in the East yard
		11	Mary Cowley, in the East yard
	July	20	Sarah Kelsey, in the North Chapel
		25	Nicholas Jarvice, in the West yard
		28	Mary dau. of Benj. & Elizabeth Taylaw, under the Gallery
	August	4	Amey Neale, in the West yard
		16	Anne Knight, in the middle Isle
		20	Elizabeth Peterson, in yᵉ Middle Isle
		21	William Wytch, in the West yard
		25	John Naseby, in the East yard
		26	James Osborn, in the East yard
	October	1	Lewis Wilson, in the Middle Isle
		4	Richᵈ Whittington, under yᵉ Gallery
		20	Anne Gore, under the Gallery
		27	Sarah Shipside, in the East yard
	November	26	Penelope Tyers, in the West yard
	January	14	Margaret the Daughter of John and Elizabeth Waugh, in the Chancell
	February	12	Richard Nickson
		13	Samuel Sadler
		16	John Hine, Clerk of Sᵗ Peters. By his Desk
	March	7	Elizabeth Sculthrop, Wife of John Sculthrop
		14	Barbara Emes Wife of John Emes
1714		25	Brigett Searle Wife of Mʳ Edward Searle, in the Chancell
		30	Richard Beck servant to Mʳ Justus Beck
	April	22	Thomas Alcock, at the Entry of the North door
	May	19 1*	John Bull, in the East yard
	June	29	Martha Hunsden, under the Organ
	July	6	Charles Powell, in the West yard
		29	Mary Bull, in the East yard
	September	26	Benjamin Wilson, in the middle Isle
		27	Walter Treadway, in the middle Isle

* Sic.

Years.	Month.	Day.	Names.
1714	August	10	Mary Griffin, by the Engine
	October	15	Elizabeth Sadler, in the South Isle
	November	1	Anna Looker, in the West yard
		27	William Wetherly in the West yard
		26	Jacob Hayes, in the West yard
	December	23	William Woodney, under the organ
	January	4	Stephen Lepie, Lodger, in the West yard
		28	Margarett Parsons, in the West yard
		29	Hannah Prime, in the middle Isle
	February	9	Anne Treadway, in the middle Isle
		27	Thomas Marriott, in the East yard
		28	Elizabeth Hine, in the East yard
	March	1	John Robins, in the West yard
1715		25	William Ferris in the East yard
	May	1	Phillip Davis, in the West yard
		6	Dianah Whighthead, under the Organ
		8	Henry Hertford, pewterer, in ye East yard
		12	Susanna Wife of Josua Lutman, in ye E. yard
		13	Mary dau. of Edwd & Mary Maber, under the Organ
	June	12	Jasper son of Roger & Rebecka Walter, in the West yard
		15	Elizabeth dau. of John & Elizabeth Marriott, under the Organ
	July	2	John son of Samuel & Hannah Whighthead, under the organ
		10	Sarah Rising, under the Organ
		25	Elizabeth dau. of Robert & Elizabeth Langdale, between the Ally & South door
	August	4	Anne Oland from St Magnus parish, in the East yard
		28	Rebecka Foulks Wife of John Foulks, in the West yard
	September	8	Ann dau. of W^m & Jane Roger, Lodger, in the West yard
		17	Elizabeth dau. of Gilbert Page, in the North Isle
		23	Martha Shrike, in the West yard
	October	11	John son of Thomas & Frances Wals, Lodger, in the West yard
		17	John Sculthrop, Barber, in the West y^d
		20	Mary Bertlemew, servant, in ye West yard
		23	Susanna Skinner, in the middle Isle
		24	Robert Hanson a Child, in ye West yard
		25	Mary Backhouse, Widow, in ye South Isle
	November	11	Martha wife of Richard Dratgate, under the **great pew**
		13	Bridgett Bringhurst, in the Chancell
		13	George Bass, Servant, in the West yard
		16	Samuel Siser, Lodger, in ye West yard
		23	Anne Freeman, Widow, in ye West yard
	December	7	Samuel Pinching, Lodger, in ye West yard
		27	Mary Jones, Sexton, in the West yard
		31	Susanna Pomroye, at the Tower door
	January	7	Henry Hertford, in the East yard
		16	William son of John Barrington Shoute, in the South Chapel
		17	Robert son of Samuel & Bridgett Beachcroft, by the sidesmens pew
		22	Thomas Cook, Lodger, in ye East yard
	February	4	Mary Parsons, in the West yard
		6	James Sparkes, in the West yard
		8	John Martin, in the East yard
		8	Thomas Kinmist, Lodger, in ye East yard

Years.	Month.	Day.	Names.
1715	February	15	Rodah dau. of Walter & Rodah Tredway, in the middle Isle
		20	Elizabeth wife of Thomas Wilcox, at the South door
		29	Elizabeth dau. of John & Eliz. Bainham, in the East yard
	March	1	Richard Smart, Lodger, in ye W. yard
		21	Anne wife of Edwd Bull, in the South Isle
		24	Mary wife of John Lambert, in ye W. yard
1716	April	4	Edward Bull, Fishmonger, in ye South Isle
		8	James & Martha son & dau. of Jos. & Martha Windham, in the Chancell, by the corner of the first pew on ye north side
		30	John Moore, Lodger, in the East yard
	May	9	Elizabeth Wife of John Waugh, D.D., Rector of this Parish, under the Communion Table
		29	Richard Harrison, a Stranger, against the great Vestry door
	June	2	Joseph Carroll, in the South Chapel
		17	Benjamin Shute, Linen draper, in the South Chapel
		29	Samuel Penny, Lodger, in the E. yard
	August	10	William Stockall, in the East yard
	September	11	James Jarvis an Infant, in the East yard
	October	15	William Pomroy, under the Organ
		28	Mary Lee, widow, under the Organ
	November	1	Richard Smyth an Infant, in ye West yard
		4	Anne Chidly an Infant, in ye West yard
		15	Moses Robins, in the West yard
	December	6	Joseph Gale, a Stranger, in ye North Isle
		11	Martha Chansey, in the North Isle
	January	2	Elizabeth Barnardiston, by the South door
		11	Thomas Weale, a Servant, in the West yard
		13	Richard Knight son of Richd Knight, Middle Isle
		22	Patronella Burton, in the West yard
	March	10	Thomas Phillips, servant, in ye West yard
		17	Mary Cartwright an Infant, in ye West yard
1717		30	Luke Davies an Infant, in the West yard
	April	1	Peter Kelsie, in the North Chapel
		15	John Marriot, Infant, under the Organ
	May	3	William Hardy, Barber Surgeon, East yard
		8	Mary Palmer, Widow, under ye Organ
		23	Joseph Bellinger an Infant, in ye West yard
		28	Joseph Mitchell, in the West yard
	June	8	Mary Fletcher a Child, in ye West yard
	July	3	Mary Margeson a Child, in ye West yard
		26	Robert Hanson, Butcher, in the East yard
		26	Matthew Taylor, porter, in ye East yard
	August	7	Frances Ellets, in the East yard
	September	5	Richard Sparks, Barber, in ye West yard
		15	Sarah Buckston, in the West yard
		25	John Swallow, in the West yard
	October	6	John son of Roger Walter, in ye West yard
		10	John Mills, merchant, in ye middle Isle
		25	Calamy Bayly, in the West yard
		30	Anne Tredway, a Child, in ye middle Isle
	November	19	Martha wife of James Branch, under ye Organ
	December	11	Edward Pott a Child, under ye Bell
		19	Shewter Carol, in ye South Chapel
		20	Mary Thorneton, in the middle Isle
		20	John Thomas, Merchant, in ye middle Isle
		29	Edward Nash, Chandler, under ye Organ

Years.	Month.	Day.	Names.
1717	January	12	Jonathan Wootley, in the West yard
	February	12	James Branch, poulterer, under yᵉ Organ
		13	Sarah Browne an Infant, in yᵉ West yard
	March	3	Josiah Lutman, a Glazier, in yᵉ West yard
1718	April	6	Francis Crisp, in yᵉ West yard
		29	Elizabeth wife of John Sparks, in yᵉ E. yard
		30	Mary Virgin a Child, in yᵉ West yard
	May	3	Mary Saunderson, a Stranger, in yᵉ N. Isle
		4	John Gore, an Apothecary, between the doors
		11	Roger Fennimore, in the East yard
		13	Captain Edward Teddeman, in yᵉ West yard
		14	Isaac Tomkins, a servant, in yᵉ East yard
		16	Samuel Ferris, an Infant, in yᵉ East yard
		20	Thomas Son of Tho. & Eliz. Hunsden, by yᵉ Font
		22	Richard Day, in yᵉ East yard
		24	Phebe dau. of John & Rebecka Pannell, in the North Isle by the back Stone
	June	9	John Buckston, in the West yard
		18	Mary Peters, in the West yard
		24	Thomas Hunsden, under the Organ
		26	Robert Garbrand, in the South Chapel
	July	5	Mrˢ Anne Bendish, in yᵉ South Chapel
		18	William son of Robᵗ & Martha Fitzhugh, in the South Chapel
	August	17	Thomas Mitchell, in the West yard
		25	Absolom Peters, in the West yard
	September	5	Anne Ley, in yᵉ paved passage
		15	Matthias Gainsborough, in yᵉ East yard
	October	5	Denisha Elwis, Widow, by yᵉ bellfry door
		13	Susanna Waring, in yᵉ Chancell near the Ministers pew
		30	Jos. Chandler, in yᵉ West yard
	November	14	James Vincent, Servant, in yᵉ West yard
		28	Isabella Adams, in yᵉ North Isle
	December	3	Anne dau. of Thomas & Eliz. Hunsden
		15	Charles Strefield, in yᵉ East yard
		24	Elizabeth Amerr, in yᵉ West yard
	January	4	Hugh Stafford, a stranger, in yᵉ East yard
		8	Martha Dufrisnay, in yᵉ middle Isle
		15	Samuel Gryffin, in yᵉ South Chapel
		24	Jane Bannister, servant, in yᵉ West yard
	February	12	Mrˢ Eliz. Barrinton, in yᵉ South Chapel
		19	Elizabeth Lenthall, in yᵉ East yard
	March	2	James Branch, West yard
		9	Mr John Withinbrook, under yᵉ Organ
1719	April	1	Mr Samˡˡ Caneton, behind yᵉ Pulpit
		10	Mr John Thomas, by yᵉ North door
		20	Thomas Shorsby, East yard
	May	13	Bridget Palmer, over agˢᵗ yᵉ Desk
		15	Martha Windham, in yᵉ Chancell
		31	John Colt, North Isle, agˢᵗ yᵉ middle pillar
	June	5	Charles Baily, East yard
		10	Susanna Bolton
		14	Henry Lucy, in yᵉ paved passage
	July	10	Jane Kimmis, East yard
		21	Elizabeth Quintry, West yard
		21	Mr William Weale, North Isle
	August	8	Mrˢ Elizabeth Jackson, under yᵉ Organ

Years.	Month.	Day.	Names.
1719	August	9	Pagett Shoresby, East yard
		13	Joseph Rook, East yard
		28	Mrs Lewis Greenwell, South Isle
	September	1	Sarah Arthur, East yard
		10	Elizabeth Cokey, West yard
		29	Rebecka Pannell, North Isle
	October	4	Martha Loadman, Pentioner, West y^d
		16	Thomas Garbrand, in ye South Chapel
		18	Sarah Stringall, in ye west yard
	November	1	Hugh Winn, in ye Middle Isle
		29	William Parker, in ye West yard
	December	3	James Right, in ye West yard
		15	Samuel Porter, in ye paved passage
		20	Henry Harrison, in ye East yard
		29	William Hutton, under ye Organ
	January	3	Thomas Fowler, under ye Organ
		19	Anne Dratgate, in ye South Isle
		23	Elizabeth Cantrell, in ye East yard
	February	1	Anne Norris, under ye organ
		2	Charles Mackleen, in ye East yard
		15	Sarah Duncomb, in ye East yard
		19	John Radhams, in ye North Isle
	March	13	Francis Clifton, in ye East yard
		20	Henry Middleton, in ye West yard
		21	Anne Fairweather, servant
1720		26	Elizabeth Unwin, in ye South Chapel
	April	17	John and Jane Laytham, in ye East yard
		18	Jane Clifton, in ye East yard
		24	Penelope Povey, in ye East yard
	May	4	Martha Norman, in ye East yard
		28	James Windham, in ye Chancell
	June	8	Thomas Fowler, in ye South Isle
		24	Dorothy Masters, in ye West yard
	July	29	Elizabeth Lewin, in ye West yard
	August	6	Barbara Hunsden, under ye Organ
		21	Thomas Bennett, in ye East yard
	September	11	Martha Newdick, in ye South Isle
		28	George Castell, in ye East yard
		30	Benj. Meryman, in ye East yard
	October	7	Richard Fitzhugh, in ye South Chapel
		16	Christopher Martin, in ye West yard
		30	Samuel Marriot, under ye Organ
	November	2	Hannah Fennimore, in ye East yard
		21	Mary Jarvis, in ye East yard
		25	Susanna Simons, in ye East yard
	January	1	Edward Maber, under ye Organ
		11	Anna Maria Barnardiston, in ye South Isle
		20	Elizabeth Gainsbrough, in ye East yard
		20	Edwd Peters, in ye West yard
		27	Mr Matth. Beck, son of Sr Justus Beck, Chancell
		29	Jacob Roberts, in ye South Isle
	February	1	Elizabeth Coker, in ye West yard
		5	William Hayward, in ye East yard
		6	John Horton, in ye West yard
		10	Jone Fespound, under ye Organ
		19	Mr Francis Wight, Reader, by ye little Vestry
		26	Elizabeth Bradley, in ye West yard

Years.	Month.	Day.	Names.
1721	February	28	Jane Coney, in yᵉ West yard
	April	19	Mary Asgill, under yᵉ Organ
		29	Loveden Hyde, in yᵉ West yard
	May	12	John Pannell, in yᵉ South Isle
		23	Thomas Morley, in yᵉ East yard
		25	Elizabeth Poole, in yᵉ Middle Isle
	June	11	William Sparks, in yᵉ West yard
		11	Mary Coker, in yᵉ West yard
		18	Susanna Bolton, in yᵉ West yard
	July	7	Mary Stanley, in yᵉ West yard
		24	Marth Reynolds, in yᵉ East yard
	August	28	Elizabeth Quintry, under yᵉ Organ
	September	18	John Rudge, in yᵉ Ch. yard
	October	3	Abraham Church, a Stranger
		10	James Wilks, in yᵉ East yard
		18	Gilbert Page, in yᵉ North Isle
		22	Willliam Weatherly, in yᵉ South Isle
	November	2	James Nicholls, under yᵉ Organ
		6	John Dollin, under yᵉ Organ
		28	Samuel Haywood, in yᵉ East yard
	December	20	John Stevens, in yᵉ West yard
		27	William Langford, in yᵉ West yard
	January	31	Thomas Brookman, in yᵉ East yard
	February	4	Samuel Howles, in yᵉ West yard
		16	Sʳ Thomas Abney, Kⁿᵗ,* in yᵉ South Chappel
		25	Sarah Bayly & Rob. Lewin, Children, E. yard
		26	John Cooper, in yᵉ North Chappell
	March	12	Jane Laytham, in yᵉ Vault, new built
		21	Matthias Bowman, in yᵉ Vault
		24	Henry Ball in yᵉ Vault
1722	April	18	Mʳ Wᵐ Greenwell, in yᵉ Chancell
		19	Mʳ Barnes (William), in yᵉ Vault
	May	7	Elizabeth March, in yᵉ East yard
		17	Edward Timpson, in yᵉ Vault
		31	Nathaniel Gower, in yᵉ West yard
	June	23	Thomas Low, in yᵉ Vault
		25	Mary Martin, in yᵉ Vault
	July	20	Elizabeth Chansey, in yᵉ North Isle
		22	Richᵈ Partridge, in the Chancell, yᵉ Gent. pew
	August	23	Eliz. Tomkinson, Churchyard
		25	Mary Wyard, in yᵉ Vault
	September	7	Mary Dalby, in yᵉ Middle Isle
		9	Martha Bettwell, in yᵉ Vault
		23	Edward Becham, in yᵉ Vault
	October	1	Robert Nicholls, in yᵉ Vault
		14	Samuel Duncombe, in yᵉ Vault
		29	Sarah Archer, under yᵉ Organ
	November	11	Hester Bartlett, in yᵉ South Isle
	December	10	Robert Newman, in yᵉ Vault
		13	Thomas Lewin, in yᵉ Vault
		21	George Pomroy, in yᵉ Vault
		27	Richard Dratgate, under yᵉ great Pew
	January	6	Robert Fowler, under yᵉ Organ
		6	Henry Flinch, in yᵉ Vault

* Fishmonger, Lord Mayor of London, 1701. See his wife's burial, May 18, 1697, and his sons', Oct. 25, 1704, and Nov. 12, 1707.

Years.	Month.	Day.	Names.
1722	January	11*	Sarah Strangway, in ye Vault
		13	Samuel Belden, South Chappell
		13	John Gazey, in ye Vault
		22	Christian Hanson, in ye Vault
		28	John Hine, by ye Clerks desk
	February	1	Simon Thorowgood, North side of ye Chancell
		7	John Page, in ye North Isle
		12	Thomas Billingham, in ye Vault
	March	19	Mary & Eliz. Twins, in ye Vault
		12	Alice Langdale, in ye Vault
1723		26	Robert Morris, in ye Vault
		29	Mary Langford, in ye Vault
	April	2	John Cliffton, in the Vault
		12	Nath. Lewin, in ye Vault
		15	Joseph Barber, in the Vault
	May	7	Mr Tho. Griffin, in ye South Isle
	June	10	Robert Gainsborough, in the Vault
		21	Mary wife of Benj. Weale, North Isle
	July	1	Debora Newman, in ye Vault
		26	Thomas Gibson, in ye Vault
		31	Mary Gibson, in the Vault
	August	9	Susan Franks, in ye Vault
		25	Mary Ingle, in ye Vault
	September	5	Isaac Ferris, in ye Vault
		7	Jane Allen, North side of ye Chancell
		7	Martha Pott, under the Bell
		20	Wm Buxton, under the Organ
		27	Mary Thorowgood, Middle Isle
	October	2	Jonathan Palfryman, in ye Vault
		8	George Finch, in the Vault
		13	Jo. Clifton, in the Vault
	November	14	Earle Stanly, in the Vault
		15	Eliz. Snablin, in ye South Isle
		27	Eliz. Belden, in ye South Chapell
	December	7	Mary Lewis, in ye Vault
		22	Hannah Michel, in the Vault
		24	Eliz. Nutt, in the Vault
		31	Katherine Maber, in the Vault
	January	19	Samuel Bolton, in the Vault
		22	Thomas Luther Haywood, in ye East yard
		28	Elioner Billingham, in ye Vault
	February	5	William Windham, in the Chancell
		10	Eliz. Casier, in the Vault
		11	Eliz. Radhams, in ye South Isle
		13	Sarah Latimer, in ye Vault
		20	Lettice Edmonds, in ye Vault
	March	2	Robert Latimer, in the Vault
		9	Anne Pott, under the Bell
		19	Frances Jervis, East yard
		13	Anne Kitson, in ye Vault
		18	Dorothy Buxton, under the Organ
		23	Wm Tomkinson, East yard
1724	April	20	Anne Arrowsmith, East yard
		29	Anne Lund, West yard

* The Register from January 11, 1722-23, to March 3, 1727-28, is subscribed " Jo. Carliol, Parson Commendat';" and from March 21, 1727-28, to July 12, 1731, " Jo. Carliol, Parson."

Years.	Month.	Day.	Names.
1724	May	27	Mary Midleton, in the Vault
	June	8	Mary Martin, in the Vault
	July	3	Mary Cam, in the Vault
		17	Mary Fowler, in the South Isle
		24	Tho. Fitzhugh, in ye North Isle
	August	20	Mary Davies, in the Vault
	September	12	Charles Duncombe, in ye West yard
		12	Wm Frank, in ye Vault
	October	18	John Bainham, in ye Vault
	November	1	Diligence Constant, in ye Vault
		2	John Cole, in the West yard
		8	Christian Harriman, in ye Vault
		19	Benjamin Barnardiston, in ye Vault
		20	Tho. Rose, in ye Chancell
	December	1	Anne Ridge, in ye Vault
		3	John Rayn, in ye West yard
		22	Moye Nichols, in ye Vault
		24	James Lewis, Stranger, in ye Vault
		24	Mary Langford, in ye West yard
		27	Benjam. Meryman, in ye West yard
		29	Robert Langdale, in the Vault
	January	2	Thomas Glover, in ye Vault
		12	Mathew Pott, under the Bell
		26	Sarah Ingham, under the Organ
		29	Isaac Summerman, in ye Vault
	February	9	William Barnes, in ye Vault
		26	Edwd Allen, under y^c 3^d pew middle Isle
	March	6	Anne Kimmist, in ye Vault
		14	Jo. Ingham, under y^c Organ
		21	Jane Laurence, in y^c Vault
1725	April	2	Eliz. Topping, in ye Vault
		30	Nicholas Baker, in the Vault
	May	18	Anne Barber, in the Vault
		23	William Smith, in ye Vault
	June	3	Mr Samuel Ingle, in ye Vault
		18	Sarah Taylor, under y^c Organ
		23	Sarah Nash, in ye Vault
		23	Samuel Tredway, in ye Vault
		29	Tho. Baker, in the Vault
	July	5	Sr James Caustin, in ye North Isle
		8	John Morris, in ye Vault
		9	Mary Stephenson, in ye Vault
		10	Patience Morris, in ye Vault
		12	John Stephenson an Infant, in ye Vault
		14	Anne Davies, in ye Vault
	August	1	Rebecka Bragg, under ye Organ
		7	Stephen Mares, in y^c Vault
		13	James Wilford, in ye Vault
		15	Walter Allen, in ye Vault
		31	Eliz. Crosby, a pensioner, in ye Vault
	September	1	Godfry Curry an Infant, in ye Ch. yard
		10	Jo. Dorrill, in ye Vault, a Lodger
		12	Hannah Michel, in ye Vault
		14	John Sparks, in ye Vault
	November	19	Anne Latimer, in ye Vault
		30	Mrs Mary Weston, in ye Vault
	December	23	Mr Walter Tredway, in ye middle Isle

Years.	Month.	Day.	Names.
1725	January	29	Mrs Elizabeth Smith, in ye Vault
		8	William Finch an Infant, in ye Vault
		16	Mrs Elizabeth Witherly, in ye South Isle
		30	Thos Mash a Child, in ye Vault
	February	17	Mr Robt Selby, in ye Vault
	March	8	Robt Peters a Foundlin, in ye Vault
		11	Mr Thos Harryman, in ye Vault
		20	Mr Tempest Leathes, in ye Vault
1726		30	Thos Hine, parish Clerk, by his Desk
	April	4	Mrs Grace Bentley, in ye Chancell
	May	21	Anne Webster, in the Vault
	June	1	Jno Lun, in ye West yard
		2	Wm Eastwood, in ye Vault
		11	Eliz. Hews an Infant, in ye Vault
		23	Thos Kimmis a Child, in ye Vault
		29	Martha Mellows, Pensioner, in ye Vault
		30	Jane Peters, Parish Child, in ye Vault
	July	5	Edward Garbrand, ye South Chapple
		12	James Peters, Parish Child, in ye Vault
		15	Sarah Bull a Child, in ye West yard
		23	Elizth Barnes, in ye Vault
		26	Sarah Nash, in ye Vault
	August	1	John Baily, in the West yard
	September	1	Charles Solendine Boyes an Infant, in the West yard
		2	Eliz. Creamer, a Pensioner, in ye Vault
		6	Grace Flude an Infant, in ye Vault
		11	Jane Elliot a Child, in ye West yard
		13	Deborah Waters an Infant, in ye middle Isle
	October	8	Eleanor Page a Lodger, in ye Vault
		4	Anne Nelson an Infant, in ye Vault, only privately baptized
		6	Mr Barnabas Rumbold, in ye Vault
		10	Thos Ferriss an Infant, in ye East churchyard
		21	Anne Peters a parish Child, in Churchyard
		24	Henrietta Stanley an Infant, in the west churchyard, privately baptiz'd
	December	7	Mary Peters a Parish Child, Vault
		10	Mary Peregrine, a Pensioner, Vault
		27	Charity Causton, in ye North Isle
		28	Abraham Upton, Pensioner, in ye Vault
	January	6	Jno Bainham, Pensioner, in Vault
	February	2	Sarah Nichols an Infant, in ye Vault, only privately baptiz'd
		8	Eliz. Blake, Pensioner, in the Vault
		3	Rose Thompson a Child, in Vault
		12	Anne Salmon, in West Church yard
		27	Eliz. Holland an Infant, in ye Vault
	March	9	Mary Bayley a Child, in East Churchyard
			Martha Arrowsmith an Infant, only privately baptiz'd, ditto
		16	Brant Wibirt, an Apprentice, ditto
		19	Mary Bolton a Child
1727		30	Thos Hearn, Lodger, in the Vault
	May	22	John Parsons, Victualler, in the Vault
		25	Mr Isaac Causton, grocer, in ye North Isle
		26	Margaret Fitzhugh a Child, in South Chapple
	June	2	Sarah Chaunesy a Child, in Vault
		11	Jane Nichol a Child, in Vault
	July	5	Jno Peters a Parish Child, in Vault
		11	Mr Wm Brookman, Poulterer, in Vault

Years.	Month.	Day.	Names.
1727	July	23	Mrs Eliz. Smith, Lodger, in Vault
	August	28	Mr Robert Harris, Painter, in Vault
		28	Mrs Elizth Taylor, by the Font
		16	Thos Guillim an Infant, in ye Vault, only privately baptiz'd
	September	12	Mrs Hannah Thomas a stranger, in ye middle Isle
		13	Margaret Cock a serv^t, in ye Vault
		13	Martha Higgate an Infant, ditto
		24	Sam^{ll} Gower an Infant, in Church yard
	October	22	Thos. Fowler a Child, in ye South Isle
		28	. . . . a poor Woman accidentally killed by a cart, in ye Vault
	November	3	Elizth Rayn a Lodger, in ye Vault
		12	Miles Sutton a Servt, in ye Vault
		15	Margaret Copten, Pensioner, in Vault
		15	Theophilus Peters a Foundlin, in Vault
		24	Mr Thos Prime, Attorney, in the middle Isle under the great pew
		26	Mr Benja. Taylor, stranger, by ye Font
	December	12	Mrs Elizth Rose, Stranger, in ye Vault
		26	Jno Curtis, Stranger, in ye Vault
		26	Mr Richd Knight, Vintner, in ye Chancel
		29	Elizth Tomkinson an Infant, in ye Chancell
		30	Mr James Coulter a Lodger, in ye Vault
	January	7	Mr Edward Coker, Lodger, in ye Vault
		7	James Peters a Foundlin, ditto
		19	Jno Gregory an Infant, in ye Vault
		20	Mary Willson an Infant, in ye Vault
	February	13	Abraham Upton, Pensioner, in ye Vault
		27	Mrs Ursula Smith wife of James Smith, in ye South Isle
		27	Katharine Lockington a Servt, in ye Vault
	March	2	Henry Kelsey, Esq., a Stranger, in the North Isle
		8	Joanna Hickman, Lodger, in the Vault
		21	Thos Duncombe an Infant, in ye Vault
1728	April	15	Diana Peters a Foundling, in ye Vault
		24	Nathanael Gower, in ye Vault, a Child
		25	Mrs Sarah Brerewood a Stranger, in the Chancell
		30	Marg^t Peters a Foundling, in ye Vault
	May	10	Jno Carver, M.D., Lodger, in ye Vault
		10	Mrs Joan Howard, Stranger, in Vault
		14	Jno Tomkinson an Infant, in ye Middle Isle
		21	Elizth Matthews an Infant, in ye Vault
		27	Anne Ridge an Infant in ye Vault
	June	26	Carolina Lunn an Infant, ditto
	July	4	Wm Cam an Infant, ditto
		17	Mary Mellows, Pensioner, in ye Vault
		28	Mr Cullum Wickes, in ye South Isle
		30	Jno Peters a Foundlin, in ye Vault
	August	3	Richd Stebbin an Infant, in Middle Isle
		22	Mr Jonathan Allen, in the Vault
		23	Mrs Elizth Dingley, Lodger, in the Vault
		31	Jno Colby an Infant, in the Vault
	September	10	Jno Higgate an Infant, ditto
		15	Richd Saggar an Apprentice, in the Vault
		21	Hannah Smith, Pensioner, ditto
		29	Anne Peter a Foundlin, in the Vault
		29	Mark Thompson a Foundlin, in ye Vault
		29	George Bubb a Child, in the Vault

Years.	Month.	Day.	Names.
1728	September	29	James Fowler an Infant, in ye South Isle, privately baptized
	October	7	Elizth Brance, Stranger, in the Vault
		18	Francis Woodley an Infant, in the Vault
		19	Anne Griffith, Pensioner, in the Vault
	November	9	. . . . a poor man found dead in the Street, the vault
		26	Robt Peters a foundlin, in the Vault
	December	11	Judeth Macklecan an Infant, in the Vault
		11	. . . . a poor man found dead in the Market, the Vault
		18	Jno Macklecan a youth, in ye Church yard
		26	Mary Peters a foundlin, in ye Vault
	January	25	Rachel Peters a Foundlin, in the Vault
	February	8	Mrs Susannah Salmon, in ye Vault
		4	Mrs Mary Barber, in the Church yard
		5	Richard Thoroughgood, Esqr, Stranger, in the Middle Isle
		9	Mrs Mary Brookman, in the Vault
		11	Sarah Asplin a poor woman found dead in the Market, in the Vault
		18	James Peters a foundlin, ditto
		19	Anne Farrer an Infant, ditto
		25	Thos Sedgewick a Servt, in the Vault
		26	Mr James Page, in the North Isle
	March	1	Jno Hannay, a Servant, Buried in ye Vault
1729		30	Josiah Brock a Lodger, ditto
	April	2	Joseph Duncomb an Infant, privately baptiz'd, in ye Church yard
		14	Sam^{ll} Stovy a Stranger, in the Vault
		29	Martha Arrowsmith an infant, in the Church yard
	June	18	Jeremiah Bentley an Infant, middle Isle
	July	4	Jane Morer a Pensioner, in the Vault
		11	Edward Thos Parker an Infant, privately baptized, in the Vault
		17	Mr Wm Walter, in West Church yard
		21	Mary Chauncey a Stranger, in the North Isle
		23	Hannah Barber an Infant, in ye West Church yard
		24	Jno Goodwin a Child, in ye East Church yard
	September	7	Michael Thompson an Infant, ye Vault
		7	Mr Philip Davies a Stranger, ditto
		12	Mr Edward Hilliard, in the Middle Isle
		19	Berriman Beachman an Infant, privately baptiz'd
		25	Richd Davis a young Child, in ye Vault
	October	3	Joseph Fendoll a Stranger, in ye West Church yard
		6	Peter Monneret a natural Child, in ye Vault
		12	Mrs Anne Bowman, in the Vault
		26	Mrs Dorothy Evans a Lodger, in the Vault
	November	9	Wm Stretton a Lodger, in the Vault
		11	Sarah Smithegoll, in ye West Church yard
		18	Henry . . . . a Parish Child, in ye Vault
		26	Jno Barnes an Infant, in ye Vault
		29	Samuel Colby an Infant, in the Vault
	December	2	Dorothy Barnes a Child, in the Vault
		13	Walter Peters a Foundlin, in the Vault
		14	Thos Fitzhugh a Stranger, the South Chappell
		23	Mary Peters a Foundlin, in the Vault
		30	Thos Hilliard an Infant, in the Vault
	January	4	Henry Connell an Infant, in the Vault
		11	Joanna Clark a Lodger, in the Vault

Years.	Month.	Day.	Names.
1729	January	16	Elizth Smith, a Stranger, in the Vault
		16	Sarah Peters a Foundling, in the Vault
		21	Wm Blundell a Child, in ye West Church yard
	February	7	Wm Bentley an Infant, in the Vault
		8	Mrs Susanna Pott, in the Bellfry
		9	Jno Cutler a Child, in the West Church yard
		16	Mary Fitzhugh, in the South Chappel
		18	Anthony Nichols a Youth, in the Vault
	March	22	Anne Ingham a Child, under the Organ
1730		29	Henry Burridge, in the Middle Isle
	April	19	Mrs Hannah Hillyard, in the Vault
		26	Mrs Mary Broad, Stranger, under the Organ
		26	Geo. Waters an Infant, in the middle Isle
		27	Jno Keys a Pensioners Child, vault
	May	5	Sophia Higgate an Infant, in ye Vault
		8	Stephen Thornley, Esqr, in the middle Isle
		13	Elizth Looker, in the West Church yard
		24	Mrs Anne Ridge, in the Vault
		28	Mrs Elizth Tomkinson, in the middle Isle
	June	8	Jno Peters a Foundlin, in ye Vault
		4	Mrs Anne Farrer, in the Vault
	July	14	Susannah Nichols an Infant, ditto
		25	Jeremiah Arrowsmith, private baptism, in the West Church-yard
		26	Frances Stebbin an Infant, in the Middle Isle
		31	Jno Tayler an Infant, in the Vault
	August	2	Elizth Sparkes, in the Vault
	September	8	Dorothy Hillyard an Infant, ditto
	October	8	Jno Clarke a Servt, ditto
		28	Jervoice Finch an Infant, ditto
	November	8	Wm Abbet a Greengrocer, ditto
		9	Martha Cox an Infant, privately baptiz^ed, ditto
		10	Nathanael Thompson an Infant, vault
	December	2	Maria Kimist an Infant, ditto
		22	Mary Johnson, under ye Organ
	February	3	A poor man found dead in ye Market, Vault
		23	Jane Bull an Infant, privately bapt., Vault
		25	Ann Barnadiston an Infant, in ye Church by the South door, under ye Engine
	March	19	Isaac Thornley, Esqr, middle Isle
		22	Charity Adams, North Isle
1731	April	5	Mary Willson a Child, vault
		21	Wm Trymmer an apprentice, vault
		28	Nathanael Prime, middle Isle
	May	6	Mary Aris, Lodger, vault
		31	George Waters an Infant, middle Isle
	June	18	Sarah Unwin, the South end of ye Communion Rails
		27	Elizth Gower a Child, vault
	July	12	Jno Pritchard an Infant, priv. bapt., Vault
		14*	Robt Godson a Lad, in the Vault
	August	30	Jane Day, in the North Isle
	September	23	Mary Marshal, in ye middle Isle
		30	Hannah Hine, in the East yard
	October	9	Thos Kimist an Infant, priv. bap., Vault

* The Register from July 14, 1731, to November 7, 1736, is subscribed "Jno Higgate, M.A., Curate."

Years.	Month.	Day.	Names.
1731	October	19	Richd Stockall, East Churchyard
	November	5	Mary Willdey, Vault
		17	Jn° Joues, West Churchyard
		24	James Barber an Infant, priv. bapt., ditto
		26	Elizth Mackadams an Infant, ditto
		27	Harman Macklecan an Infant, East Churchyard
	December	3	Susan Johnson from ye Bull Inn, Vault
		17	Maria Thorowgood, in the Chancell
		24	Joseph Caryl, in the South Chapel
		30	Robt Hart, Parish Clerk, in ye East Churchyard
	January	3	Mary Gasey an Infant, the West yard
		18	Wm Bayford a Lad, the East yard
		18	Elizth Bowyer, the same place
		19	Thos Gasey, Victualler, the West yard
		20	Dorothy Bentley an Infant, Vault
	February	2	Alice Wheeler a serv^t, West Church-yard
		7	Josiah Sanders, Woollen draper, in ye Vault
	March	19	Mary Paget a Pensioner, in ye East yard
		22	Susanna Fernley, ye same place
1732		29	Sarah Abney, in ye South Chappel
	May	4	James Smith, in ye South Isle
		5	Peter Causton, in the North Isle
		11	Wm Mayson, under ye Organ
		12	Wm Howard a Pensioner's Child, in ye West yard
		26	Wm Westall an Infant, in ye East yard
	July	12	Benjamin Brett, Haberdasher, in ye Vault
	August	7	Mr Martin Barnes, Inholder, in ye South Isle
		28	Joseph Blagdon an Infant, Vault
	September	19	Joseph Fowler an Infant, South Isle
	October	1	Elizth Mears an Infant, priv. bapt., in ye East yard
		23	John Stebbin an Infant, in the middle Isle
		30	Joseph Bentley an Infant, in the Vault
		31	Wm Woodley a Parish Child, same place
	November	28	Mrs Henrietta Kelsey, in the North Chapple
	December	11	Dorothy Lewen, in the middle Isle
		19	Joseph Blagdon, an Infant, in ye Vault
		24	M^r Jn° Hoyle, under ye Organ
	January	12	Jn° Barber an Inf^t, in the Vault
		19	Thos Hine, in the East yard
		19	Sarah Nelson a Child, in the Vault
		23	Sam^{ll} Fowler, an Infant, in the South Isle
		25	Elizth Thorogood, in the Chancell
		27	Wm Howard, a Parish Child, Vault
	February	11	Mrs Lois Thornbury, in ye Middle Isle
		20	Katharine Ireland a Parish Child, in ye West yard
		22	Wm Moyser, Servt at ye Spread eagle Inn, East y^d
1733	March	28	James Hillyard a Child from the Bull Inn, W. yard
	April	21	Marg^t Collins, under the Organ
		25	Sarah Arthur, in the East yard
	May	10	Jn° Franks, Vintner, middle Isle
		11	Jane Windham, Lodger, in ye West yard
	August	9	Wm Whythill, Lodger, ye same place
	September	4	Jn° Blundell a Child, ye same place
		7	Mary Blagdon an Infant, Vault
		26	James Stebbin a Child, middle Isle
		30	Thos Brown, in the East yard
	October	20	Mary Woodley a Pensioner's Child, Vault

Years.	Month.	Day.	Names.
1733	October	23	Mr Geo. Knapp, Lodger, vault
		25	Elizth Barnard a Child from ye Workhouse, West y^d
		28	Ann Nelson a Child, Vault
		31	Richd Lunn, Fishmonger, West yard
	November	16	Elizth Knight, in the Chancell
		16	Marg^t Bartlet, in the South Isle
		21	Ann Marcy, from the Workhouse, West y^d
	December	18	Wm Blomfield, Lodger, East y^d
		23	Thos Turner a Child, East yard
	January	6	James Hodgson, in the East y^d
	February	2	James Peters a Foundlin, in the West yard
		3	Geo. Chapman an infant, East yard
		3	Dorcas Turner an Infant, East yard
		5	Elizth Turner a Child, ye same place
	March	5	Mrs Catharine Hill, in ye South Isle
1734	April	23	Isaac Peters, West yard
	May	4	Mrs Mary Cotton, under the Organ
		25	Thos Twomley, in the West yard
		31	Elizth Day a Child, East yard
	June	2	Mary Filewood, West yard
		18	Thos Wilkinson a Servt, in the West yard
	July	9	Thos Higgate an Infant, priv. bapt., Vault
		9	Ruth Jones a Servt, Vault
		24	Sarah Blagdon Infant, Vault
	August	28	Martha Bestow, West yard
	September	1	Ann Meadows Infant, East yard
		15	Marg^t Allcock, under the Organ
	October	1	Grace Bentley Infant, priv. bapt., Vault
		7	Ann Barnard, Pensioner's Child, West yard
		11	Jno Ingham, Attorney, under the Organ
		16	Mary Springham, Lodger, West yard
		20	Mary Wright, Servt, West yard
	November	2	Robt Day an Infant, priv. bapt., East yard
		3	The Right Revd Dr Jno Waugh,* Lord Bp. of Carlisle, & Rector of the parish, under the Communion Table
		18	Martha Davis, East yard
	December	29	Jno Barber, ditto
	January	9	Sarah Hare, West yard
	February	2	Mrs Elizth Marriot, under the Organ
	March	2	Mrs Dorothy Hillyard, in the middle Isle
		7	Mr Robt Rowland, in the South Isle
		24	Mr Robt Hill, South Isle
1735	April	6	Cook Stebbin an Infant, middle Isle
	May	4	James Pointing, Victualler, in the East yard
		7	Elizth Keys a Pensioners Child, West yard
		16	Mrs Sarah Whateley, Stranger, in the Vault
		16	Ann Farman, in the East yard
		28	Mr Matthias Gainsborough, in the Vault
	July	18	Elizth Nelson a Child, Vault
	August	3	Mr Jasper Waters, Middle Isle
		24	Jno Blagdon, Infant, Vault
	September	2	Mary Harris a Lodger, West yard
		9	Joseph Radaway an Infant from ye Workhouse, ditto

* Appointed Rector of St. Peters, 1704; Prebendary of Lincoln; Dean of Gloucester. Appointed Bishop of Carlisle 1731. Died at the age of 79. See burial of his wife, May 9, 1716, and of his daughter, Jan. 14, 1713.

Years.	Month.	Day.	Names.
1735	September	25	John Stanley, West yard
	October	2	Hannah Barber an Infant ditto
	November	2	Jn° Chittoe, Child, East yard
		7	Wᵐ Whitaker, Lodger, West yard
		29	Mary Dear a Stranger, East yard
	December	2	Thoˢ Hutchinson, Butcher, East yard
		24	Mʳˢ Martha Pott, Vault
	January	1	Ann Hawkins ⎫ both from the Workhouse, W. yard
		1	Samˡˡ Peters ⎭
		5	Aaron Fawkes a Servᵗ, West yard
	February	14	Joseph Rodaway from yᵉ Workhouse, West yard
		17	James Antin a Servᵗ, East yard
		24	Mary Goodwin a Stranger, East yard
		28	Henry Cornwallis, Esqʳ, Lodger, Vault
	March	10	Jane Bristow a Servᵗ, Vault
1736		25	Sarah Peat a Pensioner's Child, West yard
		27	Jn° Eames a Chrisom, West yard
	April	5	Jane Hine a late Clerk's wife, Middle Isle
	May	1	Jn° Lycett, Mariner, West yard
		4	Mʳ Richᵈ Arthur, East yard
		17	Mʳˢ Elizᵗʰ Burridge, Middle Isle
		18	Thoˢ Peters & Richᵈ Spark Infᵗˢ, both from yᵉ Workhouse, West yard
	June	6	Mary Godwin, Lodger, East yard
		20	Wᵐ Nelson a Child, Vault
	July	4	Mʳˢ Elizᵗʰ Ferriss, Middle Isle
		30	Wᵐ Nichols a Youth, Vault
	August	11	Philip Peters a Foundlin, West yard
		14	Lewis Anthony a Chrisom, West yard
		17	Joseph Brookman a Servᵗ, Vault
		20	Mʳˢ Elizᵗʰ Annable a Stranger, East yard
		21	Susannah Peters a ffoundlin, West yard
		26	Sarah Blagdou an Infᵗ, vault
	September	5	Mary Blagdon an Infᵗ, vault
		13	Ann Stebbin, priv. baptis'd, middle Isle
		14	Mʳˢ Martha Adams, Stranger, North Isle
		19	Wᵐ Andrews, priv. bapt., Vault
		21	Mʳ Edmund Page, North Isle
	October	22	Jane Windell, Lodger, West yard
	November	7	Jane Filewood, the same place
	December	19*	Mʳˢ Sarah Bull, in the West yard
		27	Mʳˢ Ann Rosier, in the East yard
		29	Sarah Jackson, West yard
	January	2	Wᵐ Elliot, West yard
		23	Mʳˢ Elizᵗʰ Angel, under the Organ
	February	5	Sarah Turner a Child, West yard
		11	Mʳˢ Dorothy Bentley, in the middle Isle
	March	2	Charles Ayres, priv. baptiz'd, Vault
		4	Mary Turner an Infant, East yard
		13	Abigail Trantum, Vault
		18	Mʳ John Pott, under the Bell
		24	Emma Hutchins, from yᵉ Workhouse, West yard
1737	April	2	Rachel Salmon, in the West yard
		3	Anne Beauchamp, in the West yard

* The Register from December 19, 1736, to April 8, 1744, is subscribed "Richᵈ Thomas, M.A., Curate."

Years.	Month.	Day.	Names.
1737	April	8	Sarah Cary, in the Middle Isle
		12	Hannah Wingfield, in yᵉ West Yard
	July	9	Mary Grenewell, in yᵉ South Chapple
		18	Mary Trueman, in yᵉ East yard
	August	4	Thomas Dratgate, in yᵉ South Chappel
	September	8	Elizabeth Blagdon, in yᵉ Vault
	October	31	John Marriott, under yᵉ Organ
	November	2	Ruth Davies, in yᵉ East yard
		17	Mary Gold, in the Vault
	January	2	Humphrey Stebbing, in yᵉ Middle Isle
		10	Susannah Allen, in yᵉ Vault
		11	Joseph Wright, under yᵉ Organ
		12	James Lloyd, under yᵉ Organ
		22	Jane Day, in the East Yard
	February	19	John Bennet, in yᵉ East yard
		20	Mary Pickard, in yᵉ South Chappel
	March	1	Elizabeth Crouch, an Infant
		1	Robert Gower, in yᵉ Vault
		5	Mary Bayley, in yᵉ West yard
		12	Wᵐ Fernley, in yᵉ East Yard
1738	April	27	Elizabeth Salter an Infant pensioner
	May	11	John Arnold, in yᵉ East Church yard
		20	John Bennet an Infant, in yᵉ same
	June	12	Martha Drafgate, in yᵉ South Chappel
		19	Anne Ingham, under yᵉ Organ
	July	5	Walter Yate, in yᵉ Vault
		5	Mary Westall, in yᵉ East Church Yard
		16	Robert Smith, in yᵉ South Isle
	August	2	Mary Jones, in yᵉ West Church Yard
		8	James Bartlett, in yᵉ South Isle
		16	Margaret Turner, in yᵉ East Church Yard
	September	16	Mary James, in yᵉ West Church Yard
	October	1	Dorothy Lewin, in yᵉ East Church Yard
	November	5	Charles Aires, in yᵉ East Church Yard
	December	4	Charles Nelson, in yᵉ Vault
	January	21	Henry Aires, in yᵉ East Church Yard
		27	William Lloyd, under yᵉ Organ
	February	1	Elizabeth Bainham, in yᵉ West Church Yard
		18	William Hemming, under yᵉ Organ
1739	March	25	Frances Radle, in yᵉ West Church Yard
	April	1	Daniel Perrey an Infant pensioner
		7	Anne Langmore, in yᵉ Vault
		28	. . . . A poor Woman Suddenly
	May	4	Sarah Mathews, in yᵉ East Yard
		10	Mary Hunsdon, under yᵉ Organ
		26	Anne Bailey a Pensioner, in yᵉ West Yard
	June	3	William Hunt, in yᵉ West yard
	August	2	Elizabeth Wilson, in yᵉ West Yard
		4	Richᵈ Foster an Infant, in yᵉ East Yard
	September	15	Joseph Hughes, in yᵉ South Isle
		16	Elizabeth Hughes, in yᵉ East Yard
	October	5	William Potter, in yᵉ East Yard
		28	Jonathan Gale, in yᵉ East yard
	November	2	Peter Peters a foundling, in yᵉ West Yard
		24	Eleanor Storey, in the Vault
	December	10	Sarah Stebbing, in the Middle Isle
		26	Anne Looker, under yᵉ Organ

Years.	Month.	Day.	Names.
1739	January	13	Alice Bennet, in yᵉ East Yard
		24	Anne Bentley, in yᵉ Middle Isle
		25	Mary Andrews, in yᵉ East Yard
	February	8	Elizabeth Grantham, in yᵉ East Yard
		10	Sarah Bazire, in yᵉ Vault
		14	William Martin, in yᵉ Middle Isle
	March	2	William Church, in yᵉ East Yard
		9	Sarah Lawton, in yᵉ West Yard
		9	Rebekah Elliott, in yᵉ West Yard
		10	Katharine Sharrett, in yᵉ East Yard
1740		30	Richᵈ Godwin, in yᵉ Vault
	April	18	Stuart Jones a pensioner Infant
		20	William Fernley, in yᵉ East Yard
		20	William Graves, in yᵉ East Yard
		25	Thomas Gardiner, in yᵉ West Yard
	May	1	Joseph Philby, in yᵉ East Yard
		7	Elizabeth Cradock, in yᵉ Chancel
		9	Dorothy Lewin, in yᵉ East Yard
		14	Anne Blagdon, in yᵉ Vault ·
		20	John Blagdon, in yᵉ Vault
		26	Cæsar Lycett, in yᵉ West Yard
	June	6	John Taylor, in yᵉ East Yard
		19	Jonah Firth, in yᵉ Vault
		22	Susannah Skinner, in yᵉ Middle Isle
	July	5	. . . . Keys a pensioner infant
		8	Charles Abbot, in yᵒ Vault
	August	8	John Andrews, in yᵉ East Yard
		4	Anne Hungerford, in yᵉ Vault
	September	21	James Nelson, in yᵉ Vault
	October	5	Jane Hockley, in yᵉ West Yard
		8	Margaret Price, in yᵉ Vault
		12	John Stearns, in yᵉ West Yard
		24	John Westall, in yᵉ East yard
		31	Elizabeth Wheeler an Infant pensioner
	November	17	Hester Keys an Infant pensioner
		30	Mary Wisard a pensioner
	January	7	James Peters an Infant pensioner
		8	Sarah Cary Aires, in yᵉ East Yard
		9	Thomas Spittle, in yᵉ West Yard
		29	William Gibbs a pensioner
	March	12	Susannah Harrobine in yᵉ Vault
		18	Anne Coulter, in yᵉ Vault
1741	April	8	Richard Capel, in yᵉ Vault
		19	James Coulter, in yᵉ Vault
		23	Anna Maria Angell, in yᵒ East Yard
		23	. . . . Marriott, under yᵉ Organ
	May	5	. . . . Stearns, in yᵉ West Yard
	June	12	. . . . Hare, in yᵉ West Yard
	July	23	Stephen Barnadiston, under yᵉ Organ
		28	Anne Forward, Middle Isle
	August	14	S. Light a pensioner
		14	John Philby, East yard
	September	5	Sarah Scot a pensioner
		7	Wᵐ Ellcock, in yᵉ West Yard
		7	Sarah Marriot, under yᵉ Organ
		7	Sarah Boulter, in yᵉ Vault
		10	Henry Nelson, in yᵉ Vault

Years.	Month.	Day.	Names.
1741	September	14	Elizth Mitcham a pensioner
		21	Hannah Peters an Infant pens^r
	October	6	Thos Kimmis, in ye Vault
		10	Anne Lewin, in ye East Yard
		15	Sarah Dawson an Infant pensio^r
	November	15	Isaac Gale, in ye East Yard
	December	3	Etheldred Cock, in ye North Isle
		15	Anne Hart, in ye East Yard
	January	5	Jno Jones, in ye Vault
		6	Elizth Marriot, under ye Organ
		12	William Orchin a pensioner
		12	. . . . Wilson, in ye West Yard
		13	Jno Bacon, in ye West Yard
		13	Mary Warwick, in ye East Yard
		16	Joseph Blagdon, in ye Vault
		21	Wm Turner, in ye East Yard
		29	Elizth Nicholl, under ye Organ
	February	1	Elizth Martin a pensioner
		1	Mary Kirk a pensioner
		4	Wm Ingham, under ye Organ
		7	Elizth Boulton, in ye Vault
		23	Wm Williamson a pensioner
	March	10	Martha Warwick, in ye East Yard
		16	John Townsend, pensioner
		21	Elizth Darlin a pensioner
		23	Susannah Marriott, under ye Organ
1742	April	20	Priscilla Perkins, in ye East Yard
		23	Emanuel Stow, in ye East Yard
		29	Eliz^h Howard a pensioner
	May	8	Jno Marriot, under ye Organ
		28	Jno Taylor, in ye West Yard
	August	20	Jane Birch, under ye Organ
		24	Thos. Fowler, in ye South Isle
	September	8	Jonas Firth, in ye Vault
		12	John Bowman, in ye Vault
		25	Wm Berry, in ye South Chappel
	October	4	John Aires, in ye East Yard
		6	Benjamin Boldwin, Pensioner
		11	Jno Barton, in ye West Yard
	November	1	George Flowers, Pensioner
		5	Mary Irish, in ye East Yard
	December	12	John Hartley, in ye Vault
		19	Mary Betson, in ye Vault
		22	Thos Johnson Lewin
		30	Margaret Vickers, under the Organ
	February	3	Thomas Prime, in ye Middle Isle
		17	Catherine Stearns, in ye East Yard
	March	6	. . . . Avery a Pensioner
1743	April	8	Mary Jones, under ye Organ
		18	Mary Coomes a pensioner
		22	Jane Harne a pensioner
		22	Mary Taylor, in ye East yard
		28	Anne Kettell, in ye Vault
	May	29	Mary Trimmer, in ye Vault
	June	2	Penelope Barnes a pensioner
		8	Rebekah Kimmis, Junr, in ye Vault
		11	Rebekah Kimmis, Senr, in ye Vault

Years.	Month.	Day.	Names.
1743	July	4	Robert Miller a pensioner
		15	Conrade Brown, in ye West Yard
		30	Richd Broughton, in ye Vault
	August	18	Joanna Hall, in ye East Yard
		31	John Marriot, under ye Organ
	September	8	William Kettell, in ye Vault
		14	James Coulter, in ye Vault
		27	Elizh Pain, Mary Sparks, & Joseph Peters, pensioners
	October	19	William Cork, in ye East Yard
	November	10	Arthur Perkins, in ye East Yard
		24	Samll Warwick a pensioner
	December	23	Rachel Hall, in ye East Yard
	January	2	George Sherwin, in ye East Yard
		12	Thos Topping, in ye East Yard
	February	2	Frances Warham, in ye Vault
		3	. . . . Waters, in ye South Isle
	March	1	Thomas Wright, in ye Vault
		12	The Revd Dr John Middleton, Rector, in ye Chancell
1744		28	Thos Tolsman, in ye West Yard
	April	8	Thos Cutler, in ye West Yard
		18*	David Dumouchel, in ye middle Isle
		18	Anne Lloyd, under ye Organ
		22	William Hunt
	May	3	Anne Nelson, in ye Vault
	June	5	Adam Gray
		24	John Godwin, in ye East Yard
		29	Thos Crouch, in ye West yard
	August	3	Mary Lewin, in ye East yard
		21	Edward Andrews, in ye East Yard
	September	6	Thos Crouch, in ye West Yard
	November	25	Daniel Davies, in ye Vault
	December	16	John Jones, under ye Organ
	January	23	Betty Andrews, in ye East yard
	February	10	Martha Miller a pensioner
		12	Mary Irish, in ye East Yard
		17	Thos Sharret, Parish Clerk, in ye East Yard
1745	April	4	Mary Cuttler, in the W. Church Yard
	May	12	John Kettle, Esqr, Windsor Herald, in the Vault
	August	25	Anne Nayler, in the W. Ch. yard
	September	3	Joseph Clark, in the Vault
		6	John Crouch, Infant, in E. Ch. Yard
		6	Anne Stevens, in the E. Ch. Yard
		12	Rebecca Caryl, in the South Chapel
	October	20	Sarah Philby, in the East Ch. Yard
	November	5	Anne Jewster, in the Vault
		10	David Davies, in the West Ch. Yard
		15	Sarah Fowler, in the S. Isle
	December	1	A Poor Man found dead, in the Vault
		18	Elizabeth Hurtford, in the middle Isle
		27	Anne Garbrand, South Isle
	January	5	Benjamin Kimmis, in the Vault
		5	Elizabeth Walker, in the Vault
	February	6	Hannah Cumby
		6	William Tomlinson
		18	John Godwin

The Register from April 18, 1744, to May 22, 1747, is subscribed " Bd Wynne, Curate."

Years.	Month.	Day.	Names.
1745	February	18	Mary Andrews
		26	Hannah Cox
		26	Sarah Warwick
		26	John Sims, Infant
1746	April	30	Susannah Johnson
	May	23	Elizabeth Peach
		23	Mary Maber, Sexton, in the N. Isle
		25	Jonathan Battishill, W. Ch. Yard
	July	15	William Jones, Infant
	September	1	Alexander-Henry Leroux, Infant, N. Isle
		19	Joyce Blagden, in the Vault
	October	17	Martha Downs aged 106, born in Somersetshire, in the Vault
	November	1	Bridget Jewell Knight, Middle Isle
	December	7	Alice Bourn, in the E. Church Yard
		8	Elizabeth Sowton, E. Church yard
	January	13	Elizabeth Pott, in the Bellfry
		30	Margaret Hutchinson, E. Church y^d
	February	12	Elizabeth Mixer, in the Vault
1747	May	12	.... a child from ye Spread Eagles
		22	Mary Blagden, in the Vault
	June	28*	.... Mitchel, in the Vault
	July	1	.... Mitchel, both pauper
	August	18	Elizabeth Cannon
	September	14	John Pembroke, E. Ch. yard
	November	29	John Chetto, E. Ch. yard
	December	10	John Golding, the Vault
		18	Two Pensioners, the Vault
		18	Mrs Pardie, W. C. yard
		27	Sarah Jordan, W. Ch. yard
	January	1	Will. Brown, Pensioner
	February	11	Samuel Boyce, East Church yard
	March	13	Thomas Sweetland, in the Vault
		20	John Stanley, in the Vault
1748	May	20	Hannah Smith, in the Vault
		26	Mary Butler, in the Vault
	June	17	Frances Stebbing, in the Middle Isle
	September	20	Mary Kennon, Infant, East Church yard
	October	2	Robert Leroux, under the Organ
		4	Mary Dungate, West Ch. Yard
		12	The Bagpiper
	December	3	Joseph Hemmings, in the Vault
		20	Mary Stanley, in the West Ch. Yard
		21	Mary Shickle, in the Vault
	January	19	Phillip Chiver, in the Vault
1749	April	29	Richard Harrise, in the Vault
	May	8	Edgar, in the South Isle
		12	Anna Benigna Syms, in the West Ch. yard
		15	Joseph Walker from the Spread Egle, in the Vault
		18	George Whitehead, in the Vault
		27	Widow Wilson, in the Vault
	June	16	Edward Westall, in the East C. Yard
		25	William Walker, in the Vault
	July	26	.... Capel, Widow, in the Vault

* The Register from June 23, 1747, to December 28, 1764, is subscribed " Willm Shackleford, M.A., Curate."

Years.	Month.	Day.	Names.
1749	August	8	George Glover, in East Ch. Y^d
		8	Jane Boseley, in the Vault
	October	6	Wm Eames, in East Ch. Y^d
		20	Isaac Alston, West Ch. Y^d
	November	27	Ann Crouch, East Ch. Y^d
	December	1	Robert Cottle, in the Vault
		31	Gilbert Blewett, in West Ch. Y^d
	January	19	.... Axford, widow, in the Vault
		24	Edward Hayle, in the Vault
	February	7	Joseph Mapham, in West Ch. y^d
		14	Thomas Gosling, ⎱ in East Ch. y^d
		13	Thomas Huett, ⎰
	March	23	Joanna Mapham, in West Ch. y^d
1750	April	8	Rebecca Nash, in West Ch. y^d
		16	Thomas Asquith, in North Ch. y^d
		17	Thomas Shackleford, North Ch. Y^d
	July	1	Gabriel Keys, Pensioner
		13	Charles Mathews, North Ch. y^d
		14	.... Allon, under the Organ
	August	21	.... Bulley a Pensioner
	September	4	John Marriot, under ye Organ
		5	Sophia Long, South Chapple
		10	Thomas Page, in ye Vault
		23	Robert Wareham, in ye Vault
		23	.... Hicks, in ye Vault
	October	25	Eliz^th Davis, in the vault
		29	Abigail Beauchamp, West Ch. y^d
	November	21	Ann Owen, in the Vault
	December	23	Frances Gower, in the Vault
	January	3	Phœbe Walton, South Chapple
	February	7	Robert Laverick, vault
	March	24	Sarah Mapham, West Ch. y^d
1751		25	Sarah Mixer, vault
	May	9	Thomas Webster, in ye Vault
	September	29	Charles Stewart, in ye Vault
1752	March	30	Ann de Staville, in ye middle Isle
	April	19	William Knight, in ye middle Isle
	July	7	Thomas Preston an infant, ⎱ Vault
		7	Ann Chivers an infant, ⎰
	August	26	Henry Tailsworth, vault
	October	7	Miss Emelia Gladman, vault
		18	Miss Hannah Mico, vault
		31	Miss Eliz^th Page, vault
	November	19	Richard Knight, middle Isle
		22	M^rs .... Chancey, North Isle
	December	1	Richd Page an infant, Vault
1753	February	18	John Nelson, vault
	March	12	Miss Eliz. Pindar, North Isle
		23	Rebecca Farmer, vault
	June	15	Miss Hannah Binks, East Ch. y^d
	July	13	Benjamin Weale, North Isle
		24	James Eldridge, East Ch. y^d
	September	4	John Wareham, infant, vault
		5	Robt Higgs Mott, infant, vault
		16	Willm Pott, infant, vault
	October	14	Ann Smith, vault
	November	6	Mary Dawson an Infant, vault

Years.	Month.	Day.	Names.
1753	November	14	Edward Allen, Esqr, E. Ch. y^d
		25	Thomas Lewin, E. Ch. y^d
	December	7	Elizth Page an Infant, Vault
		28	A poor woman found dead
		30	Ann Berry, vault
1754	January	3	Ann Eve, Ch. y^d
		16	George Robinson, Ch. y^d
		27	Wm Hainke, Ch. y^d
	February	17	. . . . Mansfield an infant, Vault
		17	John Peter a foundling
		24	Grace Aires, Ch. y^d
	March	17	John Glover, Ch. y^d
	June	15	John Beckwith, East Ch. y^d
	August	17	Joseph Graves, W. Ch. y^d
		23	Joseph Mantle, W. Ch. y^d
		25	Samuel Peachy, vault
	September	1	Samuel Peachy an infant, vault
		22	Willm Maynard an infant, vault
	December	25	Ann White, West Ch. y^d
1755	January	11	Francis Bull, West Ch. y^d
		15	Richard Sadd, West Ch. y^d
	February	5	Thomas Cunningham, W. Ch. y^d
		17	Martha Tailsworth, vault
	April	6	Mathew Baxter, W. Ch. y^d
		13	Mary Timson, vault
	June	11	Thomas Asquish an Infant, vault
		22	Ann Hare, W. Ch. y^d
	July	1	. . . . Pearse an infant, W. Ch. y^d
		30	Grace Cook, vault
	August	7	John Berry, vault
	September	30	John Brailsforth Bonduck, W. Ch. y^d
	October	2	Mary Cornelius, vault
		12	Mary Smith, vault
		17	Elizabeth Warner, vault
	November	12	Elisha Farmer, vault
		13	Mary Howard, E. Ch. y^d
		14	Margaret Robinson, W. Ch. y^d
		16	Susannah Walter, W. Ch. y^d
		17	Susannah Warner, vault
		28	Edward Mabor, North Isle
		30	Sarah How, vault
	December	10	Elizth Basset Mantle, W. Ch. y^d
1756	January	7	Ann Walwyn
		11	Margaret Marriot
		14	Ford Beauchamp
		19	Mary Whitaker
		28	Grace Cook
		29	Ann Hayden
	March	21	William Lindsey
		25	Catherine Harris
	April	17	Susannah Jenkins
		20	Robert Stebbing
	May	24	Love-Venus Rivers
	June	8	Jane Dunn
		27	Margaret Robinson
	July	11	Sarah Callow
		16	William Pearce

Years.	Month.	Day.	Names.
1756	July	21	Susannah Wix
		22	Edyth Hainke
		25	Ann Goodwin
	August	12	Mary Hutchinson
	October		Robert Warham
	November	4	William Ferris
		16	Mary Webster
		17	Edward Jorden
1757	January	2	Amelia Cooper
		4	John Cartwright
		27	Willm Pennant Long
	February	10	Meethabel Walwyn
	March	1	Mary Conniger Dias
		1	Benjamin Mansfield
		14	Susannah Gurnell, } infants
		14	Thomas Gurnell, } infants
		29	John Cuttel an Infant
		30	Susannah Boyce
	April	10	Rebecca Mansfield
	May	12	Hannah Chivers an Infant
	June	12	Catherine Steel
		23	John Chetham
	July	10	Sarah Cuttel an Infant
	August	16	Thomas Alexander
		28	James Hendrie
	October	24	Joseph Blagdon
1758	January	13	Henry Briggs
	February	17	Edward Homeward
	March	24	Sarah Hare
	July	16	Sarah Lawrence
	August	6	Benjamin Boulter
	September	22	Mary Carter
	October	16	Esther Glover
	December	31	Mary Duncomb
1759	January	7	Amelia Cooper a child
		18	Rebecca Hanson
	February	1	John Beech a child
		19	Mary Crisp
	March	8	John Barber a child
	May	13	Robert Mott a child
		7	John Phillips
	June	3	Henry Ford a child
	July	16	Jane Wilshier
	August	8	Alexander Charles Warham
		15	John Cope
		16	Edmund Jephcoat an Infant
		18	John Ransford
	September	6	Mary Boulter
	October	28	Mary Ann Cuttel
	November	19	Sarah Bull
	December	11	Eliz^th Wallis
		29	Sarah Page
1760	January	6	. . . . Mansfield a child
		12	Ann Oxland
		12	Joseph Clark
		20	John Phipps
	February	24	Willm Stebbing

Years.	Month.	Day.	Names.
1760	April	6	Mary Jarvis
		14	Willm Hickling
	June	15	Sarah Bell
	April	25	Robert Jarvis
	June	17	Dorcas Turner
		20	Catherine Serle, in the Chancell
	July	1	William Dickens a child
	August	8	John Gisborn
	September	15	William Lawrence a child
	December	22	Henry Kelsey, north Chapple
		28	Susannah Frank, north Isle
1761	February	1	Elizabeth Smith, East Ch. yard
		11	Sarah Nicholson, Ch. yard
		15	Mary Hill, vault
	March	5	Sophia Long, vault
	April	3	Richard Garbrand, vault
		26	Robert Stebbing, middle Isle
	May	11	Ann Tovey, Vault
		31	John Hare, West Ch. Yard
	June	26	Jane White, East Ch. y^d
	August	2	Stephen Chanter, West Ch. y^d
		29	Thomas Johnson, middle Isle
	September	4	Mary Parker, Vault
		21	Henry Thompson, W. Ch. y^d
	October	13	Frances Sophia Young, Ch. y^d
	November	1	William Brown, Vault
		8	Nicholas Marwyn, W. Ch. y^d
		18	Henry Joly, Middle Isle*
	December	6	Joseph Orpwood, Ch. y^d
		13	Ann Pace, Ch. y^d
1762	January	3	John Brown, Vault
	February	11	William Gurney a Child, Ch. y^d
		13	John Thompson a Child, Ch. y^d
		16	John Kindon, Ch. y^d
		21	Ann Fernley, Ch. y^d
		26	Thomas Chivers, Ch. y^d
	March	2	Robert Lawrence a Child, Vault
		3	Samuel Thompson a Child, Ch. y^d
		7	Susannah Wickham, East Ch. y^d
		11	James Thompson a Child, Ch y^d
	April	2	The Revd James Tunstall, D.D.,† Treasurer and Canon Residentiary of St Davids, and Vicar of Rochdale, Lancashire, in the Chancel
		4	Elizabeth Clark, Ch. yard
		21	John Rigby, Middle Isle
		27	Thomas Yates, West Ch. y^d
	May	6	Henry Dawson, an infant, Vault
	June	7	Thomas Otley, an infant, Ch. y^d
		8	John Page, an infant, Vault
		17	Rebecca Gower, Vault

* In the margin is this note:—"It appears to me by the annexed Affidavit and Certificate that Henry Joly in this Registry named, and John Mary Henry Joly in the said Certificate mentioned, are one and the same identical person. (Signed) Willm Shackleford, Curate and Register."
[Certificate in French, and an Affidavit in English inserted in the Reg^r.]

† Fellow and Tutor of St. John's College, Cambridge, and Public Orator of that University. D.D., 1744. Chaplain to Archbishop Potter, presented to Rochdale in 1757 by Archbishop Hutton. Died March 28.

Years.	Month.	Day.	Names.
1762	July	23	William Walter, Ch. y^d
	September	15	John Robins, East Ch. y^d
		27	Elizabeth Angel, middle Isle
	October	12	Henrietta Thompson, E. Ch. y^d
		28	Willm Jones, Ch. y^d
	November	1	John Beazley, Ch. y^d
		3	Martha Frith, Vault
		18	Elizth Lamb, Ch. y^d
	December	1	Ann Clements, Vault
1763	January	2	Rachell Woodhead, North Isle
		3	Thomas Hickling, Vault
		10	Charles Chauncey, North Isle
		15	John Owen, Vault
		15	Mrs. . . . . Jordan, North Isle
		28	William Gower, Vault
	February	1	Mary Hare, West Ch. yard
		3	Robert Hickling, East Ch. y^d
		22	John Vickers, West Ch. y^d
		28	Hester Avery, East Ch. y^d
	March	27	Mary Orpwood, Ch. y^d
	April	24	Captn Richard Knight, Middle Isle
		27	Mary Cogan, Midd. Isle
	June	26	Stephen Venn, Vault
	August	11	Ann Gladman, Vault
		24	John Westal a Child, East Ch. y^d
	September	6	Martha Swain a Child, West Ch. y^d
		22	James Swain a Child, West Ch. y^d
	October	6	Richard Maynard a Child, Vault
	November	1	Owen Williams a Child, p.*
		6	Thomas Pitman, Ch. y^d
	December	16	John Sommers Maynard, Vault
		27	George Bain, Ch. yard, p.*
1764	January	21	A poor woman, Casual
	February	12	Sarah Avery, East Ch. y^d
		26	Frances Long, Vault
	March	4	Sarah Hilton a Child, E. Ch. y^d
		19	Richard Beasley, p.*
		22	Mary Morton a Child, Church y^d
	April	21	John Lawrence a Child, Vault
	June	4	Thomas Beasley, p.*
		15	Ann Townsend a Child, Vault
		16	John Day Kensall, a child
	September	25	Deborah Lansdown, Ch. y^d
	October	14	Thomas Crooke, E. Ch. y^d
		14	Willm Angel, E. Ch. y^d
		25	Mary Taylor, E. Ch. y^d
	November	4	Elizth Bull, W. Ch. y^d
	December	1	Ann Jay, Ch. y^d
		8	Sophia Dawson, Vault
		15	Frances Pitman, Ch. y^d
		23	George Evans, Ch. y^d
		28	Mary Oliver, Ch. y^d
1765	January	31†	Paul Elliot, E. Ch. y^d

* Pauper.

† The Register from January 31, 1765, to August 4, 1770, is subscribed "Edwd Tinley, Curate and Reg^r;" from August 6, 1770, to December 13, 1772, "E. Tinley, Curate"; and from January 17, 1773, to December 16, 1774, "Edwd Tinley, Register."

Years.	Month.	Day.	Names.
1765	February	7	Ann Knight, Middle Isle
		10	John Swain, W. Ch. y^d
		20	Elizabeth Douglass, Vault
	March	8	Randolph Tooke, North Isle
	April	25	John Page, Vault
	May	27	William Chandler, Vault
		80	Mary Swain, W. Ch. y^d
	June	27	Ann Hicks, Ch. y^d
	July	8	Daniel Walker, Vault
		17	Thomas Walker, Vault
	August	8	John Greatrex, Ch. y^d
	September	3	Edmund Morris, Ch. y^d
		19	Richard Williamson, West Ch. y^d
	October	1	Sarah Rutland, Ch. yard
		6	Joseph Vaux, Vault
		24	Jane Grimes, Ch. yard
		24	William Brown, Ch. yard
		26	Robert Brown, Ch. yard
	November	18	Rebecca Evans, Ch. yard
		24	Elizabeth Crouch, South Isle
		25	William Gower, Vault
	December	12	George Brannet, Ch. yard
			Dennis Kehne, Ch. yard
		12	Rice Griffith, Ch. yard
			John Morgan, Ch. yard
			James Streater, Ch. yard ⎫
			A man unknown, Ch. yard ⎬ Accidently killed
			A youth unknown, Ch. yard ⎭
		16	John Mills, North Isle
		81	Ann Fleming, Ch. yard
1766	January	14	Wm Shackleford, Curate of this parish, was buried in the Churchy^d by the Rector Dr Thomas, but was omitted setting down. I have therefore here put it in the margin.*

Witness my hand,
E. Tinley, Curate,
March 25th 1766.

		20	Rev. William Shackleford M. A., E. Ch. y^d
	March	4	Price Brooke Sampson, under the organ
		9	. . . . Ford, E. Ch. yard
	April	8	Rebecca Scott, Ch. yard
		20	Ann Fenn, Vault
	May	8	Benjamin Tovey, Vault
		4	Dorothy Townsend, Vault
		11	Mary Page, Vault
		28	John Lernoult Vaux, Vault
	June	24	Martha Thatcher, Vault, poor
		26	Benjamin Tovey, Vault
	July	20	Thomas Long, Vault
		28	Frances Kelsey, North Isle
	September	11	John Nash, Ch. yard
	October	27	Thomas Preston, Middle Isle
	November	11	Rebecca Pyefinch, Vault
		14	Thomas Robins, East Ch. Yard
1767	January	3	Dorothy Buck, Ch. Yard

* This entry is in the margin.

Years.	Month.	Day.	Names.
1767	January	13	Francis Kensall, Ch. Yard
		19	Edmund Morris
		25	Willm How, Ch. Yard
	April	23	James Avery, East Ch. Yard
		26	Katherine Wells, West Ch. Yard
	May	5	Mary Branwhite, d^o
	June	29	Peter Francis Thomegay, Ch. y^d
	July	10	William Cowley, under ye Organ
		10	Sarah Page, poor
		26	Sarah Thompson, Ch. y^d
		26	Rebecca Wix, Ch. y^d
	August	30	George Michael Eaton, Ch. y^d
	October	4	Elizabeth Martha Anthony, Vault
		18	Elizabeth Bent, Ch. y^d
		18	Richard Grimes, poor
	November	27	Richard Serle, Chancel
	December	17	. . . . Burgess, poor
1768	February	19	Dorothy Collett, Chancel
		27	Thomas Thompson, Ch. y^d
	March	2	William Hickling, D^o
		27	Mary Hilton, D^o
			Sarah Browne
	May	15	Katherine Kelsey, North Isle
	August	5	Ann Baker, Ch. y^d
		18	Wm Wix, Ch. y^d
	September	27	Margaretta Phillips, Vault
	November	6	John Barber, Vault
		12	John Butler, Ch. y^d, Parish Clerk
	December*		Alice Elton, Vault
1769	January	3	Mary Murvyn, Ch. y^d
		22	John Williams, Ch. y^d
		26	Katharine Thompson, Ch. y^d
	February	1	John Hardy, Vault
		2	Jane Cork, Middle Isle
		11	Wm Kensall, Ch. y^d
		12	Charles Townsend, Vault
		16	Alice Mary Greatrex, Vault
	March	4	Robt Ley, Vault
		9	John Staples, Ch. y^d
		10	Martha Wix, Ch. y^d
		21	Eliz. Nash, Ch. y^d
		26	Mary Jones, under the Organ
	April	13	Ann Tinley, Vault
		17	Edmund Pead, D^o
		18	Dorothy Thornton, d^o
	May	8	Thomas Stebbing, d^o
		26	Henry Blatchlay, Ch. y^d
		30	Thomas Grape, Vault
	June	10	Bladuny Friend Grosvenor, Vault
		17	Ann Angell, } mid. Isle
			Catherine Angell, }
	July	1	Richard Hatt, Ch. y^d
		19	Mary Bandy, South Isle
		24	James Grimes, Vault

* Sic.

Years.	Month.	Day.	Names.
1769	July	24	Elizth Hind, d°
	September	13	Joseph Greatrex, d°
	October	7	James Thomas Tuck, Ch. y^d
		8	Sarah Lovegrove, d°
		22	Sarah Bulmer, Vault
	November	8	James Grape, Vault
		24	Elizabeth Arters, Vault, poor
		30	Boddington Peacock, Ch. y^d
	December	20	Wm Thornton, Vault
		21	Thos Dyster, Ch. y^d
		23	Susanna Grimes, Vault, poor
1770	February	13	James Gilman, Vault
	March	12	Mary Jeffs, poor, Vault
	April	5	Jn° Stevenson, Chahcel
		16	Eliz. Brown, under the Organ
		30	Robt Kensall, Ch. y^d
	May	1	Jane Hallowell, d°
		9	Thos Caryl, South Isle
		13	Mary Brown, poor, Vault
		21	Elizabeth Shackleford, Ch. y^d
		27	Ann Brown, Vault
	August	4	Jn° Lloyd, under the Organ
		6	Jn° Spurr, Vault
		7	Ann Roberts, Ch. y^d
		28	Mary Thompson, Vault
	September	6	Jonathan Garland, Vault, poor
	October	4	Wm Woolfrey, Ch. y^d
		26	Mary Baxter, Ch. y^d, poor
		26	Edward Tinley, Vault
	November	10	Ann Wilson, Vault
		22	Herbert Pyefinch, d°
	December	30	Maria Lucas, d°
1771	January	7	Hannah Dare, Ch. y^d
		15	Ann Hill, d°
		20	John Jarvis, d°
		28	John Tuff, d°
	February	3	Elizth Palmer, Vault
		17	Joseph Hombler, Ch. y^d
	March	1	Wm Bulmer, Vault
		8	Sarah Barber, d°
		18	Christian Hardy, South Isle
		24	Jn° Harrison, Ch. y^d
	April	4	Eliz. Little, d°
		5	Ja^s Merryfield, d°
		28	George Hilton, Ch. y^d
	May	4	Elizth Morgan, Ch. y^d, poor
		7	Mary Vrignaud, Ch. y^d, poor
	July	12	Sarah Caryl, South Isle
		28	Jn° Wm Grisbrook, Vault
		31	Jn° Tovey, North Isle
	August	28	Elizth Greatrex, Vault
		30	Edward Wix, Church Yard
	October	16	Mariana Tinley, Vault
		25	Thomas Cogan, Ch. y^d
	November	3	Amy Greatrex, Vault
		6	Wm Brunt Day, Ch. y^d

Years.	Month.	Day.	Names.
1771	November	24	Mary Rigall, d°
		25	Susanna Day, d°
	December	5	Urania Kensall, d°
		15	Wm Lowther, Vault
1772	January	11	Margaret Walter & John Walter, under the Organ
		15	Robert Ley, Vault
		29	Orlando Watts, Ch. y^d
		30	Sarah Cowley, under the Organ
	February	6	Hannah Beckett Grimstone, Ch. y^d
		14	Alice Robinson, middle Isle
		16	Paul Thos Dyster, Ch. y^d
		18	W^m & Ann Urling, Ch. y^d
		28	Elizth Tunstall, Chancel
	March	1	John Aynge, South Isle
		3	Thos Grape, d°
		8	Thos Rigall, Ch. y^d
	April	5	Rebecca Flude, South Isle
		9	Wm Avery, Ch. y^d
	June	11	Sarah Brooker, Vault, poor
		11	Wm Cogan, Ch. y^d
	August	15	Jn° Taylor, Vault, poor
	September	17	Jn° Bruker, Vault, poor
		21	George Ley, Vault
		23	Sarah Thompson, d°
		30	James Samson, under the Organ
	October	6	John Jones, d°
		25	Wm Buswell, Vault
	November	6	Elizth Grape, d°
	December	4	Thomas Kensall, Ch. y^d
		10	Paul Elliott, d°
		13	Thomas Bent, d°
1773	January	17	Elizabeth Mott, Middle Isle
		17	Alexander Bell, South Isle
		28	Richd Eaton, Vault
	February	2	Wm Dyer, Vault, poor
		19	Sarah Bulmer, Vault
	March	16	Maria Hoffman, Vault
	April	12	Francis Bacon, d°
		24	Samuel Hatt, Ch. y^d
	June	20	Elizabeth Buckle, under Organ
		29	Thomas Penny, Ch. y^d
	July	2	Thomas John Loveday, d°
	August	26	Josiah Randall, d°
	September	10	John Lovegrove, d°
		10	Joseph Greatrex, Vault
	December	15	Saml Hilton, Ch. y^d
		26	Robt Brown, Vault
		31	Jane Angell, Middle Isle
1774	January	2	Elizabeth Paise, Ch. y^d
	February	2	Dorothy Robinson, poor
		2	Nathanael Wright Blaksley, Vault
		13	William Harris, Vault, poor
		18	Helena Tinley, Vault
	April	8	Sarah Wood, Ch. y^d
	May	6	Mary Kensall, d°
	June	11	Edmund Cooke, under the Organ

Years.	Month.	Day.	Names.
1774	August	30	Burkitt Fenn, Vault
	September	15	Francis Wigram, Ch. y^d West
	October	20	Mary Brown, Vault
	November	15	Thomas Rigall, Ch. y^d
		24	William Lawrence, Vault
		25	James Bispham, South Isle
	December	3	Susannah Avery, Ch. y^d
		6	Humphrey Penny, Ch. y^d
		16	Jane Brown, Ch. y^d

INDEX OF NAMES.

A.

Abbet, William, 132.
Abbot, Charles, 137; Christopher, 38; John, 108, 113; Priscilla, 38, 83; Sarah, 38.
Abell, Colleberry, 78.
Abine, Ann, 90; Thomas, 90.
Abney, Edward, 115; James, 91, 97; Sarah, 3, 97, 99, 110, 133; Sir Thomas, 110, 115, 117, 126; Thomas, 3, 91, 92, 97, 99, 117.
Abrathat, Ann, 91; Richard, 90.
Achmotie, *alias* Acmoody, Anne, 10; Elizabeth, 8; George, 8, 10; Helen, 8, 10.
Ackland, Charles, 53; Headley, 54; John, 52-54; Mary, 52-54; Mary Harrison, 53; William, 52.
Acres, James, 29; Mary, 29.
Acton, Ann, 96, 110; Edward, 96; Richard, 96, 110, 115, 117; Robert, 96; William, 65.
Adams, Alice, 62; Anne, 60, 91; Anthony, 70; Barbara, 68; Charity, 132; Deborah, 37; Dorcas, 2, 4, 5, 93; Elizabeth, 20; Henry, 37; Isabella, 124; James, 4, 91; John, 2, 4, 5, 20, 88, 93; Katherine, 12; Lydia, 5; Martha, 135; Mary, 37, 69, 71, 74, 84, 93; Robert, 2; Sarah, 92.
Adamson, Hannah, 26; Sarah, 26; Walter, 26, 115.
Adee, Anne, 26; John, 26, 27, 117; Richard, 27; Susanna, 26, 27, 117.
Adey, Rebecca, 86.
Aguttar, Richard, 83.
Ainesworth, John, 109; Mary, 109.
Aires, Charles, 40-42, 44, 81, 135, 136; Grace, 41, 142; Henry, 44, 136; John, 41, 138; Judith, 58; Mary, 40-42, 44; Sarah Carey, 40, 137.
Alchorne, Elizabeth, 73.

Alcock, John, 86; Margaret, 134; Thomas, 121.
Alder, Elhana, 4; George, 1; John, 1, 2, 4, 88; Mary, 1, 2, 88, 95; Mr., 90; Susan, 4; Thomas, 95.
Alexander, Thomas, 143.
Alford, Ann, 13-15, 17, 18, 20, 105; Benjamin, 13; Edmund, 18; Elizabeth, 20; James, 15, 103; John, 14; Mary, 17, 105; Thomas, 13-15, 17, 18, 20, 103, 105.
Allen, Anne, 6; Edward, 22, 111, 128, 142; George, 22, 111; Jane, 127; John, 6; Jonathan, 130; Joseph, 86; Katherine, 22; Mary, 69; Richard, 74, 82; Susannah, 136; Walter, 128; William, 74.
Allett, John, 117; William, 117.
Allibone, Henry, 107.
Allison, Thomas, 88, 91.
Allon, ——, 141.
Allston, Isaac, 141; Peter, 72.
Allum, Elizabeth, 24, 113; Richard, 24, 113.
Allyn, Frances, 79.
Alsop, Mary, 59.
Alvey, Thomas, 115.
Amerr, Elizabeth, 124.
Amey, Joseph, 77.
Anderson, Anne, 16; Daniel, 16; Mary, 17.
Andrews, Anne, 41, 105; Betty, 42, 139; Edward, 42, 139; Elizabeth, 76; George, 114; John, 40-42, 101, 137; Mary, 17, 18, 20, 40-42, 137, 140; Oliver, 11, 12, 99, 101, 105, 107, 109; Rebecca, 12, 99; Richard, 107; Sarah, 20; Susannah, 11, 12, 99, 109; Thomas, 17, 18, 20, 96, 100; William, 135.
Angell, Anne, 38, 40, 41, 50, 147; Anne Maria, 41, 52, 137; Catherine, 52, 147; Christian, 65; Elizabeth, 36-39, 48-54, 135, 145; George, 53;

Jane, 54, 149; John, 36-41, 49; Richard, 36; Susannah, 37; Thomas, 39; William, 38, 48-54, 145; William Sandall, 51.
Anger, Henry, 64; Thomas, 91.
Annable, Elizabeth, 135.
Anstruther, Elizabeth, 68 *n*; Sir Robert, 68 *n*.
Anthony, Elizabeth, 51, 52; Elizabeth Martha, 51, 147; George, 51, 52; Lewis, 135.
Antin, James, 135.
Antrobus, Daniel, 56.
Appleby, Ruth, 66.
Appleyard, Anne, 15, 16; Elizabeth, 15; John, 15, 16; Susanna, 16.
Archer, Abigail, 100; Mary, 86; Sarah, 126; Thomas, 116.
Arewater, Thomas, 77.
Arey, Ann, 11; Joseph, 11; William, 11.
Argent, Mary, 78.
Aris, Mary, 132.
Arkesden, Anne, 107; Lingham, 107.
Armitage, Anne, 68; Rebecca, 72; Robert, 95; Stephen, 96; Thomas, 96.
Armstrong, George, 66.
Arnell, Mary, 102; Uriah, 102.
Arnold, Anne, 17; John, 136; Richard, 17, 19, 20, 115; Sarah, 19; Urian, 106.
Arrold, Ann, 12.
Arrowsmith, Anne, 33, 127; Elizabeth, 33, 34, 37, 41-43; Jeremiah, 33, 34, 37, 41, 132; John, 37, 42; Martha, 129, 131; Robert, 41, 42; Thomas, 43.
Arters, Anne, 78; Elizabeth, 71, 148.
Arthur, Richard, 135; Sarah, 125, 133.
Asby, John, 18.
Asgill, Mary, 126.
Ash, William, 55.
Ashmore, Grace, 74; William, 75.

Mateire, *see* Meteire.

Matthews, Anne, 22, 23, 26, 28, 67, 111, 116 ; Charles, 141 ; Elizabeth, 130 ; George, 26, 116 ; John, 28 ; Mary, 102 ; Morley, 25 ; Rachel, 25 ; Robert, 25 ; Sarah. 22, 54, 111, 136 ; William, 22, 23, 26, 102, 111, 115, 116 ; William Gilbert, 54.

Mawe, Elizabeth, 2 ; John, 2.

May, Charles, 69.

Maynard, Benjamin, 2, 3, 88, 90 ; George, 6, 93 ; Jane, 2, 6, 93 ; John, 90 ; John Sommers, 145 ; Philip Payne, 46 ; Richard, 145; Robert, 6, 47 ; Sarah, 46, 47 ; Susanna, 2, 3, 88 ; Thomas, 46, 47 ; William, 46, 142.

Mayo, William, 73 ; Winifred, 78.

Meachell, Elizabeth, 120.

Mead, David, 118.

Meaddopp, Francis, 89.

Meadows, Ann, 38, 134 ; Daniel, 7, 14, 94 ; Elizabeth, 38-41 ; John, 14, 62 ; Joseph, 38, 80 ; Philip, 40 ; William, 39-41 ; William Christopher, 39.

Mears, Elizabeth, 133.

Medley, Elizabeth, 89.

Mein, Margaret, 60.

Mell, Easter, 72.

Mellowes, Eleanor, 34 ; Martha, 34, 129 ; Mary, 33, 34, 130 ; Robert, 33, 34 ; Sarah, 33.

Mercer, George, 50 ; Joseph, 50 ; Mary Ann, 50 ; Stephen, 71 ; Thomas, 83.

Meriton, Humphrey, 3, 93 ; John, 3, 91, 94 ; Joseph, 94 ; Sarah, 3 ; Thomas, 91.

Merrill, Ann, 1 ; Elizabeth, 1 ; William, 1.

Merryfield, James, 148.

Merton, Ann Theodosia, 48 ; Luke, 48 ; Susannah, 48 ; *see* Murton.

Meryman, Benjamin, 125, 128.

Metcalfe, Ann Maria, 39 ; Mary, 39 ; Thomas, 39.

Meteire, Hester, 4, 91 ; John, 2, 4, 90 ; Mary, 2, 4 ; Sarah, 4.

Meyer, Mary, 86.

Mico, George, 45 ; Hannah, 45, 141.

Middleton, Christiana, 67 ; Henry, 125 ; Rev. Dr. John, 139 ; Mary, 128 ; Roger, 117.

Miles, Avis, 62 ; Edward, 78 ; Elizabeth, 72 ; James, 71.

Miller, Hann, 70 ; Jane, 118 ; John, 11 ; Joyce, 11 ; Martha, 139 ; Mary, 76 ; Richard, 11 ; Robert, 139 ; William, 70.

Mills, Amos, 72 ; Elizabeth, 70, 73 ; John, 123, 146 ; Mary, 70 ; Philip, 60 ; Robert, 83.

Minard, Mary, 108.

Minshull, Daniel, 116 ; Deborah, 116 ; Harris, 116.

Mirfin, Ann, 28 ; Daniel, 28, 56 ; Elizabeth, 28 ; John, 16, 17, 105 ; Mary, 17, 105 ; Rebecca, 16, 17.

Mitcham, Elizabeth, 138.

Mitchell, Anne, 31 ; Christopher Bernardo, 55 ; Edward, 27-29, 31, 33, 34, 119 ; Elizabeth, 27-29, 33, 119-121 ; Hannah, 34, 127, 128 ; Joseph, 123 ; Josiah, 77 ; Mary, 27-29, 31, 33, 34, 119 ; Sarah, 73 ; Thomas, 29, 124 ; —, 140.

Mixer, Eliza, 43 ; Elizabeth, 43, 140 ; Sarah, 141; Peter, 43.

Moise, Elizabeth, 90.

Molden, Jane, 26, 117 ; Mary, 26, 117; William, 26, 117.

Molinen, John, 89.

Mollins, Anne, 66.

Monger, Mary, 64.

Monk, Amy, 72.

Monly, Isaac, 55.

Monneret, Peter, 36, 131.

Moore, Ann, 38 ; Bridget, 101 ; Edward, 29 ; John, 38, 123 ; Ruth, 74.

Mordaunt, John, Lord, 55 *n* ; Mary, 91 ; Osmund, 55, 91 ; Peter, 91.

More, Cornelius, 32 ; George, 32 ; Hester, 58 ; Sarah, 32.

Morecocke, Joan, 103.

Morer, Jane, 131.

Morgan, Ann, 39 ; Charles, 39 ; Eleanor, 77 ; Elizabeth, 39, 148 ; Henrietta, 34 ; Henry, 34 ; James, 79 ; John, 146 ; Sarah, 75 ; Thomas, 34 ; Zachariah, 18.

Morley, Thomas, 126.

Morris, Ann, 94 ; Dorothy, 30 ; Eleanor, 75 ; Edmond, 146, 147 ; Elizabeth, 5, 94, 98, 105, 108 ; Harry, 32 ; John, 5, 30-32, 94, 96, 98, 105, 128 ; Joseph, 98 ; Mary, 79 ; Oliver, 58 ; Patience, 31, 32, 128 ; Robert, 127 ; Thomas, 30.

Morson, Henrietta, 33 ; James, 73 ; Mary, 78 ; Thomas, 33.

Morton, Mary, 145.

Mosley, Jacob, 78.

Moss, Catherine, 50 ; Dorothy, 2 ; George, 1 ; Henry, 1, 2 ; Juliana, 1, 2.

Mott, Benjamin, 84 ; Elizabeth, 46-49, 52, 149 ; Robert, 46-49, 52, 143 ; Robert Higgs, 46, 141 ; Thomas, 52 ; William, 48.

Motteux, Catherine, 22, 111 ; Isabel Katherine, 23 ; Jane, 23, 113 ; Peter, 22, 23, 111, 113 ; Priscilla, 22, 23, 111.

Mottier, Mr., 87.

Mottram, John, 60.

Mould, Edward, 16, 18 ; Elizabeth, 19 ; John, 16, 18, 19 ; Sarah, 16, 18, 19.

Moulford, Mary, 60.

Mount, Anne, 26, 116 ; Martha, 26 ; Richard, 26.

Moy, Anthony, 17 ; Elizabeth, 103 ; Jane, 23, 114 ; Mary, 17, 23, 111 ; Richard, 17, 23, 103, 105, 111, 114.

Moyser, William, 133.

Muirhead, John Grossett, 50 *n*.

Munday, John, 86.

Munings, Nathaniel, 64.

Munrow, John, 60.

Munt, Mary, 40 ; William, 40.

Murfin, *see* Mirfin.

Murford, William, 57.

Murray, Amelia, 50 *n* ; Lord George, 50 *n* ; George, 7 ; Goodlife, 11 ; Henry, 7, 8, 10, 11, 96 ; Jane, 76 ; John, 8, 50 *n*, 96 ; Rebecca, 7, 8, 10, 11.

Murton, Elizabeth Holt, 48 ; Luke, 48, 49, 51 ; Susannah, 48-50, 51 ; William, 50 51; *see* Merton.

Murvyn, Mary, 147.

Mussell, Susanna, 71.

Muster, Anne, 110 ; John, 110.

N.

Nail, Ann, 51-54 ; Elizabeth, 41, 53 ; George, 41-44; George William, 52 ; Hannah, 40-44, 53 ; Herman, 51-54 ; John, 42, 44 ; Mary, 51 ; Sibella, 43.

Nanson, Robert, 67.

Naseby, Edward, 26 ; Elinor, 25, 115 ; Frances, 26, 27, 117, 120 ; George, 120 ; John, 25-27, 64, 115, 117, 120, 121 ; Thomas, 27, 108.

Nash, Anne, 80 ; Edward, 123 ; Elizabeth, 52, 147 ; James, 30; John, 146 ; Magdalen, 30; Martha, 52 ; Olive, 80 *n* ; Rebecca, 141 ; Sarah, 128, 129 ; Thomas, 80 *n* ; William, 52.

Nashby, John, 65.

Nayler, Anne, 139 ; Mary, 58.

Neal, Amy, 21 ; Elizabeth, 112 ; George, 39 ; Hannah, 39 ; Harman, 39 ; John, 84 ; Samuel, 61.

Neighbour, Anne, 40 ; Elizabeth, 40 ; Robert, 40.

Nelson, Anne, 38, 50, 129, 134, 139 ; Charles, 40, 136 ; Eliza-35-41, 134 ; George, 15 ; Henry, 137 ; James, 41, 137; Joanna, 39 ; John, 35-41, 49, 50, 141 ; Mary, 15 ; Sarah, 37, 49, 50, 133 ; Susanna, 86 ; Thomas, 49 ; William, 36, 135 ; William Mead, 15.

Nesby, Bridgett, 119.

Nevill, Anne, 63.

Newark, Elizabeth, 91 ; John, 91 ; Martha, 91.

ADDENDA.

London : Mitchell and Hughes, Printers, 24 Wardour Street, W.